THE MEDIA AND INTERNATIONAL SECURITY

Edited by

STEPHEN BADSEY

Royal Military Academy, Sandhurst

THE SANDHURST CONFERENCE SERIES

General Editor
Matthew Midlane

FRANK CASS
LONDON • NEW YORK

First published in 2000 in Great Britain by
FRANK CASS PUBLISHERS

Reprinted 2004
By Frank Cass
2 Park Square
Milton Park
Abingdon
Oxon
OX14 4RN

Transferred to Digital Printing 2005

Frank Cass is an imprint of the Taylor and Francis Group

British Library Cataloguing in Publication Data

The media and international security. – (The Sandhurst
Conference series)
1. Armed Forces and mass media – Great Britain – Congresses
I. Badsey, Stephen
070.4'49'355'00941

ISBN 0-7146-4848-5 (cloth)
ISBN 0-7146-4406-4 (paper)
ISSN 1483–1153

Library of Congress Cataloging-in-Publication Data

The media and international security/edited by Stephen Badsey.
  p. cm. – (The Sandhurst conference series)
  Includes bibliographical references and index.
  ISBN 0-7146-4848-5 (cloth) – ISBN 0-7146-4406-4 (pbk.)
  1. Armed Forces and mass media–Great Britain. 2. Security, International.
I. Badsey, Stephen. II. Series.
P96.A752 G76 2000
302.23'0941–dc21   99-049658

Typeset by Vitaset, Paddock Wood, Kent
Digitally printed in Great Britain by
Butler and Tanner, Burgess Hill, West Sussex

To Hugh Faringdon
– without permission

Contents

Series Editor's Preface

> In my generation, which inevitably reflected Cold War
> ways, the intellectual demands on us were modest com-
> pared with now. For the next generation the call on their
> thought processes, not least in understanding the nature
> of conflict, will be of an entirely different order.
>
> General Sir Charles Guthrie,
> then Chief of the General Staff, March 1996

As General Guthrie points out, conflict in the post-Cold War era is a far
more complex phenomenon than in that era which existed before. In
particular, it makes demands of leadership, at all levels and ranks, which
did not arise during the comparatively straightforward period of superpower rivalry which characterised much of the post-Second World War
period. If it was ever true that an officer did not need to study his
profession, it is entirely untrue today. No British officer could operate
successfully in Northern Ireland or Bosnia without an awareness of the
security and military environment in which those operations take place.

The foundation for the critical faculties on which that understanding
is based, and also for what should become a life-long study of the profession of arms, is laid at the Royal Military Academy, Sandhurst and, in
particular, within its Academic Faculty. If, in the quotation often inaccurately attributed to the Duke of Wellington, the Battle of Waterloo was
won on the playing fields of Eton, then future conflicts will be analysed
in the lecture theatres and seminar rooms of Sandhurst and its sister
military academies.

The origins of this, the first volume in the Sandhurst Conference
Series, came through the inspiration of members of the academic staff.
From the outset we decided that Sandhurst, as a military academy with a
strong academic tradition, was an ideal environment to bring together

soldiers and other practitioners with academics and theorists. Its success has provided the foundation for our second major conference, held in 1997, which will also appear as a forthcoming volume *Aspects of Peace-keeping*.

Matthew Midlane
Royal Military Academy, Sandhurst
January, 2000

Editor's Preface

This book owes its origins to the international conference on 'The Media and International Security' which took place at the Royal Military Academy, Sandhurst between 27 and 29 September 1995, involving leading journalists, academics, civil servants and members of the British and other armed forces. This conference came at a particularly important time in Britain for the development of ideas about the relationship between the news media and armed forces as an international security issue. Some papers from the conference have since been modified for this book; and some further papers have been added to complete the book and to bring it up to date for publication. Versions of some of the papers have already been published elsewhere: thanks are due to Ashgate Publishing Limited in respect of Professor Edward Braun's contribution; to the Carnegie Foundation for Nik Gowing's contribution; to the editors of *Despatches: The Journal of the Territorial Army Pool of Information Officers* for Major-General Cordingley's contribution; and particularly to Brigadier R. D. S. Gordon CBE MA, until recently the Director of Public Relations (Army), and his staff. Although some of the contributors are past or present members of the British armed forces or Ministry of Defence, the opinions expressed in their respective contributions are those of the authors alone, and not those of any organisation or institution. For convenience, any ranks or appointments given are those held at the time of speaking or writing.

At the time of the conference the Commandant of Sandhurst was Major-General J. F. Deverell; without his support and that of his predecessor, Major-General H. W. R. Pike, the conference would not have taken place; and without the continued support of his successor, Major-General A. G. Denaro, this book would never have been completed. The conference organising committee was chaired by Matthew Midlane, Director of Studies at Sandhurst, with Dr Ian Stewart, Edward Flint, Dr Duncan

Anderson and Dr Stephen Badsey as members. The three departmental heads of the Academic Faculty – Mr John Allen of the Department of Communications Studies, the late Dr John Pimlott of the Department of War Studies, and Dr Francis Toase of the Department of Defence Studies and International Affairs – and their staffs all provided support. Those who spoke at the conference also included John Keegan OBE, Colonel Jonathan Bailey, Gill Samuel, Dr Susan L. Carruthers, Dr David Miller, John Allen, Dr G. D. Sheffield and Professor J. E. Spence. Additional displays and assistance were provided by Martine de Lee, Acting Curator of the Sandhurst Collection, by Andrew Orgill, the Sandhurst Librarian, and by members of the Sandhurst staff. The Conference Facilitator was Phylomena H. Badsey. Sandhurst public relations and protocol were overseen by Major (Retd) I. C. Park-Weir.

The editor's thanks are due for help, both with the conference and with production of this book to Keith Chaffer, Alison Cox, Pat Alner, Yoland Richardson, Christine MacLennan, and particularly Marian Matthews. Supervision of the book was begun at Frank Cass by Robert Easton, and seen to completion by Hilary Hewitt and Andrew Humphrys.

Notes on the Contributors

Dr Stephen Badsey MA (Cantab.) FRHistS is a senior lecturer in the Department of War Studies at RMA Sandhurst. Among his works are *The Gulf War Assessed* (with John Pimlott), *Modern Military Operations and the Media* and *The Media and UN 'Peacekeping' Since the Gulf War*.

Matthew Midlane MA is Director of Studies at RMA Sandhurst.

General Sir Michael Rose KCB CBE DSO QGM ADC Gen. was United Nations Protection Force (UNPROFOR) Commander, Bosnia-Herzogovina Command, 1994–95. He is the author of *Fighting for Peace*.

Lieutenant-Colonel R. C. L. Clifford MBE is Chief of Media Operations at the Headquarters of the NATO Allied Command Europe Rapid Reaction Corps.

Colonel T. J. Wilton MBE was Chief of Information at the Headquarters of the NATO Allied Command Europe Rapid Reaction Corps during its deployment to former Yugoslavia, 1996.

Peter Taylor is a freelance television documentary maker. In 1995 he received the Royal Television Society's prestigious Judges' Award for his lifetime's coverage of the Northern Ireland conflict.

Richard Connaughton MPhil (Cantab.) is an honorary research fellow of the Centre of Defence and International Security Studies, Lancaster University. His books include *Military Intervention in the 1990s* and *The Nature of Future Conflict*.

Kate Adie OBE is the Chief News Reporter for BBC Television. She was the winner of the 1990 BAFTA Richard Dimbleby Award, the Royal

Television Society's News Awards in 1981 and 1987 and the Judges' Award in 1989, and the Monte Carlo International News Award in 1981 and 1990.

Dr Ian Stewart MLitt is a senior lecturer in the Department of Communications Studies at RMA Sandhurst. He is the editor (with Susan L. Carruthers) of *War, Culture and the Media*.

Professor Edward Braun is Professor of Drama at Bristol University. He is the author of *The Director and the Stage* (1982), and was Chairman of the Bristol Old Vic Trust 1987–92, and of the Gulbenkian Enquiry into Director Training 1987–89.

Sean McKnight MA is Deputy Head of the Department of War Studies at RMA Sandhurst, and a Senior Research Fellow at the Institute for the Study of War and Society, De Montfort University.

Brigadier A. M. A. Duncan DSO OBE commanded the Prince of Wales's Own Regiment in Bosnia, 1993, as part of the United Nations Protection Force (UNPROFOR).

Colonel G. R. Coward OBE was United Nations Protection Force (UNPROFOR) Military Spokesman in Sarajevo 1994–95.

D. J. Pickup MPhil FRGS is a senior lecturer in the Department of Defence Studies and International Affairs at RMA Sandhurst, and a lieutenant-commander in the Royal Naval Reserve Public Relations Branch.

Major-General Patrick A. J. Cordingley DSO commanded 7th Armoured Brigade in the 1991 Gulf War. He is the author of *In the Eye of the Storm*.

Professor Philip M. Taylor PhD MA FRHistS is Head of the Institute of Communications Studies at Leeds University. His books include *Munitions of the Mind, War and the Media: Power and Persuasion in the Gulf War* and *Global Communications, International Affairs and the Media since 1945*.

Nik Gowing is an international television news presenter and analyst of the role of the media and information handling in conflict management. He is a governor of the Westminster Foundation for Democracy, a Visiting Fellow in International Relations at Keele University, a board member for the British Association for Central and Eastern Europe, and a member of the Director's Strategy Group at the Royal Institute of International Affairs in London. In 1981 he received a BAFTA award for news coverage.

Dr Philip Towle MA is Director of the Centre of International Studies, Cambridge University, and a Fellow of Queens' College, Cambridge University. His works include *Naval Power in the Indian Ocean, Estimating Foreign Military Power, Pilots and Rebels: The Use of Aircraft in Unconventional War* and *Pundits and Patriots: Lessons from the Gulf War.*

Introduction

STEPHEN BADSEY

THE MEDIA AND INTERNATIONAL SECURITY

It is a considerable understatement that the decade of the 1990s saw a major transformation in all aspects of international security, particularly as they related to Great Britain: whether as part of Europe, or as part of the wider world, or as part of the North Atlantic Alliance and NATO. Many of the changes in Britain's international security role which have taken place since the end of the Cold War, and the likely changes for the future decade, were reflected in the British government's Strategic Defence Review of 1998. These included the introduction of the concept of 'defence diplomacy': a heightened awareness of the national and international political contexts in which military operations may be carried out. Above all, there was a recognition that military activities as an aspect of international security covered, and were likely to cover, a much greater range of functions than fighting wars as they had been traditionally understood in the earlier part of the twentieth century. Although Britain retained the capability to participate in a conflict such as the Gulf War of 1991, such military operations were expected to be the exception rather than the rule. As a reflection of this belief, the restructuring of the British armed forces initiated by the 1998 Strategic Defence Review was specifically intended to provide Britain with an enhanced expeditionary capability.

In the same decade, the role of the international news media on military operations, that is to say the actual day-to-day functioning of armed forces in carrying out their tasks, also took on an altogether new significance. This also was partly a reflection of the changing nature of military deployments. As it happens, the news media which play the largest part on the international scene almost all belong to NATO countries, in particular the United States and, to a lesser extent, Great Britain. Their new significance is especially important on expeditionary

xvii

military operations, also recognised by NATO in 1994 in the 'Partnership for Peace' initiative as the kind in which it would most likely be involved. The same trends and ideas were reflected in the restructuring of the United Nations Organisation in 1997–98. Before 1991 it was extremely rare for any of the five permanent members of the United Nations Security Council (the United States, the Russian Federation, the People's Republic of China, France and Great Britain) to be involved in UN peacekeeping. But, in the course of the 1990s, all except the People's Republic of China sent forces on at least one such operation. Again, this has posed new problems and new issues for the relationship of the news media with such events and organisations. In 1995 the then United Nations Secretary-General, Dr Boutros Boutros-Ghali, went so far as to describe the television news station Cable News Network (CNN) as 'the sixteenth member of the [UN] Security Council'.[1] As many of the chapters in this book reveal, part of the problem has been describing and defining what constitutes that very over-used term 'peacekeeping', about which disagreements between the news media and other institutions have sometimes been a source of friction. One of the justifications for the title of this book is that it deals not only with the military–media relationship, but with the manner in which that relationship has changed – and is changing – in the face of a new international security environment.

The major problem facing anyone seeking to understand these new relationships is that almost every aspect of the very complex equation has changed, and continues to change very rapidly. There is a new political structure and security environment; a new structure to the world's news media organisations; new media technologies; new military technologies; and new concepts and theories of what constitutes military force and its uses. One appropriately baffled American journalist has described the result, for all concerned, as like 'driving fast without a road map'.[2] The most challenging aspect of any discussion of the present and continuing relationship between the media and international security is the size and diversity of the interest groups and academic disciplines which seek to be accommodated within it. There is a strong sense that in the face of political, social and technological developments since the early 1980s, the practical relationships between the media and the armed forces are changing in some fundamental way. This may or may not be part of what has been claimed as a recent and continuing 'revolution in military affairs'. However frustrating this new military–media relationship might be for those involved in it, there is nothing more exciting for those studying it in academia than the thought that we may be present at the creation of a new intellectual discipline, as different from the media studies of the 1980s as nuclear physics has become from the physics of the nineteenth century. This is the justification, if one is needed, for bringing together in this book members of the academic community with practising media and military professionals, in order to better explore the new relationship between the media and international security. The chapters by Professor Philip Taylor and Dr Philip Towle in particular show just how valuable academic contributions to the debate may be.

The perspective of this book and its contributors is a British one. Whether or not there is a specific 'British way in war', there is beyond doubt a specifically British approach to the practical problems of mounting military operations in a wide variety of international security environments; and there is also a specifically British mass news media which go to report on those operations; both of which are often viewed with some admiration by other countries. At the end of the 1990s, it was a point of pride among journalists of the British Broadcasting Corporation (BBC) that they had wrested dominance of the world news television market from CNN, and that the famous or notorious 'CNN effect' should be renamed the 'BBC effect'. But, oddly, while airforces rather than armies and navies have been at the forefront of doctrinal developments since the 1991 Gulf War concerning concepts such as 'information warfare', they have played little part in the corresponding and closely associated debate over the media and military operations. The predominance of contributions from the Army to this book – with the additional welcome chapter from Lieutenant-Commander David Pickup of the Royal Navy – reflects not so much its Sandhurst origins, as the respective interest shown in this issue by the three services in the 1990s.

Readers will also note the large number of references in the individual chapters of this book to the Vietnam War (or Second Indochina War) of 1961–75. It is not surprising that the largest, longest and most controversial war of the second half of the twentieth century should feature heavily in modern preoccupations about international security issues. Still, for those unfamiliar with issues of defence doctrine, the extent to which the experiences and doctrines of the United States dominate NATO and British perspectives may come as something of a revelation. More importantly, the argument that the Vietnam War was in some way lost on the television screens of America remains a live one. Extensive and thorough academic research has failed to show any particular connection, and certainly not the direct causal relationship claimed by many who criticise the American press in the Vietnam War. However, the strength and passion of the convictions of those who were there at the time, that there was *some* causal link between the way the War was reported and the American defeat, remains enough to send dutiful academic researchers back to the sources once again.[3]

THE ROLE OF THE NEWS MEDIA

The role of the mass news media which are independent of direct control by the state is one of the fundamental ideas of Western pluralistic democratic culture. The idea that the media should *not* be under direct government control is very strongly held, for exactly the same reason that many other political systems maintain that they should: that the role of the mass media in influencing and helping form opinions and viewpoints is critical to the functioning of government, and so represents a form of power. Many of the chapters in this book explore the existence and nature of this form of power, including the critical idea of how it is perceived by others. In democracy as in any pluralistic system, it is held that power should be dispersed rather than kept under any central control. This can, and does, create problems when the armed forces of democratic countries are deployed to countries with a different tradition of behaviour towards the media. The simple idea that the international media must abide by the laws of the host country is often appealing to the armed forces themselves, as it relieves them of problems of control and censorship. However, it is in practice usually politically unacceptable to the media and to other institutions, and to public opinion at home. This was seen in the first months of the American and Coalition deployment to Saudi Arabia in 1990 for Operation 'Desert Shield', the defence of Saudi Arabia following on from the Iraqi occupation of Kuwait. Major-General Patrick Cordingley has contributed to this book a stark account of the kind of media pressures he found when commanding a brigade in the Gulf War, and which any commander may reasonably expect to face in the future.

But despite its origins in Western European political thought, it would be wrong to see this notion of the independence of the media as being any longer a purely Western idea, or as part of one competing political theory among many. Rather, the notion of the independence of the press has become a fundamental part of international law, reinforced by a number of pronouncements from the UN and the International Court of Justice, as well as Article 19 of the Universal Declaration of Human Rights. As a symbol of this, the UN itself deliberately chose to promulgate its present declaration on the importance of free and independent media in 1991 at Windhoek in Namibia, rather than in Europe or the Americas. The 'Declaration of Windhoek on Promoting an Independent and Pluralistic African Press' – the 1991 Windhoek Declaration – to which many of the countries of the world are signatories, remains the fundamental statement on the issue in international law.[4]

Theorists of the manner in which the media might influence public opinion in any country prefer to use the term 'propaganda' in an ethically and morally neutral sense – not to represent lying as such, but for any message deliberately created and intended by one group of people to have an influence on another.[5] In this sense, the argument is often made that 'everything is propaganda', and from one perspective that is true, in that very little information generated by the mass media or otherwise is completely value-free. However, most methodologies for approaching this issue distinguish between information provided by an institution which might also have its own general reasons for doing so, as against systematic targeting of one specific group by another in order to produce a specific effect. Generally, the normal function of the mass media in Western democratic pluralist society falls into the first category; and in many countries including Great Britain there is legislation to prevent it from doing otherwise. What can happen when the mass media of any country are harnessed to the specific role of hate propaganda is vividly revealed by Richard Connaughton's contribution to this book, together with some of the problems which this can pose for peacekeeping. In contrast, Peter Taylor's contribution on Northern Ireland – a story with which he has been involved for so long as to himself have become an important part of it – shows the manner in which independent news media can play a positive role over time in bringing about reconciliation and peace.

THE MILITARY, THE MEDIA AND CIVIL SOCIETY

Although much of the media–military relationship of the 1990s was indeed new, much of it also can be better understood with reference to the recent past, and in some cases the lessons of centuries before. The concept of independent media is so critical in Western liberal pluralistic society that it pre-dates universal franchise democracy, in Great Britain itself by about two centuries. Particularly if a broad definition is taken, the origins of the media and of propaganda may be traced far back into history, certainly to pre-Roman times. However, most people would accept the claim of the *Nieuwe Tijdenghen*, published in Antwerp in 1605, as the world's first newspaper, appearing about 150 years after the introduction of printing into Europe. Terms such as 'journalist' appeared about 50 years later, and recognisably modern newspapers of a kind that exercised real political influence made their appearance during the course of the eighteenth century. By no means the first of these, although the most important for much of the nineteenth century, was the *London Daily Universal Register* of 1785, which became *The Times* three years later. Emerging European political thought of this period, which found its expression in the ideals of the American Revolution, placed heavy stress on the concept of 'civil society', and on good government being a constant interaction between the rulers and the ruled. Newspapers were originally founded to help fulfil this function, and to represent various interests within civil society. They were sponsored by advertising, which still forms an important part of the revenue of most of the mass media, and were seen chiefly as a forum for political and social debate. Their origins in this period help explain particularly the unique place of the mass news media in both the constitutional law and political practice of the United States. There remains just one major instrument of United States law on the issue of the free media and their relationship with government – the First Amendment to the Constitution (the first clause of the 1791 Bill of Rights):

> Congress shall make no law respecting an establishment of religion, or prohibiting the free exercise thereof; or abridging the freedom of speech or of the Press; or the right of the people peaceably to assemble and to petition the Government for redress of grievances.

Although there have been other pieces of legislation, including most obviously the Freedom of Information Acts, and lower court rulings, all sides have persistently shied away from forcing either a Supreme Court test case or further Congressional legislation. This means that, while the whole issue of relations between the media and the armed forces in particular is swathed in ambiguity, the balance of the law is definitely on the side of the media. The position is rather different in other democratic countries such as Great Britain, or France, which has specific privacy laws. But, the domination of the United States within NATO, the media world, and as a superpower, has inevitably caused American behaviour to be seen as a model or a benchmark.

In practice the role of the modern news media as representatives of public opinion in this sense has always been controversial. There is a constant debate as to whether the media are in reality free either from the control of governments or of other interest groups. What is quite clear is that the media have never been free from the *influence* of such groups, and indeed this may be seen as part of their purpose. A particular point is the extent that the news media owned largely by international corporations can truly claim to represent public opinion in any one country, such as Great Britain. Dr Ian Stewart's chapter details aspects of the relationship between British governments and the BBC: a highly respected news organisation whose relationship with successive governments has been one of the most useful indicators of the state of British civil society.

The kind of issues and ambiguities revealed are part of the nature of civil society: ideas and functions of power are blurred and ambiguous; there is constant interaction between them, and considerable debate as to how that interaction should function. In short, the role of the media within a pluralistic democratic society is part of a process to be worked through within a set of general parameters, rather than a fixed set of rules. This is one of the arguments for diversity in the mass media. Indeed, an argument which has been used against free and independent media in totalitarian countries is that, since – naturally – the whole of the country is completely united behind the government, it would be artificial to allow separate newspapers, which would in turn foster the creation of an equally artificial dissent. (This argument was actually used by the editor of *Pravda* in Moscow in the middle 1980s in an interview for British television.)

It has been argued plausibly that even Britain's almost unique and notoriously trivial mass-circulation tabloid press has an important role to play in reporting military actions, since it reflects and represents mass popular emotional responses to the events.[6] For those imbued with the basic ideas of classical military thought, there are clearly echoes here of Clausewitz's 'remarkable trinity' of warfare. Even so, the major theorists of warfare and military doctrine of the past are not very helpful concerning the relationship between the mass media and the armed forces. Although the phenomenon of the independent war reporter arose in the West, and has been a constant factor of military operations for more than a century, neither British nor American military thought has addressed this issue in any systematic manner until quite recently. The mention in General Rose's thoughtful chapter of the effects of media coverage 'compressing' the Jominian 'levels of war' goes to the very heart of traditional European and American thinking about warfare and the way in which it is conducted. Classical Clausewitzian thought recognises the vital role of public opinion in any military operation, but Clausewitz himself does not develop this concept into any discussion of the relationship between the armed forces and the media itself. It is, however, interesting to note that Clausewitz was an admirer of the British parliamentary system of his era, recommending it for his native Prussia.[7]

Marxism–Leninism, of course, approaches the issue entirely from the perspective that everything is indeed propaganda, and that controlled mass media are some of the instruments of power to be used by the state, in peace and war. The role of 'agitation and propaganda' (or 'agitprop') in support of military operations is well described in a few pages of V. K. Triandafillov's *The Nature of the Operations of Modern Armies*. Interestingly, Triandafillov also claimed that Soviet propaganda work of his time would be made easier because the Soviet message was based on fact and the self-evident truth of its statements.[8] That *their* propaganda always tells the truth, and that *their* facts are the only accurate facts, is a very common position held by military men, who are often not able to understand the scepticism of the rest of the world, including its news media, towards their position.

One of the new features of modern international security has been the proactive approach of the armed forces towards the media. The sophistication of 'media operations' mounted by the Allied Command Europe Rapid Reaction Corps (the ARRC) detailed by Lieutenant-Colonel Clifford and Colonel Wilton in their invaluable contribution to this book shows just how seriously the matter is taken. It has again been a feature of recent military operations, although once more one with a considerable history, that there have been occasions on which armed forces have needed practical media skills of their own, in order to generate news or information of their own as part of the conduct of a military operation. This can range from propaganda directed against an enemy on the battlefield, to entirely benign posters and radio broadcasts informing victims of a natural disaster of the location of relief and rescue services, or warning of land mines. The capability to produce such simple information materials was a feature of most countries' armed forces during the Second World War. For various reasons including financial economy, the activity was phased out in all major Western countries between the 1950s and the 1970s. It has had to be revived again in quite recent times, chiefly because of the changed nature of probable military operations. At present, by far the largest and best equipped of these military information units is the United States 4th Psychological Operations Group, which was first deployed for the 1991 Gulf War, and which has a wide range of technology and professional skills available to it.

As several of the chapters in this book make clear, it is well understood that such activities often need to be co-ordinated with the otherwise separate issue of the armed forces' relationship with the media. This can be an area of some tension. To suggest that the media should investigate for themselves rather than accept military statements at face value can seem to the armed forces like an accusation that they are lying, or that they do not know best how to deal with difficult circumstances. When this happens, issues of military pride and a sense of integrity can come to the front very rapidly, to be met by an equally strong pride and professionalism from the members of media, who have been known to react very badly if they consider that their trust has been breached or that they have been 'managed' too strongly. General Rose, in his memoirs *Fighting for Peace*, has given a candid account of his own outraged response to one reporter who suggested in print that he had been less than truthful.[9] Kate

Adie's thought-provoking contribution to this book also sets out some of the problems faced from the other side by a top reporter when dealing with the armed forces.

So, on operations, armed forces have found themselves generating information in two ways: both directly through their own information units, and indirectly by interaction with the national and international media. This kind of information campaign was pursued very successfully by the United Nations Implementation Force (or IFOR) to former Yugoslavia following the 1995 Dayton Accord. It was obviously of critical importance to the success of the IFOR mission that the two messages being put out, by direct means to the people themselves, and by indirect means to the media, supported each other rather than conflicting.[10] The contrast between the approaches to the media in former Yugoslavia by the original United Nations Protection Force (UNPROFOR) of 1992–95 and by IFOR constitutes an important case-study. IFOR – benefiting greatly from UNPROFOR's previous experience – had the strategy and the resources, and above all the political and military context, to pursue a successful media campaign as part of its wider campaign of bringing peace and stability to the region. This is in no way a criticism of UNPROFOR, which worked under conditions that often verged on the impossible. Colonel Gary Coward's chapter reveals both the commitment of the UNPROFOR media staff, and the problems under which they laboured compared to the later IFOR. Brigadier Alaistair Duncan's chapter, which draws directly on his own experience as a battalion commander with UNPROFOR, shows the very high level of professionalism that was brought to the task.

THE MILITARY–MEDIA RELATIONSHIP

In the absence of a detailed tradition in military theory on the media, and in keeping with the broader concepts of the nature of democratic civil society, much of the new relationship between armed forces and the news media has developed through practice and pragmatism, and through historical experience. If there could be said to be a fundamental position among British – or international – news reporters of military operations, it may be described as an obvious desire to report the news and the facts as best they can, but also to be accepted as part of the wider institutional structure. This includes the fact that international news media organisations, and their reporting and editorial staff, are no different from the rest of humanity in their relationship to the core values of international law and conduct. United Nations peacekeeping deployments have received considerable practical support from international news media teams. But equally, the international news media can also be very critical indeed if they feel that a peacekeeping operation is not living up to their own expectations. This was a persistent problem of all sides in the UNPROFOR deployment to the states that constituted the former Yugoslavia. In Kate Adie's chapter of this book, her vivid account of experiences in Bosnia is a reflection of the close associations and the tensions that can form between the reporters and soldiers in such circumstances; while Nik Gowing's summing up of the position on all sides over several such operations shows just how deep-rooted opinions can become.[11]

Notoriously, reporters are only as good as their sources, and maintaining reasonable working relations with those sources is part of their skill. When reporting in dangerous situations, and particularly with armed forces of their own nationality – or in a special case such as UN peacekeepers – media professionals are concerned not to reveal anything which might threaten their own forces. Naturally, this position could be abused by armed forces, who might argue that *any* reporting of their activities is potentially life-threatening. This argument is at least as old as the American Civil War (1861–65), in which it was used unsuccessfully by Major-General William T. Sherman, who did not wish actions such as his burning of the city of Atlanta to be widely publicised.

If there can be said to be a fundamental military position in respect of the media, in the past it has usually been a desire for secrecy and security, reinforced by a considerable array of punitive military regulations. In reality, these regulations have never stopped senior officers developing what have often been close informal contacts with the media, as part of the general interaction of society. General Rose's description of his own early contacts with Kate Adie and the BBC are part of a tradition of such relationships with news reporters going back well into the nineteenth century. These informal relationships, built up at home and in peacetime, can often be militarily valuable on operations. The general point to emerge from all this deliberation, and the experience behind it, is that any absolute position on both sides is, and always has been, unrealistic. Military attempts to claim that media coverage is in all cases a form of spying for the enemy are as ridiculous, and as politically naive and ineffective, as media claims that they have an absolute right to unlimited access, and to report whatever they wish. Between these two extreme positions lies the real world in which military relations with the media actually take place.

The whole issue of the impact of the media on military operations – including warfare in its traditional sense – has its origins chiefly in the double revolution in communications which was a feature of the wider

Industrial Revolution in the first half of the nineteenth century. The development of railways and telegraph communications transformed much of the industrialised world, and in particular the manner in which it fought its wars. Indeed, a recurring part of the story of the new relationship between the media and international security has been the manner in which technological developments have upset old and established certainties and relationships. In 1851 Reuters set up the world's first major news agency in London, based on the telegraph. The very idea of 'news' in the modern sense came from this development; and the belief that reporting from the battlefield to the newspaper might take place fast enough to have some impact on the conduct of the war itself, in particular by giving information to the enemy, or by provoking public demands for a change in strategy, became a considerable military concern in the second half of the nineteenth century. The Crimean War (1853–56) earned William Howard Russell of *The Times* the title of the world's first 'war correspondent', something that he actively disliked. The American Civil War may be counted as the first war fought by a literate democracy, and the Franco-Prussian War (1870–71) probably counts as the first war in which the speed of reporting from the battlefield became a critical issue for newspapers. The newspaper term 'scoop', meaning to report important news faster than anyone else, dates from only a decade later.[12]

By the end of the nineteenth century, governments and their armed forces were convinced that some kind of control over the media would be necessary in wartime, chiefly on grounds of security. Very much as a century later, there was fear that newspaper-owning magnates could exercise political power beyond the ability of governments to control. Indeed, the American newspaper tycoon William Randolph Hurst (on whose life the film *Citizen Kane* is loosely based), did much to provoke the Spanish–American War of 1898. The 1899 Hague Convention on warfare made the first recognition of the duality of the military–media relationship: reporters would receive non-combatant status with armies, but only if they were registered or accredited. The idea of formal military censorship in wartime, which had been developing in the second half of the nineteenth century, became part of legislation in many countries including Britain just prior to the First World War. Again, one of the ambiguities of the relationship which has persisted to the present day is that both government legislation and military regulations provided a wide range of powerful controls and punishments for members of the armed forces who dealt openly with the media; but in practice many senior officers maintained close contacts with the press, and its power was such that only very rarely were such regulations actually enforced.

The military–media experiences for the First and Second World Wars were remarkably similar, as might be expected of two very large industrialised wars fought barely 20 years apart, in each case for the survival of both state and society. The whole philosophy of both wars was the harnessing of every aspect of British society to the war effort, and the media were no exception. It is, however, important that the harnessing of the news media as an arm of state propaganda was negotiated and controlled at high political levels, and for broad strategic aims. Very much as the experience of Vietnam convinced the American armed forces that the media were suspect, so the late nineteenth-century experience had also left a residue of prejudice against the media on the part of military authorities. In both wars it took the British military authorities about two years to accept the idea of reporters and cameramen with the fighting forces (an experience shared by most other belligerents), and even then only under strict control and censorship. The reporters themselves, anxious both to win the confidence of the military authorities and to play their part in winning the war, practised self-censorship to a degree that, with hindsight, many found unsettling.[13]

The onset of the Cold War, and for Britain the retreat from Empire, meant that, on the whole, the same basic approach continued on all sides towards the role of the news media in wartime. In particular, issues involving the media remained the business of the higher levels of politics and command, and there was an assumption of a shared interest – or patriotism – between the national government and the national media which underlay any immediate disagreement or confrontation. It was also important for Britain that, during this entire period, no government committed British armed forces to any major military operation which did not enjoy a reasonable level of popular support, and an equally reasonable chance of a politically acceptable victory – with the single massive exception of the 1956 Suez Crisis.[14]

The big change came in the 1960s with the emergence of television to replace newspapers as the dominant news medium, and with the American experience in Vietnam, which was to prove so influential on British thinking. Just as changes in journalism and politics weakened the older assumption of shared values, so changes in military and civil communications technology meant that reporting from the battlefield could now affect the details of military operations as well as strategy and politics. The armed forces became increasingly concerned about their image in the media, and rightly so. As Professor Edward Braun's chapter, analysing various fictional portrayals of the Army on British television in this period shows, the relationship between this image and political reality had become a close and complex one. By the 1980s, and in many ways in contradiction to their own experience in the 1982 Falklands War, the

British armed forces had come to share the American belief that television in particular was so powerful that some kind of direct military control over war reporting was once more necessary. What is important is that news media organisations also accepted this view, and that the result was the voluntary media 'pool' system seen in the 1991 Gulf War, and mentioned throughout this book.[15]

Also, as reflected in many of the chapters of this book, the relationship between the armed forces and the media during the 1991 Gulf War remains one of controversy and debate, and again rightly so. But as Sean McKnight points out in his thoughtful chapter, the debate has been of a rather different nature in Britain than in the United States, reflecting a different experience which was, generally speaking, happier for all sides. This chapter is also concerned to challenge a theory which grew up with considerable speed following the Gulf War, and which has now reached quite outspoken proportions within academia, of some kind of conspiracy between the British – or American – armed forces and the media to deceive their own people into war. This chapter rightly points out the contrast between the self-investigation and self-criticism of the news media over their behaviour in covering the Gulf War, and the remarkable indifference of the Western academic world to its failures in understanding the nature of the Iraqi armed forces before the war. To this may be added an almost wilful refusal in some cases to understand what has happened to both military and media technology and its uses since the Vietnam era, and the implications of the emergence of the new relationship between the armed forces and the media.

Towards the end of the 1990s, there was some speculation among media professionals and academics that a major change in Western public consumption of the mass media might be taking place, comparable in importance to the eclipse of newspapers by television in the 1960s. This change was the emergence of 'new media' or 'new news', including such formats as local or regional 'talk radio' stations, daytime television chat shows (especially for cable and satellite multi-channel television), magazines deliberately designed for niche audiences and, above all, the increasing use of the Internet for news and communication. Whereas the trend in the 1960s had been towards homogeneity and large news media providers, the trend of the 1990s was towards fragmentation and specialised media, and increasingly towards targeting the political and social elite by news providers.

The importance of the new media in military operations was confirmed by the Kosovo crisis of March–June 1999. The ethnic cleansing of Kosovar Albanians from the province by the armed forces of the rump Yugoslav Republic (Serbia and Montenegro) produced from NATO its largest military response since the 1991 Gulf War. Again, the NATO action was very much in keeping with the changes in thinking about likely future deployments that had been discussed earlier in the decade. The use of the Internet (and other methods of electronic communications including fax transmissions) during a war dated back, at least, to the Iraqi occupation of Kuwait in 1990. But, as the Yugoslav authorities progressively suppressed the independent media – including radio stations and newspapers – within Serbia itself, the Internet became perhaps the chief means of communication and propaganda on both sides, leading to the Kosovo crisis being characterised as 'The War of the Web'.

The level of 'interpenetrability' of information created on all sides by this phenomenon was understood and predicted, but it was nevertheless remarkable to observe. While military action continued on both sides, an outpouring of political statements and rhetoric was exchanged daily through both the new and the old media. On 31 March, almost at the start of the conflict, the British Defence Secretary George Robertson announced at the daily Whitehall Press briefing on the crisis that the Internet website created by the British government (the Ministry of Defence and the Foreign and Commonwealth Office in combination) had received 150,000 'hits' (enquiries) in the previous 24 hours: 1,400 of those 'hits' had come from within Yugoslavia itself. Part of the British response was to create a Serbian-language version of this website.

Other than the new importance of the Internet, the NATO experience confirmed many of the conclusions about military–media relations which had emerged during the 1990s. It was clear that the war for 'public opinion' would be critical for both sides. As part of the propaganda war, the phenomenon of journalists from coalition countries being allowed to report (under very closely controlled conditions) from the enemy capital city under attack, which had appeared so unusually in the Gulf War, was seen again from Belgrade. In some cases this even involved the same people, notably the BBC's veteran John Simpson, who had reported from Baghdad in 1991. The preference of the United States in particular for air attacks rather than ground forces was also apparent once more, together with the difficulties for the news media in reporting impartially on such attacks, and in reconciling conflicting versions of events. Also as often before, any tensions between NATO and the international mass media – any media problems, as the military would view the issue – were secondary symptoms of military problems in strategy and achieving their desired objectives. Or, from the perspective of the media, they were doing their job well by investigating, and asking the hard questions.

After the experiences and changes of the decade which began with the Gulf War and ended with Kosovo, the lasting impression of relations

Introduction

during conflict between Western military organisations such as NATO and the international news media was of much better understanding and ease with each other in 1999 than in 1991, and much was learned on all sides about the new realities of military–media relations. But the conflicts and difficulties which are an essential part of the relationship between the military and the media have also remained much in evidence.

NOTES

1. Quoted in L. Minear, C. Scott and T. G. Weiss, *The News Media, Civil War and Humanitarian Action* (London and Boulder, CO: Lynne Rienner, 1996), p. 4.
2. W. P. Strobel, *Late-Breaking Foreign Policy: The News Media's Influence on Peace Operations* (Washington, DC: United States Institute for Peace Press, 1997), p. 57. See also C. Bellamy, *Knights in White Armour: The New Art of War and Peace* (London: Hutchinson, 1996), pp. 149–93; A. Parsons, *From Cold War To Hot Peace* (London: Michael Joseph, 1995), pp. 183–259.
3. See, for example, B. Bond, *The Pursuit of Victory: From Napoleon to Saddam Hussein* (Oxford: Oxford University Press, 1996), pp. 189–90; and M. Hudson and J. Stanier, *War and the Media* (Thrupp: Sutton, 1997), pp. 99–118.
4. 'Declaration of Windhoek on Promoting an Independent and Pluralistic African Press', United Nations Department of Public Information DPI/1142-40979, October 1991.
5. For a discussion of these issues, see, for example, the standard textbook G. S. Jowett and V. O'Donnell, *Propaganda and Persuasion* (Newbury Park, CA and London: Sage, 1992), *passim*.
6. M. Shaw, *Civil Society and the Media in Global Crises: Representing Distant Violence* (London: Pinter, 1996), p. 120.
7. C. Bassford, *Clausewitz in English: The Reception of Clausewitz in Britain and America 1815–1945* (Oxford and New York: Oxford University Press, 1994), p. 37.
8. V. K. Triandafillov (trans. W. A. Burhams), *The Nature of the Operations of Modern Armies* (London: Frank Cass, 1994, original edn 1929), pp. 163–4.
9. M. Rose, *Fighting For Peace* (London: Harvill, 1998), pp. 64–5.
10. See P. Combelles Siegel, *Target Bosnia: Integrating Information Activities in Peace Operations* (Washington, DC: CCRP, 1998), *passim*.
11. For some of these complexities, see also J. Gow, R. Paterson and A. Preston (eds), *Bosnia by Television* (London: BFI Publishing, 1996), *passim*.
12. For a summary, see P. M. Taylor, *Munitions of the Mind: War Propaganda from the Ancient World to the Nuclear Age* (London: Patrick Stephens, 1990), pp. 109–63.
13. For an overview, see M. L. Sanders and P. M. Taylor, *British Propaganda During the First World War* (London: Macmillan, 1982); G. S. Messinger, *British Propaganda and the State in the First World War* (Manchester: Manchester University Press, 1992); N. J. Cull, *Selling War: The British Propaganda Campaign Against American 'Neutrality' in World War II* (Oxford and New York: Oxford University Press, 1995).

14. See T. Shaw, *Eden, Suez and the Mass Media: Propaganda and Persuasion During the Suez Crisis* (London and New York: I. B. Tauris, 1996), and Susan L. Carruthers, *Winning Hearts and Minds: British Governments, the Media and Colonial Counter-Insurgency 1944–1960* (London and New York: Leicester University Press, 1995).
15. For a summary, see also S. Badsey, 'The Media War', in J. Pimlott and S. Badsey (eds), *The Gulf War Assessed* (London: Arms & Armour, 1992), pp. 219–46.

Part One:

The Media and Military Operations

The Media and International Security

GENERAL SIR MICHAEL ROSE

When the British Army went peacekeeping in Aden in the 1960s it was all a very simple business. In those days we were issued, if I remember rightly, with a tin helmet, a pair of starched shorts, a Lee Enfield rifle and a banner. When in trouble we unfolded the banner which had written across it 'Disperse or We Fire', and every time we fired the troublemakers always used to disperse! It was all very easy. Thirty years later peace-keepers drop bombs from F18 aircraft, and what happens then is that they get taken hostage. Life therefore has become considerably more complex. When I was asked to write the chapter opening this book, I tried to analyse in my mind exactly what was the fundamental relationship that existed between the media and those involved in peacekeeping.

The first time that I had personally been exposed to public scrutiny through the media was at the Iranian Embassy siege in London in 1981, when I was in charge of SAS operations. I was being reported on by a young cub reporter who had spent many days on top of a gantry observing the siege, and it was her first big exposure as a journalist as well. Her name was Kate Adie. She is now the chief news reporter for BBC tele-vision, and both the things she said about me at the time, and the things that I subsequently said about her, clearly have caused us both to prosper in our respective careers! Thus, if for no other reason than personal advancement, it may not be a bad thing for the military and the media to work with each other on military operations.

More seriously, I spent 12 months in Bosnia, 1994–95, as UNPROFOR (United Nations Protection Force) commander, being variously portrayed by the world's media: as a John Buchan-style hero who single-handedly saved the city of Sarajevo; as someone who presided over war criminals; and as the man who lent a helping hand to the Serbs. One photograph published in the British newspaper the *Mail on Sunday* at the time, of me supposedly retreating in the face of threats from the Serbs, was actually me calling in airstrikes against them! With media treatment like this, it is not perhaps obvious why an honest, simple soldier trying to do a difficult job should ever have anything to do with the media. The temptation must be not to sup with the Devil, however long the spoon. Nevertheless, I think that the very opposite attitude among military commanders is needed in today's world. For today, the military and the media are inextricably linked, not just in our personal careers, as I somewhat frivolously suggested, but in the whole way our different operations are carried out. For good or ill, the fourth estate has an undoubted influence on modern society which is quite different from the situation that existed before the Crimean War (1853–56). The media must now be seen by all soldiers as being centrally important to all our activities.

As Nik Gowing has already pointed out in his very thoughtful and well-researched paper for Harvard University,[1] although the media do not always have an automatic impact on the formulation of foreign policy, a close relationship does exist between the two. If images of terrible human suffering are presented to the world by television and newspapers and world leaders appear to be doing nothing to alleviate such human suffering, then a very strong moral message is being sent that 'something must be done'. This represents the moral imperative which confronts all democracies that have an interest in furthering the condition of humankind and in maintaining international peace.

If the humanitarian emergency is the result of a natural disaster such as a volcano or landslide, then it is a comparatively straightforward matter for nations and privately funded organisations to do something about it. If the disaster is the result of a confused conflict whereby a country has collapsed into a situation of civil war, such as we saw in former Yugoslavia 1992–95, then there will also be many reasons for not getting involved. These are what Sir Michael Howard calls *raisons d'état*. It may be that taking action will be too expensive in terms of both human and financial resources, or that no national interest may be involved, or that there is no clear exit strategy. Those in power, aware of these many different considerations weighing upon them, will often look for compromise solutions rather than all-out commitment. To conceal the limited scope of action available to them and to assuage public opinion, they will of course make powerful but meaningless calls for action in the UN which they secretly are not prepared to back themselves. It is also true to say that those in opposition will use any perceived public inaction as a stick with which to beat a government, and they will focus on any media images which help their cause. By using such media material, opposition parties in democracies, which do not have the same sort of responsibilities as the government, can whip up a great deal of public emotion for intervention in order to portray the government as weak. It is also the case that those within the theatre of operations who represent narrow sectarian interests, either political, religious, nationalist or a combination of all, will also seek to create false images in order to gain sympathy for their cause. All this places a great responsibility on the media. As Oscar Wilde once said, 'truth is never pure and rarely simple'.

One very specific point about the media in international security operations is that one of the differences which now exists between a General War and Operations Other Than War (OOTW) is the compression that occurs between the strategic level, the operational level and the tactical level.[2] When a soldier of a forward unit in a fire trench speaks to a media person in a General War, what they say to each other does not usually have major strategic impact, but it certainly does in the form of conflict we have seen in Bosnia. What happens on the ground can, often in a very short period of time, be seen around the world and debated on the floor of the UN Security Council. Often partial, manipulated or incorrect snippets of information are transmitted around the world, and these are used to develop policy which in turn affects those on the ground working for peace. We have to learn to live with this compression, but it places a tremendous onus on governments to delay policy making until a full and accurate picture has emerged.

Therefore, because the form of conflict in the world today is changing, the military and the media need to change their approaches to public information policy. In the chaotic 'new world disorder' that confronts us, the issues being fought over are often more ancient than the personal memories of the people in the region and remain wholly incomprehensible to outsiders. Distortion and manipulation are not only a way of life but a means of survival. In these circumstances morality has no meaning. The traditional image of the honest hack chewing on a stubby pencil and doing his best to report the truth is today as hackneyed and inaccurate as the press images of me as the hero of Sarajevo were during my time in Bosnia.

In the search for a new approach, the first thing we have to do is establish whether there can ever be common cause: common goals between the media and the instruments of authority which are trying to create conditions of security and order, for example the United Nations and its peacekeepers who are tasked with carrying out the international mandate. In a General War, where a country is fighting for its survival, the media are clearly much more likely to give support to its armed forces. This even happened in the Falklands Conflict of 1982. But, in Operations Other Than War, where the national interest is less evident and the issues are less focused, media reporting is likely to be based on different moral and

5

political perceptions. For example, the media may not wish to support the sort of humanitarian relief and peacekeeping mission that we have seen in Bosnia, if they believe that such a peacekeeping mission may, if successful, ultimately lead to unjust peace or the division of the country. Equally, the moral basis for the delivery of humanitarian aid may not be supported by the media and international community when such aid might serve to prolong the war.

These moral issues were evident in a discussion that I once had in Bosnia with a reporter from a national UK newspaper, who personally declared to me that he was actively seeking to undermine the mission of the United Nations in Bosnia by falsely describing the situation. He took this position because he believed that it was the moral duty of the West to fight for the Bosnian Muslim people. I asked him whether his policy might not entail many more deaths than were actually occurring in the country. He said that he didn't care about that at all, as an unjust peace simply could not be allowed. Such an attitude was clearly in direct opposition to the UN peacekeeping mission, and the UN needs to understand how to combat such attitudes.

In this connection, I believe that no human being, particularly one who is a member of a stable, orderly, civilised society, in which human rights, the dignity of men and women and of both large and small nations, are respected, can escape or walk away from his responsibility for helping less fortunate nations and people to achieve the same kind of standards of security and civilisation that we currently enjoy. I take these words, quite deliberately, from the Charter of the United Nations, which in its time has been an enormous influence for order and good in the world, signed and made effective in San Francisco on 24 October 1945. Not even journalists can exclude themselves from this moral obligation, or from supporting the human race!

Whatever the moral basis of reporting, it is clear that reporting by the media is going to be extremely important in the sort of conditions that we have seen prevailing in former Yugoslavia, where nations collapse and deep-rooted problems arise. We live in a world today of some 4.5 billion people, of whom roughly 1 billion have never seen a doctor or received any medical treatment; 1 billion do not know how to read or write; 1 billion do not have safe drinking water or an adequate diet. By the year 2050 projections based on economic growth and agricultural resources indicate that there will be 10 billion people in the world, and that the proportion of the world's population living in such deprived and oppressed conditions will be much greater. At the moment we see the problems that we have around us becoming increasingly hard to solve by the political and purely military means that we have at our disposal. In the future I believe that it is going to be impossible. Alliances and military technology simply will not be able to solve the problems that we are going to face in the next 50 years or so. It will be people's attitudes which count, and the influence of the media in this area will be critical.

Nor should media reporting ever provide the sole basis for policy making, although such reporting will always play an important part in alerting the world to injustice and human disaster. It is too haphazard and inconsistent in the quality of its coverage and reporting. For example, I was in Bangladesh in 1991, arriving one night in the middle of a tropical storm. When I woke up next morning there were 250,000 people dead as the result of the cyclone and tidal waves that swept the country, and another 250,000 people died of starvation or disease in the next few months. This disaster received little international media attention and therefore little aid. On the other hand, the humanitarian disaster in Northern Iraq – not only man-made but, in numerical terms, small in comparison – received enormous international aid because of media attention. Should we allow our foreign policy to be based on the 'CNN factor'? I believe not.

If the media can be an influence for good, then clearly the reverse is also true. Mischievous, propagandist or distorted reporting will always further division and conflict. When emotions are being stirred, distorted images of suffering make it very difficult for policy to be developed on a reasonable basis. Looking back at my own year in Sarajevo, I had absolutely no difficulty with the government of Bosnia operating a propaganda machine. After all, we in this country had a propaganda machine in the Second World War when *we* were struggling for survival. But, I found it surprising when considerable elements of the press in Bosnia knowingly became parts of that propaganda machine. Of course, no one denies the right of journalists (or anyone else for that matter) to question policies that are being implemented, or possess their own moral point of view, but they should at least see facts as they are, and live up to their responsibilities, by not indulging in smear tactics and deliberate distortion of fact in order to attain their aims. That, after all, was the practice of Goebbels.

Turning now to the role of the UN: Ralph Bunche, who received the Nobel Peace Prize in 1950 for bringing about the cease-fire and armistice between Israel and the Arab states of the Middle East, said that the UN was reason's voice which allowed radical change to take place without upheaval. But reason's voice also comes through the organs of the media, and the UN, without the media, is not going to have the same effect in places where violent upheaval is taking place. However, in these circumstances, the debate about the means used, the extent to which force should be used in the pursuit of the mandate, and the categorical imperatives which exist between the political and humanitarian objectives will all need much clearer definition in the future.

For the first 45 years of the UN's existence, its peacekeeping missions took place against a background of political consent. The UN acted as a third party which was required to intervene as a mediator by the two parties to a conflict. In this environment, peacekeepers were able to act impartially with a common aim in view. The media capabilities of the UN have become geared to such a benign environment. Now that public information officers are being confronted with a much more hostile environment in which to operate, one in which it is very difficult to make moral judgements, and where the information database is changing very rapidly indeed, the qualities of the UN media official operating at the high operations end of the modern 'spectrum of peacekeeping' need to be very different from those who are used to cruising the corridors of the UN building in New York. I saw some dramatic demonstrations of this while serving in Bosnia.

Yasushi Akashi, the UN envoy to Bosnia, well understood the requirement for such a change. He was the person who brought about, rather unexpectedly in some people's judgement, the peaceful resolution of the situation in Cambodia only a year earlier. He did this by using the media to talk directly to the people, to change attitudes, and to win the initiative and political high ground from the Khmer Rouge. He understood extremely well the fact that the media were central to everything that we tried to do in Bosnia. He therefore attempted to import the same mechanisms and people that he had used in Cambodia. I am sad to say that most of them did not succeed in Bosnia! There, we needed people who were able to withstand the enormous pressures and hazards of dealing day-to-day with the media, and explain short-term set-backs against the logic of a long-term strategy. To do that, people have to have experience of operations themselves, be used to a battlefield environment, and have the confidence to make immediate decisions and stick to them. Journalists are extremely good at thinking on their feet, however wrong history subsequently proves them to be. Apart from anything else, many of them have greater operational experience of war environments than the UN public information officers. The media are always going to be ahead of the UN in gathering information, and they can always disrupt the UN public information machine by asking difficult questions.

In Bosnia, in an attempt to solve the problems caused by the inadequacy of the UN public information machine, I brought in military people to run the public relations apparatus. They were the sort of people who had commanded on operations in Northern Ireland and who could

8

slug it out on the floor in a welter of accusation and counter-accusation whilst at the same time keeping in sight the purpose of the mission. I also allowed UNPROFOR personnel to provide members of the media with transport and communications facilities so that they could see and report things for themselves, rather than exclude them from UN vehicles and locations as had been the case before I arrived. What we never did was to try to put the media under UN control. That was not my purpose. What I was trying to suggest is that security forces should provide facilities in the shape of the transport resources, communications and, if necessary, security. Such a step will, in spite of some mischievous reporting, ultimately serve the cause of peace, for in the end the truth will always be able to overcome lies.

The same criticism of insufficiencies can also be levelled at national public relations structures, aid organisations and others involved in peacekeeping and humanitarian aid delivery. Although the politicians of some nations very ably supported their governments' policies towards Bosnia, in the UN there was a surprising lack of political support on occasion for the operation on the ground. It is clear that there needs to be an organised, coherent public information campaign especially among the troop-contributing nations, so that the inevitable criticisms concerning the ineffectiveness of the UN can be dealt with.

In conclusion, perhaps the world's first great war reporter was Thucydides. In his account of the Peloponnesian War, he wrote something which I have always taken as a fundamental principle, and on which I have operated throughout my military career. That is, that the first man who comes and reports from the battlefield is always the first one who ran away, and to be wary of the message that he is carrying! Journalists produce the first accounts of any military operation, and I have always treated their accounts in exactly the same way.

NOTES

1. Nik Gowing, 'Real-Time Television Coverage of Armed Conflicts and Diplomatic Crises: Does it Pressure or Distort Foreign Policy Decisions?', working paper 94-1, Joan Shorenstein Barone Center on the Press, Politics and Public Policy (Cambridge, MA: Harvard University, 1994).
2. These are technical military terms in British and NATO doctrine. 'General War' refers to a state of conflict in which the existence of a civilisation is at risk, such as in the Second World War. 'Operations Other Than War' (OOTW) is a comparatively recent coinage, officially introduced in 1994, used to categorise military operations short of actual war. The 'strategic level' refers to the military level of command which deals directly with political issues and orders coming down to it from above. It then formulates responses which are

9

passed to the 'operational level' of command, which plans and conducts actual battles, and in turn its orders are passed on to the 'tactical level', the troops in the field. The point is that in British military doctrine political orders should have no direct effect below the strategic level, and in turn actions taken at the tactical level should have no direct political implications.

2

Media Operations and the ARRC

LIEUTENANT-COLONEL R. C. L. CLIFFORD AND COLONEL T. J. WILTON

> NATO is exceptionally dependent upon positive public opinion. Political will to perform any task can never be expected unless the publics are clearly informed and sympathetic to our endeavours.
>
> General George A. Joulwan, US Army,
> NATO Supreme Allied Commander Europe (SACEUR)
> 1993–97

This chapter will examine how the ARRC (Allied Command Europe Rapid Reaction Corps) intends to achieve, and maintain in the future, the positive public opinion necessary to support the political will so vital to NATO operations. It will examine the concept of 'media operations' (or 'media ops') and look at how HQ ARRC is preparing itself for the media wars of the twenty-first century. It will chart the ARRC's progress from the hard lessons of IFOR (NATO's peace implementation force) in former Yugoslavia in 1995–96, through the following year of review when HQ ARRC refined its concepts and philosophy. But first it is necessary to look at what the ARRC actually is. Only by knowing its history, its original design and the influences and experiences that have shaped it, can its current thinking be fully understood.

THE ALLIED COMMAND EUROPE RAPID REACTION CORPS

NATO's new strategic concept for the aftermath of the Cold War, which outlined the overall concept for the Alliance, and provided a basis upon which to restructure NATO's military forces, was agreed at the Rome Summit in 1991. The emphasis moved away from the large in-place formations of the Cold War and instead focused on smaller, more flexible forces to be used in support of NATO's crisis management strategy. The resulting military structure is made up of immediate and rapid reaction forces, main defence forces and augmentation forces.

The ARRC is the land component of the rapid reaction forces. It is multinational, and comprises staff, assigned military formations and representatives from 14 nations. It supports SACEUR's crisis management options through the following range of activities:

- Deterrence, to demonstrate capability and resolve during peace and, during crisis, to show collective political will and solidarity through timely deployment;
- Reinforcement, to deploy rapidly in support of collective defence under Article Five of the North Atlantic Charter; and
- Military Operations, ranging from Peace Support Operations (PSO) through to combat operations, anywhere as directed by SACEUR.

Demonstration of Resolve

The very existence of the ARRC as a multinational corps demonstrates NATO's resolve to counter any aggression against a member state. It is expected to deploy within days to a potential trouble spot, to assist in-place national forces or delay an aggressor until the arrival of augmentation forces. After successfully conducting land operations in the former Yugoslavia, the ARRC's mission was rewritten to reflect the conduct of PSO as a core requirement, and the geographical constraints of Allied Command Europe (ACE) were removed.[1] Essentially, the ARRC must now be prepared to conduct military operations, from war fighting to PSO, anywhere as ordered by SACEUR in support of NATO's crisis management strategy.

The ARRC consists of a standing multinational headquarters (HQ) under the permanent operational command of SACEUR, and ten assigned divisions together with corps troops, provided by 13 nations, and from which the required force package for a particular mission can be chosen.[2] This is multinationality at the operational level, something that did not exist in NATO previously. In Cold War Europe, national corps were to fight along side each other as distinct entities under a NATO 'Army Group'. The operational level was a national responsibility. With the formation of the ARRC, this became a NATO responsibility. But there was no NATO history, background, experience nor doctrine on which to draw. Additionally, there is now a requirement for reaction forces doctrine, again where none previously existed. HQ ARRC now finds itself developing concepts and doctrine for both multinational corps level[3] and reaction forces operations, for combat and PSO. This has also opened up for scrutiny whole areas previously outside the core military staff functions of 'G1' to 'G4',[4] including such activities as civil affairs, civil–military co-operation, media operations and the conduct of operational level public information (PI).

The ARRC Blooded

While all this was being debated in HQ ARRC, matters on the world stage, and in the Balkans in particular, reached the point at which NATO was called upon to deploy ground troops into Bosnia and Herzegovina. On 20 December 1995, following the Dayton Peace Accord, HQ ARRC deployed to Sarajevo to assume command of the land component of the NATO-led IFOR, for Operation 'Joint Endeavour'. In a little over nine months, it had successfully implemented the military aspects of the General Framework Agreement for Peace (GFAP) established at Dayton, and provided a secure environment for the first post-war elections, which were held on 14 September 1996. The Implementation Force became the Stabilisation Force (SFOR) in November 1996, and HQ ARRC returned to its usual home in Germany. The deployment was a seminal experience, and one that has coloured much of the ARRC's thinking since, particularly in the area of information and media operations. It was also a turning-point in military–media relationships, and sparked a radical re-think of PI and operational media handling in NATO and in many of its member nations, not least in the UK.

THE IFOR EXPERIENCE

> The deployment of the ARRC to Bosnia in 1995 is now
> an important precedent and paradigm of the new business
> of media handling.
>
> Nik Gowing[5]

As the IFOR land component command, HQ ARRC was based in Sarajevo. During the preparations for and early stages of the deployment, it became apparent that not only would the media be taking a very keen interest in events, but the information that was imparted would impact on the political leaders in the area, the former warring factions, and the indigenous population. How this information was handled could significantly impact on the success of the mission. This section describes how HQ ARRC developed its information campaign doctrine 'in theatre', and implemented and refined its information-handling skills.

The Information Campaign

The overall information campaign was defined as 'The co-ordinated application of Media Operations,[6] Psychological Operations[7] (PSYOPS) and Civil–Military Co-operation (CIMIC)'.[8] The success of the information campaign required close and continuous co-ordination between Public Information (PI) and PSYOPS. This closeness initially caused some difficulties. Although there was clear doctrine on how to use PI and PSYOPS in war fighting, as discrete but co-ordinated entities, no such doctrine existed for peace support operations. However, as only 'White PSYOPS'[9] were used, the relationship caused less concern than might otherwise have been the case, and could be much closer. The doctrine for an information campaign therefore evolved throughout the operation.

The aim of the information campaign was to seize and maintain the initiative by imparting timely and effective information within COMARRC's (Commander ARRC) intent. It was based on the principle that information was a major lever, albeit with the potential for collateral damage, and that it was to defend IFOR's 'centre of gravity', which was deemed to be world opinion on the outcome of the IFOR mission.[10]

The information campaign was to be transparent, commensurate with the requirements for operational security, and proactive. It was to be based on facts, not assumptions or speculation. When mistakes were made they were admitted. Common themes and messages were developed at the highest appropriate level and disseminated throughout the command, although at no stage was a PSYOPS message to be given directly to the press. As an erstwhile communist country, control of the media throughout the former Yugoslavia was prevalent and expected. The information campaign, supported by actions, was used to counter this manipulation order to give the population 'ground truth'.

There were two drivers for the information campaign. These were the General Framework Agreement for Peace (GFAP), achieved in Dayton and subsequently signed in Paris on 20 December 1995, which gave IFOR its legal authority; and the campaign plan, produced by the Land Component Commander, which directed how the military annex of the GFAP was to be implemented.

Co-ordination

Key to the effectiveness of the information campaign was close and regular co-ordination. To achieve this there were four regular meetings. Of these, meetings of the HQ IFOR Joint Information Co-ordination Committee (JICC) were held weekly, and attended by HQ IFOR PI,

PSYOPS, Legal Adviser, Political Adviser (POLAD) and CIMIC staff. Representatives from HQ ARRC were also present and, as the operation progressed, so were those from the major international organisations (IOs) and non-governmental organisations (NGOs). This group looked forward to major milestones in the GFAP and tried to ensure that not only did the parties involved not undermine each other, but that their efforts were actively synchronised.

In addition, meetings of the HQ ARRC Perceptions Group (PG) were held weekly, with a similar agenda and attendance to the JICC, but at the Land Component level. Day-to-day management of the information campaign for planned and probable events was the responsibility of the HQ ARRC Information Co-ordination Group (CICG), meetings of which were held daily throughout the mission. These were chaired personally by COMARRC as his first scheduled event each day,[11] which enabled him to give daily close direction to the information campaign. The CICG was effectively the targeting group which decided the message, target audience, method(s) of dissemination, delivery timing and subsequent analysis.[12] It was focused on 'deep' information operations, although for the initial weeks of the deployment 'close' information operations occupied most of the staff effort. 'Rear' information operations were conducted but were not often considered by the CICG.[13]

Also, a final co-ordination group was held before the daily press conference. Initially, only HQ ARRC or IFOR gave the daily press briefings. However, as the IOs and NGOs became established, these became joint press conferences. To ensure that the international community was seen to present a united front, the pre-press conference meeting enabled the major briefers to co-ordinate their efforts.[14]

Delivery Systems

Information 'close operations' used a combination of PI and classic PSYOPS techniques. International and national print, wire, television and radio media were briefed by a wide variety of means, which included press releases, a 24-hour Corps Press Information Centre (CPIC), a daily scheduled press conference, 'one to one' briefings, and detailed background briefings to new journalists or to update those who had been out of area for some time.[15] This placed a great reliance on sufficient and reliable communications. Consequently, the CPIC was accorded a very high priority for civilian communications assets. In the latter stages of the campaign, once the civilian trunk telecommunications system was up to it, press releases and conference transcripts were placed directly into the public domain via the Internet.

IFOR also used six radio transmitters and one recording studio, which made tapes that were then distributed on a weekly basis to any of the over 60 local radio stations throughout Bosnia and Herzegovina to which IFOR had access. This was in addition to interviews, some quite lengthy, with local IFOR commanders.[16] During the early stage of the IFOR deployment there was limited terrestrial television available. This coverage improved throughout the mission and regular interviews were given. Additionally, IFOR had its own television studio and film team which produced short (four to six minutes) pieces on key issues which were then given to local television stations for transmission. Limited resources dictated that this could only be achieved weekly.[17] Leaflets and posters were also used extensively throughout the campaign. They became increasingly sophisticated as improved printing capabilities became available, both internally and as local printing capability was restored. They could be used theatre-wide or tailored to a specific location. Loudspeaker broadcasts, a crude but effective medium for very localised messages, were also employed.

Information 'deep operations' used a blend of PSYOPS and Public Relations (PR). These included an 'own brand' newspaper: the free weekly newspaper the *Herald of Peace*, which was published with a circulation peaking at 125,000 copies. The paper appeared in Serbo-Croat (both Latinic and Cyrillic) and English, and circulated throughout Bosnia and Herzegovina.[18] A monthly glossy magazine *Mirko* was published, targeted at the teenage market, together with a colouring book (on land mine awareness) aimed at the younger age groups. A wide range of promotional 'novelty' items was also distributed, including footballs, basketballs, colouring books, pens and pencils, all of which had a logo or message related to peace.

Finally, in information 'rear operations', efforts were made to ensure that troop-contributing nations (TCN) and the families of soldiers deployed were kept informed by regular articles or features in their respective national press using either military or national journalists, or both.

Problem Areas

Media reports can give a false impression through a tendency to 'tunnel vision': to report on only what is seen through a camera lens. To overcome this, military forces may need to gather their own evidence to demonstrate that what is being reported is not representative of the whole country. In Sarajevo there were a number of major military and IO headquarters in close proximity to each other. This enabled journalists to phone or visit each agency quickly and seek discrepancies or divisions. These divisions then became the basis for a story. To avoid this, close co-ordination between the military and IOs was essential. Initially there was a feeling that a number of journalists were biased. Some had been in Bosnia for a number of years and had fallen foul of one or other of the warring factions. There was a tendency to reflect this in their reporting. It took time for journalists to have confidence in IFOR reporting of incidents, especially when it praised the particular faction the journalists perceived as the 'enemy'.

In the late twentieth century, journalists with modern equipment, four wheel drive vehicles, and with internationally accepted credit cards or cash, are able to appear anywhere in the area of operations. Although accreditation procedures were in place in Bosnia, journalists were able, and allowed, to move freely around the country without military escorts.[19] Except in General War, or campaigns in which the military can control access to the area of operations (as, for example, in the Falklands Campaign of 1982), this will probably be the norm. Consequently, all soldiers must be given proper media training.

Summary

The ARRC 'Lessons Learned' report on its experience in Bosnia concluded that:

> On Peace Support Operations, a proactive, responsive and co-ordinated information campaign, with high level co-ordination of Media Ops and Psyops, is an all pervasive and major lever which can be used to shape the environment, perceptions and opinions. The information campaign played a significant part in every aspect of the IFOR mission. To be effective this campaign must be targeted, commence before deployment (to be effective on deployment) and be co-ordinated internally with staff branches and externally with the major international agencies.[20]

AFTER IFOR: PREPARING FOR THE NEXT ROUND

> Trying to predict the future in an uncertain world is not easy, but whatever happens ... the ARRC ... must be ready for any eventuality, able to carry out its mission whatever and whenever SACEUR directs.
>
> Lieutenant-General (now Sir) Mike Jackson,
> COMARRC[21]

Both the IFOR and SFOR deployments generated a frenzy of 'Lessons Learned'[22] reports by units and headquarters, organisations, study centres and individual protagonists both military and civilian, including academics, journalists and analysts. Articles, essays and books have been written about the information campaign, and strategic studies centres across the world debate the 'new' era in military–media relationships and its impact on global security issues. There is a daunting amount of 'this is how we did it/this is how you should have done it' information available to those whose job it is to prepare for the next time.

But, although the IFOR experience was a seminal one, it was the product of a very specific set of circumstances and conditions, and at a very specific time in the evolution of NATO's emerging role in global security issues. It is very unlikely to be repeated, and HQ ARRC must avoid laying itself open to the classic criticism of military organisations, that of 'preparing to fight the last campaign better'. Instead, it must look to the future and prepare for the next campaign: as COMARRC says, it must be ready for any eventuality. Of all the myriad 'Lessons Learned', three themes for media operations stand out:

- Be prepared
- Be co-ordinated
- Be proactive.

This next section will look at how HQ ARRC has built on the experiences in Bosnia, developed those themes over the intervening 18 months, and is preparing itself for the next round of the media campaign.

Although as a NATO headquarters, HQ ARRC Media Ops Branch follows the NATO guidelines for Public Information (PI),[23] one of the results of 18 months of conceptual and doctrinal development is a revision of the concept and definition of Media Operations[24] for use at the corps level. The current concept is simple:

> HQ ARRC Media Operations Branch is to be independent, fully deployable and capable of prosecuting COMARRC's media campaign in accordance with NATO PI policy in peace or on operations, regardless of Transfer of Authority[25] or Rules of Engagement.[26]

To set the scene, it is probably also worth looking at the ARRC definition of Media Operations:

> The operational function, incorporating PI[27] and PR,[28] designed to plan, direct, co-ordinate and conduct the media campaign in peace and on operations in order to support the successful prosecution of COMARRC's mission.

18

The definition of the media campaign is:

> The planned, co-ordinated and continuous use of all aspects of PI and PR to ensure the dissemination of a timely, cohesive, and positive message which presents an accurate and credible public image of the force and its mission. It is designed to gain and maintain public support so contributing to COMARRC's freedom of action in his area of responsibility.[29]

Media Operations in Peacetime

Preparation, preparation, preparation – media operations is a continuous process, and the media campaign runs through peace and operations but at a different level for each. The relative importance of PI and PR changes: the requirement for PI is generally less in peacetime and allows for training and preparation. The following paragraphs will look at HQ ARRC media operations in peacetime and how it prepares for deployment.

Selling the ARRC: The ARRC PR Campaign

'Go out young man and market the ARRC.'[30] During its year in Bosnia, the ARRC had lost its identity, subsumed by the IFOR banner. All but a few *cognoscenti* had forgotten its existence, and a marketing and PR campaign was developed to redress the balance. This was to have a number of goals. One was to raise the profile of the ARRC against the 'children of ESDI',[31] including the EUROCORPS, EUROFOR, the German/Netherlands Corps and the Franco/German Corps. Another was to inform NATO, the TCNs and the troops of the assigned formations; and also to contribute to NATO's crisis management strategy of deterrence by reminding (potential) foes of the ARRC's operationally proven capabilities, and the political commitment of NATO to use it.

HQ ARRC has developed a suite of products designed to build up a recognisable corporate image at the same time as promoting the ARRC as an organisation. This includes a video, based largely on the IFOR experience, a brochure, a quarterly journal, and an information tri-fold. HQ ARRC also has an Internet website[32] linked into NATO HQ, together with SHAPE, the subordinate NATO commands and some of the TCN and assigned divisions' sites.

The quarterly journal is aimed as much at keeping HQ ARRC's domestic audience at its home in Rheindahlen in Germany aware of what goes on in the headquarters as it is at informing the general readership of wider ARRC issues. It also acts as a forum for informed debate by the

ARRC's multinational staff officers on doctrinal matters, and offers the assigned national forces the opportunity to distribute their own articles to a wider international audience than they may otherwise have managed.

In peacetime, HQ ARRC has little to offer journalists by way of 'good copy'. It owns no soldiers, tanks, guns or helicopters, all of which are national assets. It conducts no field-training exercises, as training is a national responsibility. Consequently, Media Ops Branch is involved in very little active PI. Those events that may elicit some journalistic reaction, such as change of command ceremonies, high-level visits, exercises or discussions over the integration of 'invited nations'[33] into ARRC force structures, are dealt with as PI but very much used as part of the profile-raising PR campaign.

One of the major challenges facing the ARRC PR campaign is the non-availability of translation facilities for languages other than English or German. This is being addressed with the senior national representatives, but as of the time of writing there is still a gap in coverage of some TCNs.

Co-ordination: Unity of Effort

The need for full and early co-ordination is one of the three key 'Lessons Learned'. As noted by SACEUR at the beginning of this chapter, providing clear information to the publics is the key to gaining positive public opinion and, through it, political will. It requires co-ordination of effort at all levels, to ensure that the forces speaks with one voice. This is particularly important in coalition or alliance operations where the natural friction that is the very nature of multinationality militates against it.

Each nation has its own PI structures and policies, many of which are not only at variance with each other, but also with those of NATO and the ARRC.[34] This is not a criticism, it is a fact. Co-ordination of these disparate attitudes and capabilities cannot be achieved overnight, and HQ ARRC Media Operations Branch devotes a considerable amount of time liasing with the Public Information Officers (PIOs) of its superior NATO headquarters, and those of its assigned national formations and their ministries of defence (or the equivalent). It has also developed a good working relationship with the PIOs of EUROCORPS, among others, and the recently activated EUROFOR.

Part of the post-IFOR doctrinal development has been the production of a series of TACSOPs and TACSOIs[35] which explain the way that HQ ARRC will conduct operations, including media operations. These have been distributed to NATO and national assigned forces, and ensure a common understanding of ARRC concepts and procedures before the start of any operation.

Peace Support Operations by their very nature do not allow specific planning until they happen. One critical area, which cannot be co-ordinated until the mission is known, is the crucial link with the PIOs of the United Nations, IOs and NGOs, who will almost certainly have been operating in theatre for some time prior to the ARRC's arrival, and together with the journalists will know far more of what is happening than the military. The need for liaison, as a first step to co-ordination, has been identified as a key requirement to be started as soon as possible once authority is given.

'Our Friends the Enemy': Educating the Press

Few news offices nowadays can afford dedicated defence correspondents. The level of military ignorance amongst journalists is frightening, and it is increasing. Just as it is vital for PIOs to understand the media, so it is helpful if the media understands the military. Notwithstanding HQ ARRC's lack of newsworthy opportunities in peacetime, a great deal of effort is put into educating the press. ARRC fact sheets and press releases, complete with contact addresses and key personnel *resumés*, cascade across e-mail and fax lines to editors and journalists in print, radio and television. They may not be read, but the ARRC badge (or corporate logo) should lodge subliminally in someone's mind and the points of contact, background reference information and website details will be available should any journalist want to run a piece on the ARRC.

Personal contacts are as vital as a generally informed media. Occasionally, visiting journalists are given background briefings and interviews with the senior commanders. Once a year defence correspondents, local journalists and the international press corps from the embassy circuit in Bonn are invited to HQ ARRC for a collective background briefing session and the annual Media Ops study period always has at least one journalist as a guest speaker.

On any deployment, the 'in place' journalists will have a far better understanding of the local situation and the key players, and will probably have greater freedom of movement than the military. They are not likely to take kindly to an incoming military force imposing arbitrary constraints upon their 'freedom of action'. They are also likely to be considerably better informed, and to have well established sources of information across political or factional divides. Early liaison and background briefings are vital: to inform and educate the journalists about the incoming force, to identify and explain any new ground rules, to build on their acquired knowledge and to seek to establish mutual understanding.

Understanding the Rules of the Game: The Media Arena

Much has already been written about the challenges facing the media as we rush headlong towards the dawn of the twenty-first century. Budgetary pressures are reducing the number of specialist correspondents and deployable news teams. This leads to an increasing reliance on wire services and freelance journalists for copy. The constant 'thirst to be first' with news at ever decreasing intervals, and the ability of modern technology to let even the least trained and able 'hack' broadcast live from almost anywhere in the world, have all put great pressures on editorial staffs. This is well documented and has been summed up by the television journalist Nik Gowing as 'the tyranny of real time' and the age of 'robo-hack'.[36] How do these pressures currently facing the professional media affect the military? The two have always worked to different agendas and to different time scales. The journalist must get the story out. The military must check the facts. As Pascale Combelles Siegel has put it, 'For the journalist, immediacy can override accuracy. For the military, accuracy can override immediacy.'[37] The major difference is that the military is accountable, especially when operational security (OPSEC) or casualties are involved. The journalist can always speculate, but a military comment lends veracity and credibility and must be given wisely. This is not an excuse for doing and saying nothing. It is a catalyst for the military to improve its speed of response: to ensure that its PIOs are in a position to meet the journalistic requirement for immediacy with properly checked information to meet the military's need for accuracy. The story will out whatever, and it is beholden on PIOs to ensure that it goes out with the military view represented. This still relies as much on a revised attitude of the military mind as it does on the acquisition of the necessary equipment.

Adapt and Overcome: An Attitude of Mind

Public information officers are not journalists. Talking to them will not automatically result in a comment being published. Above all, PIOs must be trusted. Military minds must be of an attitude that looks to inform the PIO of operations that are planned or incidents as they occur and not hide unpleasant facts. This will allow the PIO to do his job: prevent a military incident becoming a public crisis. It requires considerable training and education on both sides to build up a mutual respect between the PIO and the other functional staff branches, particularly 'G3 Ops' and 'G3 Plans' who have the knowledge of planned or ongoing incidents.[38] The actual deployment is too late to start training. HQ ARRC runs a regular training schedule throughout the year for all personnel which comprises media awareness and interview techniques training. Media awareness training is included as part of the new arrivals' brief, and the annual individual military skills training package. The journalist is a demon to the military mind. Most soldiers are convinced that the sole and single purpose of every journalist is to destroy their careers. This is not necessarily the case, although there are always horror stories to lend it credence. Most of the problems stem from ignorance, and great importance is placed on explaining to the staff what the media do, what the Media Ops Branch does, and the role of every member of the HQ in the process.

Incident reporting is probably the most important area. Military PIOs must be responsive, not reactive. The discrepancies between the relative speeds of the media and military reporting chains have been well documented. Practicalities of communication hardware are a factor, but it is the initial identification and understanding of a potential incident that is vital. This is not easy in a multinational environment when not only may there be two or more languages involved, but when cultural differences also colour what may be regarded as an 'incident', which is not the same to all men. It also depends on the agenda and cultural make-up of the journalist. The ARRC cannot hope for complete success, but by developing a flexible and open frame of mind and providing regular staff updates on the 'hot topics', it should at least be able to compete on reasonably level ground.

Media-handling techniques are important for all military personnel. In the age of the open media battlefield and the 'strategic soldier', anyone is liable to be interviewed at any time with consequences reaching far beyond his immediate area. Every HQ ARRC soldier is issued with a credit card-sized *aide mémoire* containing handy hints for media encounters and the generic ARRC command and campaign themes.[39]

It is from the media that most of us get our knowledge of the outside world. Military staff officers are no different. One of the most important tasks for the Media Ops Branch is to monitor the world's media and to provide news summaries and analysis in an easily digestible form to the staff. A compilation of NATO and national products is provided daily in hard copy and electronically, and 'own language' publications are made available for non-native English speakers in the Branch library.

Quarterly interview techniques training is provided for senior officers, specialist spokesmen, and others who wish to use it. The more credible and professional the spokesman, the better the image of the force, the more credible the military and the more it is likely to get the message across. This quarterly interview techniques training is approached rather as a regular visit to the ranges to fire one's personal weapon. It is a core military skill every bit as important as marksmanship.

Preparing the Script: Planning

HQ ARRC is a planning headquarters. The Media Ops Branch has a dedicated media plans officer, who ensures that it plays its full part in the HQ planning process. Operational planning is the responsibility of G3 Plans, and is co-ordinated across the headquarters by means of the Corps Plans Group (CPG), which has representation from all functional staff branches. During the estimate process, the media plans officer is responsible for ensuring that media tasks and implications are identified from the higher commander's intent and the concept of operations. During the formulation of ARRC plans, he is responsible for identifying any media implications from intended activities and for drafting the media ops annex to the plan. The CPG is one of the main forums for the all important co-ordination and liaison with other staff branches.

Exercise planning is the responsibility of the G3 exercise planning staff. The media planner will be involved early in the exercise development phase to ensure that the correct level of media play is factored into the scenario preparation. This will also ensure that the necessary press simulation (SIMPRESS) implications and requirements have been addressed. Too often exercises are conducted in a reality vacuum. Mindful of the lessons from Bosnia, and that a deployment is too late to start practising, HQ ARRC has designed media play to provide a reality framework around any exercise scenario. A comprehensive SIMPRESS operation, under command of the exercise controller, produces video and print products mixed with 'Realworld' news. This may contain strategic disinformation and deception campaigns, as well as the reporting of more immediate stories from the ARRC area of operations. From this the G2, PSYOPS, political and media staffs try to identify themes and messages and prepare responses. The SIMPRESS organisation provides a pool of 'journalists' to attend press conferences, ask questions and interview military personnel. This exercises the Media Ops staffs, PI reporting system, and chain of command in the formulation and release of press lines. It also practises the HQ staffs at all levels in the timely passage of accurate information.

The Techno-War: The Right Kit For The Job

'Robohack' technology not only benefits impoverished freelancers, it also allows military PI staff to enter the arena similarly equipped to the media professionals. HQ ARRC Media Ops Branch has a comprehensive equipment purchase programme and is acquiring the digital technology necessary to meet the media on roughly equal terms. For any pre-planned operation or identified incident, a news response team can be quickly on the scene equipped with a camera, laptop and Internet, cellphone or military communications. This allows the military version of events, in image and print, to be sent back to ARRC Main HQ and the CPIC within minutes, to produce the timely and informed comment which may otherwise be missing from the immediacy/accuracy equation. If necessary, the same information can be transmitted to the newsrooms and wire services at about the same time as the journalists transmit their stories. This will help overcome the 'tunnel vision lens' identified in Bosnia, and may even benefit future editors faced with their own 'real time news' dilemma.

ARRC MEDIA OPERATIONS ON DEPLOYMENT

Any deployment is invariably easier than the preparation. Everyone is focused on the matter in hand, funds usually become available and there is little time for anything but the immediate. For the Media Ops staff, the focus shifts away from PR to operational PI and the peacetime preparations should allow them to enter the arena capable of conducting immediate media operations. This final section will look at the main tasks of HQ ARRC Media Ops Branch on deployment.

The Operational Media Campaign

The whole *raison d'être* of the Media Operations Branch is to prosecute COMARRC's media campaign. For Article 5 Collective Defence (combat) operations it expects to direct NATO PI operations in the ARRC's area of operations (AO) in support of the strategic NATO/SHAPE PI campaign. It will take on full augmentation, establish the Press and Information Centre and liase with 'in-place' national forces, flanking formations, together with NGOs and IOs where necessary. Although based primarily in HQ ARRC Main, the Media Ops cell would also provide PI and media support to HQ Rear Support Command and HQ ARRC Rear.[40] Most of NATO's current operational planning however is based on PSO and centred around the Combined Joint Task Force (CJTF) concept. This sees the nucleus CJTF HQ being found from HQ AFCENT or AFSOUTH with the most likely Land Component Command HQ (LCC) being formed by HQ ARRC. The remainder of this section will look at how HQ ARRC Media Ops provides PI support to the CJTF HQ.

On deployment, the Media Operations Branch splits into two functional areas: the Media Ops Cell, which is based in HQ ARRC Main, and the nucleus of the Combined Press Information Centre (CPIC). This is a theatre-level asset, comprising staff from each of the component commands (maritime, land and air) but which would usually be co-located with the LCC as the supported command. The Media Ops Cell is responsible for developing, planning and conducting COMARRC's media campaign in support of the NATO PI policy. The media planner is co-located permanently with the Corps Plans Group. The remainder of the cell concentrates on conducting current media operations from within the main HQ next to the Operations Centre (OPSCEN). The Media Ops officer runs the Media Ops Cell. He is involved in a continuous walk around the OPSCEN and outlying areas, visiting each of the functional staffs and finding out the latest information from each, identifying potential crisis and informing each of the current media and PI situation. He is the link between ARRC Main, the NATO PI cells in the Theatre HQ and the national PI cells in the assigned divisional HQs. He also forms the crucial link between ARRC Main and the CPIC, and will staff responses to questions (RTQ) around the HQ for answers. He will brief at the internal and external operational staff updates and must be fully aware of all that is going on in the ARRC AO.

Chief Media Operations is co-located with the Legal Officer and the Political Adviser (POLAD) in the Command Group. He is responsible to COMARRC for all PI and media issues in the ARRC AO. He will be in regular contact with the NATO CPIO and is responsible for ensuring that the ARRC media campaign supports the strategic PI policy. This is done through the Perceptions Group which meets on an ad hoc basis, and can comprise representatives from all staff functions as required.[41] Chief Media Ops is a permanent member of the Perceptions Group, and it is here that the detailed co-ordination of PSYOPS, Media Ops and CIMIC operations is achieved.

It was an acknowledged truism among those who took part that 'In Bosnia we worked a three day week: yesterday, today and tomorrow.' Just as it is important to keep the staff informed of global events in peace, so it is even more important on operations when attention and energies are focused into narrow functional areas. It is only by knowing the 'reality framework' in which any ARRC mission is being conducted that the wider implications of individual staff actions can be understood. It is equally important for all staff to be aware of the master messages and the overall strategic image that the force is to project.

The Combined Press Information Centre (CPIC)

The CPIC is where the Theatre Commander's PI campaign is prosecuted. It will be set up at the centre of media focus, which will invariably mean that it is co-located with the Land Component Command HQ. The NATO CPIC director will receive his strategic direction from the CJTF HQ but be given detailed guidance from, and provide detailed operational level support to, the Land Component Commander (COMARRC). Based on a cadre of permanent HQ ARRC Media Ops staff officers, it relies heavily on NATO augmentation to bring it up to its operational establishment. However, as required by the ARRC media operations concept, it will be equipped and structured to conduct immediate – but limited – PI operations without waiting for augmentation. Wherever possible, it will be located close enough to the LCC HQ (ARRC Main) to allow COMARRC, Chief Media Ops or other designated spokesmen to be readily available for conferences and interviews. On combat operations, mobility and security factors will constrain its location, but on PSO it will ideally be within at least ten minutes' travelling time of the headquarters. With the CJTF PIO some distance away in the Theatre HQ and Chief Media Ops as the LCC PIO based in ARRC Main, the CPIC Director is routinely responsible for ensuring that journalists are fully briefed. This requires secure communications to staff RTQs and embargoed media lines, and to ensure that the CPIC Director is fully appraised of the operational situation and so able to make sound judgements in the absence of detailed orders.

The CPIC contains the business end of the media operation. It will provide statements, conduct regular press conferences, provide RTQs, arrange interviews and seeks to set itself up as a 'one stop shop' for information in the Theatre AO. It comprises three main sections. The Media Relations Section is responsible for media handling, escorting and registration. The PI Section is responsible for staffing press lines and RTQs to the CJTF or LCC HQ, producing PI briefing packs, and briefing journalists on routine issues. The Information and Analysis Section is responsible for command information[42] and media analysis. High-grade media analysis was identified as key to the success of the IFOR information campaign. The days of firing off PI lines and calling it a job well done are over. Their effects must be monitored and understood. Media Ops planners are expected to know how the force and its mission are being perceived by public opinion, and to be able to test and adjust the operation as required. The CPIC is the major tool for NATO to get its message out to the public, and presents the public face of the force to the media. It needs high calibre individuals and good quality, reliable communications. Its importance must not be underestimated and it must be resourced accordingly.

CONCLUSION

In Bosnia, HQ ARRC established a level of military–media operations and PI that is generally acknowledged to have set the standard by which all others will be judged. The media has come to expect it and the ARRC must maintain that standard if it is to establish and retain its credibility on any future deployment.

Preparation and co-ordination are vital to a successful media operation. The PI lines of command, co-ordination, direction and guidance are complicated and tortuous. In an ideal world there would be clear strategic and political direction, a defined end state, and Media Ops/PIO and CPIC staffs at all levels would be in regular contact with each other. The NATO lines and the national lines would coincide, and the force would speak with one voice. It is unlikely to be so easy. Thorough preparation and continuous liaison are key to making it work. Good personal relationships are vital to avoid misunderstanding and confusion, and the importance of simple operating procedures and regular exercises cannot be overstated.

Whatever happens, military–media operations is a growth industry, and what has been described in this chapter is only the beginning. Changes in technology, military, public and media attitudes and the very nature of military activities will see them evolving further. The growth of Internet technology has put a different complexion on the traditional view of PI as indirect information, dependent on the media to pass the message to the public. The availability of websites allows the military to make its messages directly available to the public, by posting press releases, transcripts of press conferences, and photographs directly onto the web. If they want it, the public now have access to raw information without journalistic or editorial comment. The technology is also available to post press releases and statements directly onto the wire services, which account for more and more of the 'feed' for mainstream journalists. In some countries, military news services and programmes are already a regular and accepted feature of national broadcasting. Could the military soon find itself in direct competition with the professional media as a news provider?

What else may the future hold? The use of military technology openly to jam civilian radio stations in Bosnia and elsewhere and rebroadcast 'true' information has spawned a whole new lexicon of terms, such as 'media monitoring', 'compliance operations', 'media restructuring' and so on. There have even been calls for the United Nations to establish an 'independent information intervention unit with three primary areas of responsibility: monitoring, peace broadcasting and ... jamming'.[43] The traditional dividing line that kept classic PI pure and apart from the murkier aspects of information operations is being rapidly eroded. How this will affect NATO PI is another question, but NATO is working hard to adapt to the shifting sands of the military–media interface in the new world order.

As the spearhead of NATO's crisis management strategy, HQ ARRC will continue to play its full part in the process as it enters the twenty-first century, prepared and ready to meet whatever challenges lie ahead: *Audentis Fortuna Iuvat!*

NOTES

1. The ARRC's current mission states that: 'HQ ARRC is to be prepared to deploy on SACEUR's order, to an area of operation designated by SACEUR, and undertake combined, joint military operations across the operational spectrum either as a corps HQ with up to four divisions and corps troops under OPCOM/OPCON, or as a Land Component Command HQ, in order to support SACEUR's crisis management options.'
2. The ARRC's order of battle would comprise up to four of the following assigned divisions: 7th German Panzer Division, 2nd Greek Mechanised Division, 1st Turkish Mechanised Division, 1st US Armored Division, the Spanish Rapid Reaction Division, the Multi-National Division (Central) (MND(C)), 3rd Italian Mechanised Division, 1st UK Armoured Division, 3rd UK Mechanised Division. The Multi-National Division (South) (MND(S)) is not fully constituted in peacetime, but could be assigned for ARRC operations.
3. The terms 'corps level' and 'operational level' are used synonymously when denoting levels of military operations.
4. These are NATO designations for staff organisation: G1 – Personnel, G2 – Intelligence, G3 – Operations, G4 – Logistics.
5. N. Gowing, 'Conflict, the Military and the Media – a New Optimism?' *The Officer*, 7, 3 (May–June 1997), pp. 24–6, reproduced in *ARRC Journal*, 1, 1 (September 1997).
6. In 1995 the ARRC media operations mission was 'to incorporate all aspects of press, TV and radio into operational planning in order to represent the media dimension in the commander's concept'.
7. Psychological operations (PSYOPS) are defined by NATO as: 'Planned psychological operations in peace, crisis and war directed to enemy, friendly and neutral audiences in order to influence attitudes and behaviour affecting the achievement of political and military objectives. They include strategic psychological activities (SPA), psychological consolidation activities, (PCA), battlefield psychological activities (BPA) and peace support psychological

activities (PSPA).' See NATO MC 402. Because PSYOPS is in some countries a 'dirty word' and liable to misinterpretation by the media, the phrase 'IFOR information campaign' (IIC) was used to denote the use of PSYOPS.

8. Civil–military co-operation (CIMIC) is defined as: 'The resources and arrangements which support the relationship between NATO commanders and national authorities, civil and military, and civil populations in an area where NATO military forces are, or plan to be, employed. Such arrangements include co-operation with non-governmental or international agencies, organisations and authorities.' See NATO MC 411 (August 1997).

9. Officially used in connection with propaganda (a product of PSYOPS activities) the colour designation has become used in connection with PSYOPS activities generally. The definitions are as follows: 'Black: Propaganda which purports to emanate from a source other than the true one. Grey: Propaganda which does not specifically identify any source. White: Propaganda disseminated and acknowledged by the sponsor or by an accredited agency thereof.' See NATO MC 402/AAP-6 *NATO Glossary of Terms and Definitions* (English and French) 1995 (hereafter NATO AAP-6).

10. 'Centre of Gravity' is defined in British Army doctrine as 'That aspect of the enemy's overall capability which, if attacked, will lead either to his inevitable defeat or his wish to sue for peace through negotiation.' *Army Doctrine Publication Volume 1: Operations*, Army Code 71565 (London: HMSO, 1994).

11. The remainder of the group comprised: DCOMARRC, COSARRC, Media Adviser (a former US journalist contracted for one year as COMARRC's personal media adviser), Political Adviser (POLAD), Legal Officer, Chief Civil Affairs/CIMIC, Chief Information, Media Ops Spokesmen, PSYOPS Staff Officer and Deputy Commander of PSYOPS Unit. In addition, the HQ IFOR PIO regularly attended, as did other functional specialists when required.

12. The importance of analysis cannot be underestimated, and monitoring national and international television, radio, print media and the wire services was a continuous process to ensure that anomalies and errors could be corrected as they occurred.

13. Within ARRC doctrine, operations are defined in this context by time. 'Deep operations' are more than 72 hours away, 'close operations' are within 72 hours. Rear information operations were conducted, but in this case consisted of keeping troop-contributing nations informed (at various levels) of the activities of the forces. Rear information operations were typically conducted by PI staff of individual nations.

14. At a typical press conference the following organisations were represented: IFOR (normally by HQ ARRC), Office of the High Representative (OHR), United Nations High Commission for Refugees (UNHCR), Organisation for Security and Co-operation in Europe (OSCE), United Nations Mission in Bosnia and Herzegovina (UNMIBH). UNMIBH also represented the International Police Task Force (IPTF) and the International Criminal Tribunal for Former Yugoslavia (ICTY).

15. Press conferences were held primarily in the PIC based in the Holiday Inn, Sarajevo. As Republika Srpska journalists were reluctant to travel into Federation territory, a second press brief was held for them on a Monday. Wherever possible the main press conference was held in Republika Srpska

on a Tuesday. Major press conferences once a month were also held outside Sarajevo to ensure all local press had access. This was in addition to press conferences run by multinational divisions – typically on a weekly basis.

16. These interviews ranged from 'one to one' in a studio, phone-ins, and panel discussions, to hosting a popular music programme.

17. In the case of IFOR pre-recorded radio and television tapes the condition made to the transmitting authority was that it played the tape as a whole and did not edit it. Radio and television stations were monitored to ensure compliance.

18. Initially, *Herald of Peace* concentrated on informing the population of Bosnia and Herzegovina on the Dayton Peace Agreement: what it meant for the people, what IFOR's role in this was, and the capabilities it had to enforce that peace. Then, as the mission progressed, the emphasis moved to the IOs and their part in the reconstruction of the fabric of the country as well as key issues such as elections.

19. Mine awareness and first-aid lectures were held on a regular basis for journalists.

20. HQ ACE Rapid Reaction Corps: Operation 'Firm Endeavour' Lessons Learned report.

21. Forward to *ARRC Journal*, 1, 1 (September 1997).

22. The two most influential are the HQ ARRC Operation 'Firm Endeavour' Lessons Learned report, and the Joint Analysis Team (JAT) report on IFOR prepared for NATO. The JAT analysis of the PI and information campaign was directed by Pascale Combelles Siegel, whose experiences have been published as P. Combelles Siegel, *Target Bosnia: Integrating Information Activities in Peace Operations* (Washington, DC: CCRP, 1998).

23. NATO Land Forces PI guidance is contained in SHAPE's Allied Command Europe (ACE) Directive AD 95-1 and AD 95-2, and in the annual ACE Public Information Plan (ACEPIP).

24. Unless specifically identified as official NATO or national terms, the ARRC concepts and definitions relating to media operations are HQ ARRC terms only. Whilst acknowledged by NATO and the troop-contributing nations, they have not been formally agreed or approved.

25. Transfer of Authority (TOA) is defined as: 'The process by which governments hand over command and control of National forces to NATO.' For a better understanding of NATO command states, see NATO AAP-6.

26. Rules of Engagement (ROE) are defined as: 'Directives issued by competent military authority which specify the circumstances and limitations under which forces will initiate and/or continue combat engagements with other forces encountered.' See NATO AAP-6.

27. Public Information is defined as: 'Information which is released or published for the primary purpose of keeping the public fully informed, thereby gaining their understanding and support.' See NATO AAP-6.

28. The term 'public relations' (PR) is not acknowledged by NATO. For the purposes of this chapter, the British definition is used: 'The planned and sustained effort to establish and maintain goodwill and mutual understanding between an organisation and its public.' See Joint Services Publication JSP 110.

29. This is not intended to suggest that everything will be subject to a glossy 'spin'. A positive public image of the force is as dependent on fast and honest

admissions of mistakes as it is on 'good news' stories. This has been proven time and again and is one of the major lessons from the ARRC's tour in Bosnia.

30. Major-General T. J. Sulivan, COSARRC (Chief of Staff ARRC), instructions to Chief of Media Operations, January 1997.

31. ESDI: European Security and Defence Initiative.

32. This can be consulted on the Internet at page: http://www.arrcmedia.com.

33. As of the time of writing, the 'invited nations' were the Czech Republic, Hungary and Poland.

34. Few of the assigned divisions have PI representation in peacetime, although most expect to be augmented for ARRC operations. Those that do have PIOs spread them throughout the functional staff branches from G1 through G2 and G3 to G5. Some are held as a command function with permanent right of access to the commander. Most deploy with the main headquarters but few have regular contact with the G3 Ops staff. One is deployed with the Rear HQ and consequently divorced from both the action and his commander. Very few have dedicated communications of any sort and none are secure. Not all have delegated national PI release authority; some act as the commanders' spokesmen and others merely as advisers and staff officers.

35. TACSOPs: tactical standing operational procedures. These show subordinate formations how HQ ARRC intends to conduct operations and explain their role in them. TACSOIs: tactical standing operational instructions. These outline internal HQ ARRC staff procedures and identify how each functional staff area fits into the whole.

36. In a presentation to Exercise 'ARRCANE PISTE', HQ ARRC's Media Operations study period, June 1997.

37. P. Combelles Siegel, p. 51.

38. This is made considerably easier if Media Ops staffs and PIOs have either a G3 background or at least formal staff training. They will be able to talk to the G3 world in its own language and will appreciate some of the 'drivers' that influence the G3 staffs. This will build up credibility, mutual trust and respect and ultimately speed up the passage of information, thus allowing the PIOs to reconcile the journalistic requirements of immediacy with the military requirements of accuracy.

39. The ARRC's command themes have been developed for use during peace and can be used as a bridge in any situation: 'The ARRC is a *Trained and Ready Force, Proven, Multi-national* and *Prepared*.' The campaign themes are generic to any campaign and build on the command themes: 'The ARRC is *Lethal, Legal* and *Right*.' The ARRC will of course use NATO-developed master messages as part of the strategic PI campaign.

40. It is a national responsibility to deploy forces into a theatre of operations. The ARRC's deployment concept calls for HQ Rear Support Command (RSC) to be responsible for co-ordinating the reception, staging, onward movement and integration (RSOI) of all assigned forces once TOA has occurred. HQ RSC will probably be located in the main port of entry into the theatre, which may not be in the same country as the ARRC AO and HQ ARRC Main. HQ ARRC Rear may be located in the ARRC Rear Area some way from ARRC Main. There is therefore a need to co-ordinate the media message between the three headquarters. The RSC and Rear Media Advisers are Chief Media Ops assets and tasked from ARRC Main as required.

41. Work on the NATO concept of 'Information Operations' is developing. Until such time as it becomes agreed NATO doctrine, HQ ARRC will continue to use the term 'Perceptions Operations' to describe the process by which it seeks to co-ordinate and synchronise all activities in order to create the environment necessary to support the successful prosecution of COMARRC's mission. The Perceptions Group is the forum in which the synchronisation takes place.
42. Also known as troop information. Previously command information was a national responsibility. The current NATO doctrine of CJTFs and AJFs with the ARRC as the most likely Land Component Command means that HQ ARRC must have the capability to produce command information if required.
43. J. F. Metzl, 'Information Intervention – When Switching Channels Isn't Enough', *Foreign Affairs*, 76, 6 (November/December 1997), pp. 15–20.

3

Myths: The Military, the Media and the IRA

PETER TAYLOR

'Written in Blood' was a television documentary I made in the summer of 1994 to mark the twenty-fifth anniversary of the deployment of British troops on the streets of Northern Ireland in 1969. It took the form of a personal retrospective. The introduction was a series of snapshots of my experiences, including clips of Ian Paisley in 1973 telling me to 'go back to England' and culminating with a little boy with the letters 'IRA' tattooed on his knuckles. I had interviewed him 20 years ago when he was about 11 years old. Paisley ordered me back to England: but I kept coming back, as did hundreds of British soldiers. Many never came back at all. The little boy, went his way too. I met him again – 15 years later – in the Maze prison. He was serving life for the murder of a British soldier.

It was, for me, a very personal film: an emotional and political journey from ignorance to, I hope, some degree of understanding. It was a journey through prejudice, myth and confusion. Part of the confusion was trying to form a view of the warring parties based on personal encounter and experience, rather than the stereotypes with which each side conveniently brands the other. I did this more recently in *Provos – the IRA and Sinn Fein*: my television series and book that explored the Republican psyche and strategy. Accepting the stereotype is the easy way out – because it keeps the picture simple. Black is black and white is white and we all know where we are. But, of course perception depends on the individual's point of departure and that is determined by a potent mixture of allegiance, propaganda, ideology and history. Soldiers, therefore, are either long-suffering peacekeepers, or the murderous agents of British imperialism. Journalists are either covert Provo sympathisers or the mouthpiece of the British Establishment. And the Provisional IRA (or 'Provos'), who have been the catalyst of change (however uncomfortable that may seem) are either mindless terrorists and Mafiosi, or heroic young men and women prepared to make the ultimate sacrifice for Ireland. In each case, however, the reality is infinitely more complex. As General Sir Michael Rose put it so candidly in the opening chapter to this book, the media are part of the war. And if that applies to Bosnia it applies even more so to Ireland. In this chapter I will endeavour to thread my way through the minefield and challenge some of the myths.

In 1989, the twentieth anniversary of the current Irish 'Troubles', I challenged the stereotypes of the three traditions historically involved in the conflict: the Nationalists, the Unionists and the British. The trilogy of resulting documentaries was called 'Families at War'. The first programme was titled 'The Volunteer' and was the story of how and why one young man joined the IRA and the effect that it had on his family. His name was Shane Paul O'Doherty – and he was not what people expected. Shane Paul could not be further removed from the stereotypical IRA man, however romantic his attachment to Irish history. He came from a middle-class family in Derry (or Londonderry). His father was a teacher and the family was opposed to all forms of violence. It was 'Bloody Sunday' (of which more later) that drove him to join the IRA. His mother only discovered his involvement when she was cleaning out his bedroom and discovered a balaclava and bag full of bullets under his pillow. His terrified father threw the bullets into the River Foyle. The discovery tore the family apart. In 1976 he was given 30 life sentences at the Old Bailey for masterminding the IRA's letter bomb campaign in London.

But Shane Paul's case also destroyed the myth that the IRA never lets its volunteers out of its clutches and that they remain irredeemable. In gaol, he recanted, rejected violence and attacked the IRA for its inability to think beyond its military campaign. In 1989 Shane Paul was released and he has recently graduated with an English degree from Trinity College, Dublin. I believe that the sentiments he expressed, shared by some of the Republican leadership, helped create the climate in which the IRA opted for a strategy of 'unarmed struggle', however tactical that may be.

The second film in the trilogy was about the experiences of the Protestant Unionist Loyalist community – which again challenged the stereotype – and the third, 'The Regiment', was about the Army in the form of the Royal Green Jackets. Again, this challenged the Republican stereotype of the British soldier. As I said, it was the tragedy of 'Bloody Sunday' in 1972 that drove the young Shane Paul O'Doherty – and hundreds of others – to join the IRA. That day in Londonderry/Derry was a watershed in the Troubles, and more than any other single event it gave the IRA what it most needed: propaganda, recruits and a potent issue. Tragically, The Parachute Regiment ('the Paras') reinforced the Republican stereotype of the British Army by their actions that day, which left 13 unarmed civilians dead on the streets of a British city. It should never have happened, and, significantly, it never happened again. Inevitably, myths grew up around the killings, most potently that the Paras' action was deliberate, sanctioned on high to teach the Catholics of the Bogside area a lesson. In propaganda, myth soon becomes fact.

Nothing could have been further from the truth. Without diminishing the tragedy of what happened, I was anxious to dispel the myth before it became forever locked in the historical record. 'Bloody Sunday' was an undisciplined cock-up not a conspiracy. To their credit, the Army and The Parachute Regiment helped me make the film, knowing they were taking a risk. It contained two remarkable interviews. One with the still-serving Company Sergeant-Major, and the other with Colonel Derek Wilford, who was the commanding officer on the day. Twenty years on – as it then was when the film was made – both remained haunted by the memory.

Not only did the programme shatter the myth that there was a conspiracy to kill Catholics, it destroyed the notion that all those involved were callous and uncaring. The Company Sergeant-Major's apology and Colonel Wilford's regret – clearly painful to both – prompted letters of appreciation from the Bogside, saying 'thank you'. No one had ever said 'sorry' before. I think the film, in a small way, played its part in the process of reconciliation. It could not have done so without the Army's decision to assist, a decision not without its risks.

Interestingly, when I first came to look again at the films that I have made, I was not aware of the thread that I now realise runs through them. Each, in some way, foreshadows the seismic change within the IRA and Sinn Fein and the dawning realisation within the British corridors of power that bold initiatives would have to be taken if there was ever to be an end to the conflict. This came when both sides recognised that outright victory would never be achieved on the battlefield. In a word, the 'war' in the military sense, was unwinnable – for both sides. This was the theme of a BBC 'Panorama' programme I made in 1988 called 'The Long War'. The film was made at a time when the IRA had received a series of crippling setbacks: the universal revulsion to the Enniskillen bombing; the seizure of Libyan arms on board the *Eksund* (although three previous shipments had got through); and the loss of eight of the IRA's most experienced men, shot dead by the SAS at Loughgall. For the first time, the programme revealed the IRA as military intelligence saw it. The image could not have been further removed from the stereotype. I am still surprised at the number of even the Army's most senior officers who dismiss the Provisionals as Mafiosi and criminal racketeers.

The film I made that perhaps did most to challenge the stereotype of the IRA was 'Enemies Within': a rare and unique view of life within the Maze prison. It also went some way to diffusing the prisons as an issue in the province. We spent about a month researching and filming on the Republican and Loyalist wings, with, by agreement, no Northern Ireland Office 'minders' in sight. This was the first time I heard Republicans talk of the 'armed struggle' as a 'tactic' to be set aside at the appropriate moment – as with the ANC in South Africa during the same period – in favour of the 'political struggle' to reach the final resolution. That is what we have seen happening since 1998 with the Good Friday Agreement.

One of my lasting memories is looking at one prisoner's bookshelf with some surprise. He was doing life for murder. I asked him what an IRA man was doing reading Tolstoy and Hardy. He looked me straight in the eye and said, 'Because an IRA man's normal, just like everybody else.' The difference of course is that 'everybody else' doesn't go around killing people. But he made the point. Another part of the film showed prisoners going out on home leave. Again, it challenged the stereotype that the IRA has little support within the community. The prisoner we followed was Raymond McCartney, who was then the IRA's 'Officer Commanding' (or OC) in the Maze. He was serving a life sentence for the murder of the Dupont executive, Geoffrey Agate. The sequence showed him arriving home and being greeted by a reception committee led by Martin McGuinness. The shot of McGuinness is highly significant. He was clearly anxious to talk at first hand with the Maze OC. It was barely six months later that a senior MI6 officer, Michael Oatley, made contact with McGuinness, marking from the British point of view the beginning of the 'peace process'.

This was a pivotal moment in the potential resolution of the conflict. For understandable reasons, the government's discussions with the IRA leadership were conducted in the utmost secrecy. In March 1993, the most secret and sensitive exchange took place: between the man euphemistically known as 'the British government representative' (BGR) and two of the Republican movement's most senior figures, Martin McGuinness and Gerry Kelly. It was a historic encounter which, remarkably, came within days of the Warrington bombing. At the meeting, the BGR is said to have indicated to McGuinness and Kelly that a united Ireland was historically inevitable. The question of whether the meeting was 'authorised' or not remains a matter of some contention. No doubt it had maximum deniability. I do know that the Secretary of State for Northern Ireland, Sir Patrick Mayhew, knew nothing of it until six months later. The meeting and what was said were not myths but interesting reality. History alone will record whether it eventually led to peace in Ireland and the end of the British Army's 'longest war'.

In 1994 I made a further film, 'A Soldier's Tale', as part of a BBC season to mark the twenty-fifth anniversary of the Troubles. Its purpose was to provide a historical record of British soldiering in Ireland – from the mouths of those who had done the fighting and seen the dying. Again, the Director of Public Relations (Army), in consultation, made the bold decision to co-operate. From the outset, I made it clear that we wanted to paint a real picture, not a sanitised one. I think we did, warts and all. Some of it was funny. Some of it was raw. Some of it was heroic. Soldiers who had lived through the unforgettable experience later told me that was just what it had been like.

And what of the media and the myth? In the end, the audience must be the judge, but you must judge on what you see; and that does not mean condemning everything and everybody by one or two things you do not like. Sadly, we often have to pay for the sins of our colleagues. You don't judge the Army by one soldier. We, like everyone else, are there to do a job – whether it be in Bosnia, the Gulf or Northern Ireland. Often, like the messenger, we're blamed for the news. As Sir Michael Rose has said, the media are part of the war, but it is dangerous, unfair and naive to think of us as the enemy.

4

The Media of Hate

RICHARD CONNAUGHTON

INTRODUCTION

It would be wrong to believe either that the existence of the media of hate is a recent phenomenon or that today it is confined to crippled, developing states. In its short span of history, radio provides us with examples as vivid as Goebbels' radio or Cairo Radio in the 1950s. What we are discussing is an extreme form of propaganda, extreme in so far as it is targeted upon an audience known to be susceptible to its messages of hatred. Hate radio is also operating legitimately in the United States. It is odd that, today, American airwaves are permitted to carry messages which both excite and pollute. Recently, mothers on welfare have been in the firing line:

> I wonder if they've ever figured out how they multiply like that? It's like maggots on a hot day. You look one minute and there are so many there, and you look again, and wow, they've tripled.

The man who said that was not broadcasting from Hicksville USA, but presents a popular afternoon rush-hour programme in New York. The same presenter supported a man who had rung in to encourage white people to oil their guns, and, when someone called to complain about high levels of local crime, he was told to 'get a gun and do something'. Messages such as these, illegal in Canada, are not illegal in the USA because the Constitution zealously safeguards the right of free speech. It is left to a thoroughly well-developed legal system to deal with matters of incitement, slander and libel.

The link between New York and the eventual destination of this chapter in Central Africa is their common denominator of the 'media of hate'. A definition of this to embrace all current circumstances might be:

Messages formulated by opponents of existing systems; the means of conveying those messages at low risk to the authors of the messages, and the pressure of an aggrieved recipient group with a capacity to create disorder.

Radio has an omnipresence in future military operational environments. It is by far the most important and effective means of communication that is available. Properly used, its power can be harnessed to the benefit of the target population and those called upon to intervene in a troubled environment. Cambodia's UNTAC (United Nations Transitional Authority in Cambodia) experience provides a good example where a non-propagandist radio was made available to all political parties and was used as a major instrument in the civic education programme. There was therefore no justification for individual parties, including the Khmer Rouge, to establish competing services. Rwanda provides no such happy example.

A SUMMARY OF RWANDA'S PROBLEMS

Rwanda secured full independence from Belgium on 1 July 1962, but within 18 months tribal warfare broke out, continuing intermittently until the Arusha Peace Accords of 4 August 1993 sought finally to put an end to the spiral of violence. United Nations Security Council resolution 872 of October 1993 provided for the establishment of a United Nations Assistance Mission in Rwanda (UNAMIR) to monitor the cease-fire until the formation of a representative government. However, the governmental transition process fell behind schedule and on 6 April 1994, while returning from Tanzania with a new peace package, the executive jet carrying the Presidents of Rwanda and Burundi was shot down over Kigali airfield. Both men were killed. That act set in motion a prepared plan of the majority Hutus to embark upon genocide, targeting the minority Tutsis and moderate Hutus.

There were six principal elements in Rwanda's complex 1994 crisis[1] and the response to it. The first was the genocide conducted by substantial elements within the majority ethnic group (Hutu) against the minority ethnic group (Tutsi). There was not a precise division. Among the estimated half-to-one million slaughtered was a high proportion of Hutu moderates. The second was a conventional conflict conducted between the Hutu *Force Armée Rwandaise* (FAR) and the Tutsi Rwandan Patriotic Front (RPF). The conflict spanned the entire country less the south-west corner and resulted in an RPF victory and the installation of a majority

Tutsi government. This was followed by an operational-level manoeuvre of 1.5 million Hutu refugees into four neighbouring countries and the mounting of substantial and high-profile relief efforts by the host governments, the UN, the Red Cross and other non-governmental organisations (NGOs). Fourth was the presence of armed elements of the defeated army and militia within the refugee camps. Fifth was the involvement of third-party military contingents, either as part of UNAMIR I and II, or the French Operation 'Turquoise' confined to the south-west sector, or the American Operation 'Support Hope', or as national teams in refugee camps beyond Rwanda's borders. Finally, there was the unprecedented number of agencies and NGOs engaged in humanitarian activities, including 230 NGOs in Rwanda and approximately 100 in Goma, Zaire.

THE UN'S EXPERIENCE

One of the major questions to be examined in relation to the Rwanda situation is the role of international broadcasters. What, for example, had the BBC World Service done to bring unbiased reporting into the country? It does appear that Radio UNAMIR approached the BBC for permission to re-broadcast the World Service news. The BBC declined to become associated with Radio UNAMIR because it saw the UN in Rwanda as a political player with its own agenda. The BBC felt the central premise of that agenda was that the security situation in Central Africa would continue to deteriorate unless the Hutu refugees who had fled the country returned to Rwanda. It was believed that Radio UNAMIR's aim would be to encourage the refugees to return home and the BBC could not therefore become involved directly with the station. In fact, the BBC's concerns ran deeper than that.

The BBC negative feeling towards the UN developed due to the perception of the UN's Radio Rajo in Somalia 1992–94 as a propaganda tool of the UN. The subsequent UN advance on General Aideed's Mogadishu Radio reflects the linkage between political power and radio in Africa, confirming it to be by far the most effective mass medium. Invariably, the first target in a military coup is the radio station. There are only two African states which do not have their own television service but this means is, for the most part, a highly centralised luxury.[2] Newspapers are usually published in cities and tend to have little utility in a countryside where there are high levels of illiteracy. However, it is in Rwanda, a country the size of Belgium, and Africa's most densely populated country, that the most blatant use of the radio for political means occurred, and where there are important lessons to be learned for the future.

RADIO MILLE COLLINES

Hate radio does not, of course, exist in a vacuum. You have to understand the culture of a people, particularly the Hutu, used to conformity, even submission, and many living under the protection of the chiefs. In Rwanda, as in almost all African countries, the national radio had been used as a medium for broadcasting propaganda. Every day there would be discourse on the President's statements on development. Meanwhile, social inequality in the country was growing very fast due to the inflow of foreign aid which led to the creation of a local bourgeoisie. Capitalising on money provoked wide inequalities among the elite, proving to be dangerously divisive. Radio became the symbol of modernity. It was the first item that the mostly unemployed, 'no-prospects' youth would buy, so that corrupting messages went into the right ears, stimulating thoughts of violence as the last resort of exhausted minds. There are so many of these. Almost half the region's 7.5 million population is under 15 years old, and AIDS has contributed to an overwhelming sense of despair. At least 20 per cent of the sexually active in urban areas have AIDS.

The Hutu militia, the *Interahamwe*, was comprised of these young people who either had no job, no land, or who had had previous hopes of paid work but were frustrated in that aspiration. In the early 1990s there had been a flood of cheap Chinese radios arriving in the country: even then no more than 25 per cent of the population had one, and, if the regular, professional, salaried class is excluded, that figure falls to between 10 and 15 per cent. In Rwanda, the radio is called *ibitega*, one word with a depth of meaning: 'magical means to act upon someone else at a distance'. National radio had been used to give information on life, birth and death, even calling people to make specified rendezvous. The ground was therefore already fertile for the appearance of *Radio Mille Collines* (meaning 'a thousand hills').

Radio Mille Collines was originally licensed in July 1993 as an independent radio, but it was always a partisan radio supporting the majority Hutus. At the same time, the so-called Zero Network was established to plan the destruction of the minority Tutsis. *Radio Mille Collines* was undoubtedly part of that process. The willing hands of the young were turned to the gathering of funds for the somewhat vague purposes of protecting the freedom of the press, developing a culture of information and finding solutions to the many problems in Rwanda under a democratic framework. The radio had its origins in Belgium, there being strong Hutu cells operating in Brussels and Liège. Two channels were established: one broadcasting in French, the other in the local language, Kinyarwanda. The French-language broadcasts were rarely controversial, although a Belgian with an Italian name, Georges Ruggio, ran a virulently pro-Hutu political chat show, details of which percolated down among the people, leading to the flawed logic that 'if the white man says it, it must be true'.

By December 1993, the overt criticism of Belgium had become established on the Kinyarwanda channel, just as had the praise of France. The channel was having remarkable success in seducing the peasants away from the national radio which they found boring. Instead, *Radio Mille Collines* offered its young listeners a pop programme which contained hidden messages that the law of the majority was a substitute for democracy.

At the end of 1993, the UN established a presence in Kigali. UNAMIR comprised a Belgian parachute battalion and a composite battalion from Bangladesh. When the Belgians provided protected escorts to the minority Tutsis in the coalition government, *Radio Mille Collines* had a propaganda field-day. The Belgian ambassador complained to the Hutu President about the anti-Belgian rhetoric, to which the President responded, 'Tell me, Ambassador, in your country, how do you close down a democratic radio station?' What is strange is that so many of the Westerners did not see the signs anywhere near so clearly as the Tutsis who were about to be massacred. The missionaries and NGOs were giving so much of themselves that they could not see the developments under their noses. The papal nuncio had priests who spoke the local language and who told him of the levels of incitement developing on *Radio Mille Collines*. So extreme had these exhortations become that he dismissed them as nonsense without necessarily pausing to reflect upon the impact these messages were having upon the Hutus.

Rwanda was not the UN's finest hour. In January 1994 the commanding UN general officer, acting on information received, sent a most immediate signal to New York, advising UN headquarters of the movement towards genocide in the country, and requesting a change in his UN Charter Chapter VI peacekeeping mandate, and permission to conduct a cordon and search operation. Permission was denied. Despite many similar requests, permission was continually denied, so as to cultivate an impression among the Hutus that they could go about their business with impunity. The refusal of the Security Council to involve itself in Rwanda, and the reduction of UNAMIR's strength to a political presence, gave the Hutus the green lights they required. The signal for the slaughter to begin was the shooting down on 6 April 1994 of the executive jet over Kigali, killing the Presidents of Rwanda and Burundi. Immediately, barriers were thrown up in Kigali, manned by the young Hutu *Interahamwe* militia, with a radio in one hand, a machete in the other.

Radio Mille Collines increased its tempo: 'The baskets are only half full. They should be filled to the brim.' Death warrants were sent out over the airwaves. One targeted the Minister of Labour and Social Affairs who, with his mother, wife and children was murdered by the militia. The radio gave blanket encouragement to the Hutus to slaughter the minority Tutsis and Hutu moderates. Of considerable significance was the *Radio*'s encouragement 'to every man his Belgian'. The Belgian parachute battalion was the only effective, cohesive military force in Kigali. They had come from Somalia where their mandate had allowed them to use 'all necessary means'. They could not comprehend the reason why they had been so constrained in Kigali. Nevertheless, they were an obvious Hutu target upon which to inflict unacceptable casualties so as to force their withdrawal (as had happened to the Americans in Mogadishu) and thus allow the *Interahamwe* a freer hand. *Radio Mille Collines* conspired in what proved to be a highly successful tactic by accusing the Belgians of having shot down the presidential aircraft (of which the Hutu Presidential Guard were guilty). Ten Belgians escorting the Prime Minister were seized after he had been murdered. Taken to the Hutu barracks of the Reconnaissance Regiment, the ten naked men were lined up in front of the battalion. 'These are the men who murdered our President', said their commanding officer, who walked away leaving the Belgians to be cut down. The decision of the Belgians to withdraw their force came almost immediately, followed by that of the Bangladeshis to withdraw theirs. When the ten coffins arrived in Brussels, the newspapers begged the question, 'How could such an event come to pass on a peacekeeping operation?' That very same question had been asked in Central Punjab in June 1993 when relatives heard that 24 Pakistani soldiers had been killed and 56 wounded in a UN operation in Somalia. Their objective had been General Aideed's radio station.

It has been suggested that the French helped the principal *Radio Mille Collines* shareholders to leave the country. Among those was the wealthy Felicien Kabuga who was able to flee to Switzerland the day before his planned arrest. He thus avoided being called to account for his alleged crimes against humanity in the genocide which claimed up to 1 million lives. He subsequently took refuge in Nairobi, which became a hub of plotting and propaganda against the new, predominantly Tutsi government. When Tutsi forces took Kigali, *Radio Mille Collines* took to the road. The US Secretary of Defense had been converted to the need to jam *Radio Mille Collines* but politicians in Washington, fearful of transgressing the matter of freedom of speech, stopped him in his tracks. The UN was also unable to jam it, as its commander explained:

44

Linda Chalker [UK Minister for Development] promised radio stations and a jamming facility as indeed did the Americans and Canadians, but they allowed themselves to be hamstrung on the sovereign state issue even though the Hutu radio was making overt demands that the genocide continue.

It was not until mid-July that the French, who had entered south-west Rwanda, became aware of the unwelcome influence of *Radio Mille Collines*. Their commanding general admitted that 'This was a real failure of the French and an important lesson for the future. Our attention had been largely held by operational and logistical problems.' The necessary electronic means arrived soon after, and the hate radio was shut down on 17 July. The French General Lafourcade admitted that he had also requested the means to spread positive information and added, 'Be assured, we are now very much aware of the importance of a counter-radio situation.'

There is a view that if a friendly radio had been established by the intervening forces whilst the genocide was in progress that would have been acceptable, but as soon as the new government became established there were differences with UNAMIR over its hopes to set up its own radio station. The only way to sidestep the sovereignty issue at this point is either to carry on regardless or to establish a continuous test broadcast. The stakes are too high to be weak. The Red Cross has said that 'There is no more powerful medium for reaching refugees than radio, and the louder the voice of reason on the airwaves, the less room there is for propaganda.'

Militarily defeated, the Hutus embarked upon an operational-level manoeuvre to take 1.5 million of their supporters out of Rwanda, principally into the border area of eastern Zaire. *Reporter Sans Frontières*, a radio service funded by UNHCR, established *Radio Gataschya* (meaning 'swallow' – as in 'returning home') to counteract what the militants were saying to the refugees in the camps. But, the truth of the matter was that it was not safe for them to go home. In addition, UNAMIR refused to co-operate, because of concerns of impartiality but also because it had a different perception of the truth.

Perhaps surprisingly, it was Germany which had run the national radio for the former, defeated Hutu government. All that was required to bring the radio back on the air was a battery and some diesel oil. The USA's representatives said they would supply these, but when Washington staff heard of this they were told to disassociate themselves from their offer. In fact the help was secretly rendered. What concerned Washington was, if the national radio were to be used by the new Tutsi government to initiate a new round of genocide, they did not want the USA identified with having brought the radio station back to life.

BURUNDI AND ITS PRESS

What has been discussed thus far is the operation of radio services. That is the major, but not the exclusive instrument in the media of hate. In now extending this study into the field of newspapers, an explicit opportunity becomes available to challenge readers to reconsider some of the basic assumptions they may have made concerning the nature and influence of the media in Third World conflicts. For the extension of this examination we look at Burundi, a crowded country the size of Wales, lying to the immediate south of Rwanda. There are also radio issues there, but the important lessons have already been teased out of the situation in Rwanda. In fact, the Hutus had a so-called hate radio broadcasting into Burundi from Uvira in Zaire, but hate newspapers had a higher profile in Burundi than in Rwanda. Rwanda and Burundi are sometimes regarded as twin states, but they are not identical twins. The ethnic mix is much the same, a substantial 85 per cent Hutu majority and a Tutsi minority. In Burundi, however, the Tutsis have never relinquished power. In the democratic elections of 1993 they lost heavily in the polls but, through the means of a creeping coup they regained power, not least because of the predominantly Tutsi army.

There were five extremist newspapers in Burundi – three Tutsi, two Hutu – but the most extreme were Tutsi: *Le Carrefour des Idées* and *La Nation*. The material was written by militants, not proper journalists, and the papers were financed by individuals, businessmen or politicians. The material they wrote was virulent and unsubtle in its threats. Lists of so-called Hutu activists in Tutsi papers were not designed to improve their popularity. An article in the February 1995 edition of *La Nation* had its intention made perfectly clear. It reads (in translation):

> The Secretary-General of the United Nations, Dag Hammarskjøld was killed in Katanga (now Shaba) in 1961. There was a violent reaction but no follow-up to his death. The French Ambassador to Kinshasa was assassinated by the Zairian army last year. France was up in arms but threats were stifled. These two foreigners were not killed without reason. It was as a result of their interference in the internal affairs of Zaire. Today, Burundi risks being

46

enveloped in conflagration by two foreign diplomats – the Mauritanian Ahmedou Ould Abdallah, Special Representative of Boutros Boutros-Ghali [then UN Secretary-General] to Burundi and Robert Krueger, US Ambassador to Burundi. These two diplomats have not come here to represent Boutros Boutros-Ghali or Clinton. They represent a Frodebu [Hutu party] lobby which wishes to silence all that section of the nation opposed to Frodebu. Both wish to overthrow the government of Kanyenkiko. Burundian patriots advise them to go home as soon as possible. If not, they must be shown that Burundi does not want them by demonstration, or other means.

SUMMARY

What it is hoped we have shown is the media of hate's potential to destabilise. As a result of the destabilisation in both Rwanda and Burundi hundreds of thousands, mostly Hutus, became refugees, more than Africa has ever known. Their refugee camps were not unlike guerrilla training camps and arms flowed into the hands of the impressionable young spoiling for a fight. International preventive diplomacy is an essential prerequisite to dampen down emotions and address the causes of dissent. The last thing Rwanda and Burundi need is a media of hate to ignite the blue touch paper.

Solutions that need to be found lie in the dilution of the effect these messages can cause by addressing the problems which give rise to them. This is why it is so much more important to tackle the message rather than the means. After all, it is relatively straightforward to switch the latter off. The sense of impunity evident in both states has so obviously to be countered. How could Kenya have provided refuge for one of those prominent in the Rwandan genocide? How can virulent stories be published unchallenged in Bujumbura papers? People were aggrieved because so many were refugees unable to return home, a home where the rule of law barely existed, where there were no prospects for the numerous young encapsulated in a demographic time bomb, and where a handful of individuals held sway over both suffering states. Prevention is preferable to cure but, if the search for a cure becomes unavoidable, it is to be hoped that those called in to sort out the mess have two communications strategies: one to introduce a friendly, non-propagandist radio service, and another to jam radios the sole purpose of which is to incite violence and disorder.

47

NOTES

1. For greater detail of the military/humanitarian conduct of this operation, see R. M. Connaughton, 'Military Support and Protection for Humanitarian Assistance, Rwanda, April–December 1994', *The Occasional*, paper number 18 (Camberley: Strategic and Combat Studies Institute, 1996); or Cambridge University's Global Security Programme through the Internet.
2. Television has greater relevance in the more developed countries and in this context 'developed' is used relatively. For example, in former Yugoslavia, the various national forces fought to gain control of the television networks. Having lived in a regime where the control of communications was the key to the control of the population, they required no convincing of the need to control the media, which became a most decided media of hate.

Part Two:
The Media View of the Military

5

The Media Portrayal of the Military

KATE ADIE

Any views that I have on the portrayal of the military by the media will share the characteristics of television news: they are highly selective, necessarily simplified, suspected of some bias, and delivered by a reporter that people may find slightly irritating! But, unlike my personal opinions, television news does command the attention every night of at least one-quarter of the population, and in times of national crisis the figure rises even higher. These days, there is undoubtedly a sensitivity among media-aware politicians about those stories which dominate the major news bulletins; a sensitivity which, due to the urgent style of these stories, certainly has the *appearance* of influencing swift and perhaps rather hurried political action. For the purposes of this chapter, however, I want to concentrate not on the political impact of television news but on what the viewers are getting; on the kind of news story which involves the military, how that story is selected, how it is put together, and finally on some thoughts about image making.

First, lest anyone should think that journalists are constantly wrestling with the principles of media–military relationships as we go on the air at nine o'clock each evening, let me explain that the most profound comment I have ever heard in the BBC television newsroom on the portrayal of the military in Bosnia was, coming after a complicated and politically sensitive statement delivered by an UNPROFOR (United Nations Protection Force) officer, 'That blue beret doesn't fit, does it?' A trawl through BBC television news bulletins for the first eight months of 1995 shows that, apart from the war in Yugoslavia, the British armed forces and the Ministry of Defence keep a fairly low profile when compared to other high-spending departments of state; and that defence is not a particularly newsworthy issue when compared to health, education and welfare. Other than a few officers involved in the Gulf War or in operations in former Yugoslavia, who have appeared regularly on television in the last few years, senior figures in the military world are quite unknown to television viewers, including such important people as the Chief of the Defence Staff. There has also been a recent decline in the television coverage of traditional ceremonial events involving the armed forces, and not even Trooping the Colour is the headline story that it used to be.

What constitutes television news is often even at variance with news coverage by serious newspapers. Taking a look at the top three stories of the BBC six o'clock and nine o'clock news bulletins of 1995, the Balkans dominated our own coverage, but that was in flat variance to the serious press. Their top three headlines were just not our headlines. Television, with its element of sensationally up-to-date information and its predilection for exciting pictures, favours war. There is also a strong national element in television coverage. The financial resources of all media organisations, even the BBC, are finite, and it makes a big difference to the coverage of a war if British troops are involved. Back in 1992 the BBC made a policy decision to devote considerable energy and funds to maintaining a permanent BBC news presence in the Balkans, and this had a big effect on the frequency with which stories about the region appeared.

But, other than simple convenience, the reason for concentrating on the top three BBC television stories in detail is that virtually by definition they are likely to be more comprehensive than other stories, and to include comments or snippets of interview. They are also definitely hard news stories, rather than diary events, or features, or just quirky tales. Also, it seems that a growing phenomenon among television viewers is that they are 'snacking' on news. That is to say that viewers sample news bulletins throughout the day, and that in the evening they may only want headlines rather than the full course of a 28-minute programme.

The British armed forces started off 1995 very quietly in media terms, despite there being several thousand British troops in former Yugoslavia and the BBC having both radio and television correspondents in Sarajevo. Not one British military story made it onto the front of the news for a month. But, although winter was a relatively quiet time in Bosnia, pictures of war were certainly running on our bulletins. They were coming from Chechnya, to which some former members of the Sarajevo press corps had already migrated, sending back the same kind of pictures which they had once sent from Bosnia. This illustrates the point that resources are finite, and that not many news companies can afford to run operations in two or more dangerous areas simultaneously. The costs of sending the media to war safely (or as safely as possible) are horrendous. Armoured vehicles can cost well over £60,000, and a good bullet-proof jacket costs just under £1,000 or so. In a hostile environment where journalists need sophisticated equipment which was not designed with encounters with

120mm mortars in mind, running costs are high. It may seem trite to suggest that one foreign war is enough in each bulletin, but the editorial pattern of American television networks in particular endorses this, and indeed sometimes their television news bulletins can have a distinctly isolationist feel. In the four years of the war in former Yugoslavia most American networks ran very few foreign news stories, with very little complaint from their viewers. If in future British news companies intend to base their programming on a more popular and tabloid style of news, then this will probably not have very wide horizons. The very successful tabloid press we have in this country, which scarcely featured Bosnia in its coverage throughout this period, might became a model for British television in the future.

Back in the Balkans, once the fighting in Gorazde became news, television pictures became instantly available by satellite dish as several freelance local crews were operating right in the centre of that city, supplying the kind of frightening pictures which show that high risks are being run. Those kinds of pictures were more common in the early stages of the war; but after 75 or more journalists died covering the story there was less desire to go that extra mile for the picture. One of the reasons why coverage of the (wrongly termed) 'safe areas' of Gorazde, Bihac and Srebenica was so sparse was because of the danger under which journalists worked: and not only the general danger of a war zone but very specific threats to themselves, including deliberate murder. With no kind of officially approved escort into such areas on offer from either the local people or the UN, to get into those safe areas foreign journalists were faced with a lengthy overland journey on foot through hostile and sometimes lethal territory. By 1995 few journalists thought such risks were worth the candle, and even fewer editors were willing to shoulder the responsibility for such adventures.

Whether the UN itself had any mandate to effect the free movement of the press is a moot point. In reality the policy on the ground always depends very much on individual attitudes and decisions, and in Bosnia this had an effect on our coverage. For a start, no one was quite sure what the UN rules were; there was a lot of paper on the subject, but it amounted to no more than rubbish. Most British commanders, even if they thought they knew what the rules were, preferred to pursue their own discretion. They did not object to the press coming along on operations, even difficult and dangerous ones; they gave them armed escorts, and found them places inside armoured vehicles for safety, in complete contradiction to a specific UN edict on the subject; and they gave background briefings in great detail on the military situation.

But, despite the presence of British troops, several weeks of 1995 passed with only the occasional reference to Bosnia and no lead stories on our own television bulletins. In one way this was good news for the British military, as it meant that there were no accidents or incidents, because injury or death in a war zone will usually get attention. There is an interesting comparison here between British and French political approaches and television coverage. With the situation in Bosnia seeming so intractable at times, French politicians found it expedient to have the Foreign Legion constitute a large part of their troop contribution, because the death of a foreigner causes fewer ripples in the French media. With no BBC television mention of troops in Bosnia, five other stories made it into our top three on screen, all with a common theme: in Cyprus a British soldier was involved in a fatal car accident; in Belfast two Scots Guards were gaoled for murder; the Army disciplined soldiers of The Parachute Regiment for assault; and the retirement of Sir Sandy Wilson (who had commanded a brigade in the Falklands War) took place. Also, the controversial case of Private Lee Clegg of The Parachute Regiment appeared once early in the year. Crime, violent behaviour and scandal are normal news fodder.

One of the factors which selects a story, although not necessarily a military story, from the daily stew is if a 'fall from grace' appears. When the pillars of society lean from the straight and narrow there is usually a journalist lurking nearby. In Britain the victims of this conventionalised approach are often vicars or other members of the clergy, who are somehow traditionally never expected by newspaper editors to get into sports cars, have the acquaintance of young, blond women, or to indulge in anything remotely exciting. But all professional members of society are targets for the press should they be caught straying. In this world of changing values, in which most people have little connection with service life unless they have personally experienced it, all members of the armed forces still seem to have high standards demanded of them by the general public, which associates the military with disciplined behaviour and with self-control, and in return entertains some kind of respect for them. So the occasional scandal or case of criminality among the armed forces makes far more headlines than a comparable case in civilian life. The newspaper fixation with the military experience also leads to a large number of 'fall from grace' stories which are headed 'Former Soldier …'; and an enormous number of people seem to qualify as 'ex-SAS'. (It is often a fact buried down the page of the story that the individual left the service about 20 years previously!)

The combination of tradition, war-making and status which feeds into our image of the armed forces is actually very British. It is not encountered in many other European countries, even among those which are members of NATO. In most countries service in the military seems to be regarded as just another sort of job, and therefore as nothing special. In Britain the armed forces are still somewhat separate from the rest of society and often actually live apart from the rest of us, which has produced arguments about granting them separate treatment in respect of such issues as equal opportunities for women and the treatment of homosexuals. The military are one of the very few groups which actually qualifies for that overused cliché much loved of editors, 'a close-knit community', and they have a hierarchy of deference and obedience totally unknown now in any other part of society. Foreign journalists are quite baffled by this. In the Gulf War and in the Balkans my non-British journalist colleagues were very curious about the status and image of British troops, which they found very different to their own. I was with a group of American correspondents at a gathering of young British Army officers during the Gulf War; 'Why are they all talking about school?' one television reporter demanded afterwards. On another occasion, in the desert, the Americans were flummoxed by the appearance of British commanding officers. 'If they are in the same Army', my colleagues wanted to know, 'why are they all wearing different clothes, especially that man with a knee-length jumper with a huge rat knitted on it?'

In this context of how separate the British armed forces are from the rest of society, I should mention the kind of story which the Army likes to promote about itself, but which is not shown to a mass news audience. This is the 'good news' piece of public relations, which begins 'You should come along and see the jolly good work our chaps are doing!' I still get many telephone calls which start like that, and they are all wasting their time. National television news is 'hard news', and there is usually fierce competition for which of a dozen or so stories get into each bulletin. Even so, a remarkable amount of official energy is directed to trying to sell these stories to the national news media, and while they might have stood a chance some years ago, for better or worse things have moved on. Although things are changing, I still encounter people who are charged with carrying out a press role for the armed forces who seem not to have noticed what is actually on the news these days. In my own experience, the civilian and part-time practitioners of this role employed by the military are particularly old-fashioned and amateurish.

For the armed forces, the other side of this issue is that television news is fascinated by war. That does not mean that television excels in coverage of such matters. It is neither comprehensive nor incisive; it lacks detail; it lacks reflection; it lacks a context; it has problems of access; it has problems of verification of material. It tends to sensation but it stops well short of the full horrors: a major problem to those of us who report from war zones. A BBC editor demanded of me 18 months ago that I excise every shot of dead bodies from a story which I had compiled near the town of Prozov in Bosnia. I thought this was unreasonable when the story was that of the massacre of 38 elderly people, and their corpses were lying around about us. A voice squeaked down the phone from London, 'You can't have dead bodies on the news, you know!' I replied, 'This is war!' 'So what?' said the voice. There are a lot of problems in trying to convey the reality of war.

Nevertheless, after the quiet start of the winter, the six-month period March–August 1995 saw one-third of all BBC major news bulletins include footage from Bosnia or Croatia, frequently as the lead story, which was much greater coverage than the newspapers gave to the Balkans. Although there was not necessarily a British military element to all these bulletins, a high proportion did feature British troops and their activities, either in the background or as a reference to the political and diplomatic stories. Many of the senior positions in UNPROFOR in 1995 were filled by British officers. Also, British forces were placed in some of the more difficult and active areas, and were considerably more proactive than the contingents of some other contributing nations. Or, as one Dutch correspondent returning from a village near Vitez one night remarked to me, 'Your lot are at it again and they are a bit miffed that the BBC is not there.'

In Bosnia the UN promised the media a 'transparent' operation, based on the claim that they were going to tell everything and tell the truth. As we might have guessed, this turned into a new definition of the word 'transparent'. The press soon learned that large amounts of information were being withheld, that an emphasis was creeping into briefings that was intent on excluding sensitive matters, and that it was not unknown for two dozen British Warrior IFVs (infantry fighting vehicles) to thunder past your front gate at midnight, just two hours after the battalion commander has lied to you about turning in for a good night's sleep. The UN bureaucracy itself still does not have a policy towards the media in wars and complex emergencies; quite possibly this is no bad thing in itself, as it allows countries such as Britain to follow their own policies more successfully. But meretricious statements, deception and false information are as much a part of the UN's armoury as that of any government, and in some cases even more. Many member countries of the UN, some of which had troops involved in Bosnia and other recent UN operations, believe in violently enforced censorship and have a contempt for enquiry which leads them to imprison or shoot journalists. Countries which have the same kind of relationship between the government, the press and the armed forces which we enjoy in Britain are very few in number, and even fewer as members of UN operations. At least so far, NATO as a collective organisation also has no coherent policy towards the media, as it also includes some countries whose attitude towards the media is far from that expected in Britain.

The UN has had a good line in nonsense in recent times too. There is hardly a journalist who has served in Sarajevo who has not spent time on the floor, under the furniture, listening to someone in a blue beret shouting above the sound of explosions to tell them that 'the cease-fire is holding'. One of my own notebooks includes a line from a UN spokesman chiding us for failing to appreciate the quieter atmosphere of the city with 'only 2,012' firing incidents. Having decided that the UN was not exactly playing the game of transparency and open journalism, the next source for most journalists was according to national preference, and there were immense variations between what some of the troop-contributing nations would tell us. In fact, the hacks took to drawing up a cruel league-table of UN national contingents as sources of information. Without going into further detail, I should say that the Ukrainians featured prominently as always worth visiting, scoring no points for information but scoring high for the liver-rotting quality of their hospitality; the Turks were disinclined to tell the UNPROFOR force commander anything, never mind the British contingent down the road. But, working this way, journalists were soon confronted with a moral dilemma when two sources of information failed to run in parallel, or even contradicted one other. Did we follow the UN line and jeopardise our relationship with a national contingent, or did we try to find a compromise? It was frequently a nightmare.

Well, no reporting of a war ever works perfectly, and we were not very surprised. But, since 1991, after the set-piece nature of the Gulf War with the idea of media pools, new experiments in media–military relations and particularly the experience of the Balkans have changed our ideas completely. With apologies to all those who have written position papers and worked out how to organise media pools for the next war, they are now out of date. The British have been feeling their way through this experiment as best they might, with no media pools, an uncontrollable number of journalists roaming around, and problems with UN information which was often uneven and also out of date. The detailed background briefings from the British themselves provided a substantial amount of information for the international press to work on, and were very welcome. I say this because there was (eventually, and after some months of experiment as to how they were going to run the briefings) a very definite allure of the British press briefings held in Vitez. Nobody else held that kind of regular briefing, none of the other contingents. I was personally lambasted by the French General Morillon early on in the deployment of the UN troops. 'Why are all these stories about the British?' he asked, and we replied,

'Because the British tell us things the French don't!' General Morillon's answer to this was not to institute press briefings, but to appear everywhere himself on television.

These briefings were extremely valuable, but chiefly for the print journalists. Television does not like being reduced to briefings. We need pictures, and the very distinctive style of some of the British Army's press briefings did not quite lend itself to the 'Nine O'Clock News'. While British journalists had little problem being addressed by a young officer delivering prep school jokes, some of our foreign colleagues were puzzled that these came from a man wearing a rugby shirt, with a dog under his arm. (Before anyone in the Ministry of Defence starts a witch-hunt, I should add that the information and analysis given by this young officer's sharp brain were possibly the best we had in three years.)

But we needed pictures, and, lo and behold, the Ministry of Defence sent Warrior IFVs to Bosnia! Camera crews found these armoured vehicles fascinating. They proved an irresistible image, curiously reminiscent of the warhorse of old going into battle. Pictures were taken by camera crews on Warriors, in them and underneath them as they rolled over the road. The Warriors also share many of the same characteristics as generals, being stylish, slightly threatening, making a lot of noise and looking good on camera. An extraordinary amount of footage has been shown of these Warriors and not just on British television, often well beyond their specific relevance to any story.

The British Army contingent for UNPROFOR was soon found by most of the international press to be more approachable than most other contingents. Their bases were moderately accessible and so were their soldiers. Compared to other UN contingents, the British were amenable, mainly due to one factor which makes the Ministry of Defence blench: the British soldiers talk to journalists. Admittedly, they may not always deliver gems of intelligence, but their openness was striking at all levels, and very human reactions to a grim situation are what have produced memorable moments of television. Ours is above all an intimate medium: truthful and candid observations, whether from a general or the youngest private soldier, lodge in the mind of the audience. Carefully prepared statements and nicely organised media facilities, all the public relations in the world, all of these pale beside the words of a professional soldier expressing his honest opinion. However, trying to get this accepted is an uphill task, and squawks of fear enshrined in the words 'personality cult' are heard from Whitehall. As a journalist, I find this attitude old-fashioned and singularly out of touch with modern communications. The armed forces need their personalities. For better or worse we live in the age of the personal. An anonymous institution is seen as hostile and uncaring;

the phrase 'No comment' excites contempt rather than respect for reticence.

Above all, to discourage personal communication is a sign that you lack confidence in your people. This disparaging attitude is still exercised through endless mutterings down the line that publicity of any sort cannot be good for the career, that people in uniform are not to be trusted; civil servants from the quaintly named Government Information Service hover around at interviews, coughing with disapproval or interfering with leaden comments and insulting interpretations of the soldiers' remarks. *How dare they?* This has been annoying me, and all my colleagues, for years now. Each time we have made our protests, and each time nothing has been done. In the 'media war', the military's best weapon is their people, and they very rarely let their own side down. While realising that this method of approach is harder for the bureaucrats to control, fraught with problems of a personal nature, and shot through with those terrible issues of individual emotion, those in command of modern armed forces have got to come to terms with it. The audience has already done so, and it likes what it sees. Ask British television viewers what they remember of British troops in Bosnia and they will recall not the military manoeuvres, or the negotiations, or the statistics, but the faces and the voices under the blue berets.

Having stated boldly that the military should have confidence in their own troops, it is only fair to ask if the military should have any confidence whatsoever in the media. The media may indeed have preconceptions about the military, prejudices that operate before a story is even written or embarked upon. Of course we are all the product of our own culture, with greatly varying experiences. For the ordinary British hack the armed forces are a bit of a mystery. The structure, the jargon, the atmosphere engendered by discipline, all of this is a puzzle. Our view of the Army in particular is still likely to be conditioned by the views expressed 30 years ago (about the time that many people who are now senior officers were joining the Army) in Anthony Sampson's *The Anatomy of Britain*, which portrayed officers as often idle, ignorant and self-satisfied, and restricted to a narrow social group. Today, younger journalists are often surprised to encounter university-educated young officers from a wide range of backgrounds. It is a measure of how hard old journalistic attitudes can die that in Bosnia it was the talk of the press pack that officers in a Yorkshire regiment actually had Yorkshire regional accents, rather than the cut-glass caricature that had been expected.

Despite our individual prejudices, the media do not set off to report military stories with a set agenda. There are individual cases of journalists who either have their own specific purpose and task, or have had one set by their editor, and the military are right to complain about these. But they are easily spotted, and they are in the minority. The British press as a whole has no particular way of approaching a story, far less one which will damage military security; and it has no great axe to grind. It is, after all, not very likely that editors of the Sunday or weekday tabloids will have paid their hacks to go all the way to central Bosnia to report in detail on the tactical aspects of the international security environment. The television people do not set out in the morning with a political or personal crusade in mind. Any correspondent who gets too personally involved with any one story comes in for scrutiny from his editors, his colleagues and the audience. Television news is a middle-of-the-road animal; it only feels fully justified that it is doing its job when it is knocked down by the political traffic coming from both directions.

But, I must keep repeating, television news does want pictures. This sometimes means going and getting virtually the same picture every day, much to the amazement of soldiers puzzled by this repetitious behaviour, because the bulletins demand today's images wherever possible. It also means going into areas of war zones where one should not normally go. It staggers and appals a number of people in the services when they find out just how far journalists are prepared to venture. Time and again in Bosnia soldiers have expressed horror at what they see as mindless risk-taking by journalists who have only a certain amount of personal protection, limited knowledge of fieldcraft, no good grasp of procedures and no idea whatsoever about things that go bang. To which we reply, 'You do your job and we'll do ours.' We work in parallel, each along our very own line. That is the basis for a good working relationship: if we end up convinced that we are both equally mad, then we are getting along all right. And if we can develop a healthy trust for one another, then so much the better.

Covering Bosnia did present a number of ethical problems for the media. Because of the scale of the danger, which included not just accidents and cross-fire, but deliberate targeting and murder of the press, the journalists found themselves seeking shelter with the military. When Lieutenant-Colonel Bob Stewart of the Cheshire Regiment first offered to escort us through a difficult area in 1992, the reaction of the press was one of absolute incredulity. It seemed a highly peculiar offer, not in line with UN policy, and apparently intended to compromise our journalistic independence. We all stood there outside the camp in Vitez complaining, 'You must be joking! Why bother with us? And why should we bother with you?' A matter of weeks later, most of the press were expert at throwing themselves lemming-like into the back of a Warrior. The extremely nasty nature of the conflict pushed the journalists into very close contact with UNPROFOR (or at least some of it, as a number of contingents offered no such facilities or protection), and the British gained much more national and international coverage and publicity as news spread that they would take you under their wing. Inevitably, such close contact has its drawbacks. To what extent were the journalists in any way beholden to the military, either to the British or to the UN? Did the press begin to feel that the warring factions were all hostile and that the UN was friendly? Did associating with the UN taint the journalists in the eyes of the locals? Should journalists show loyalty to the armed forces of their own countries, especially if those journalists acquire information that the armed forces could use? For wars in which your own country is fighting as a participant these questions are well rehearsed, both among journalists and as part of the military–media relationship. But, in a peace-support or peacekeeping operation there are very few official guidelines; few journalists have got their ideas worked out; and there is not much agreement as to the direction towards which we should be heading. Personally, I have no definite answers at the moment; I can only recognise that this is not an easy area, and that it is going to need a lot of flexibility on the part of those involved in military–media thinking to come up with workable and principled ideas.

Let me return to the importance of being portrayed at all in the media. There was a time when institutions were faceless, when words from on high were handed out by a minion or conveyed through a considered letter to *The Times*. Reticence was respected. Not decades ago a governor of the Bank of England referred to my request for an interview on camera as 'a rather vulgar idea'. However, whether we like it or not, a considerable part of any institution's image now is the image of its leading individuals, or, at a pinch, its spokespersons. Television has been criticised (probably quite rightly) for demanding or creating a narrow set of criteria for a successful appearance. The kind of image favoured by television is highly conventional, even soothing, something that gives confidence. As public relations companies like to say, 'television comes into the living room'. So, one talks about 'collateral damage', not the raw realism of war. Our stories simplify: reporters are rarely granted more than two-and-a-half minutes to encompass the situation. Applied historically, such criteria would have had severe consequences for the careers of most military men. If the fears of timorous civil servants about a 'cult of personality' had been allowed to prevail, not one of the heroes of British military history would ever have emerged. Even so, the brilliance, ruthlessness and the complexities of leading men who face possible death do not fit easily into a 15-second sound bite and the two-minute summary. Even a reasonably pithy quote beginning 'England expects this day that every man ...' would

61

probably be scrutinised unfavourably by today's news editors if it were to be delivered by a one-eyed man who was minus an arm, and who was known to be publicly associating with a woman not his wife! Today's clever soldiers might like to contemplate the challenge of summarising the complexities of military theory in one sentence for an audience which has just been riveted by half an hour of watching 'Neighbours' or any other soap opera. And if television makes monstrous demands, radio is not much kinder. The brevity of bulletins, the constant updating of stories, the concept of rolling news, all combine to compress and simplify, although it is never our intention to distort or misrepresent. We work within the conventions of speed and brevity which might easily drive military people to the conclusion that the entire process should be avoided or ignored, or at least touched only with the bargepole of public information channels. Yet, they can no longer stand aloof from us. Part of our democratic process these days is contact and communication via television. Whether we like it or not, a considerable amount of policy making, politicking and shaping of public opinion is conducted through individuals who appear in the media. No organisation which needs public support can afford to stay silent. Whatever the armed forces say and do on the small screen may be their only means of being portrayed effectively.

I believe that in the last few years the military have been learning this lesson on the battlefield and on operations, partly because people who are taking vital decisions on a daily basis are not frightened of making up their minds about what to say to a mere journalist. But, away from the battlefields, in times of peace, the military silence on this subject has been much greater. Of course there are rules which exist to cover the military–media relationship, but perhaps some of these deserve a little revision. It also seems to me that some matters of enormous significance to the military are presently discussed in public without reference to the views of those most involved. Taking a random sample of major stories involving the armed forces over the last few years, issues such as cutbacks in the services, their intended role and strength in the future, homosexuality and the armed forces, and the services' attitude to women have all lacked one vital ingredient: that has been the experience, attitude and judgement of the men and women who are serving in the armed forces now. I know of no other organisation whose present and future is discussed in the sole context of the opinions of outsiders, journalists, MPs, disgruntled former members, or completely mad old fossils in armchairs. While acknowledging that there are some difficulties, it is time to reconsider the reticence, a good deal of which is fuelled by Whitehall's traditional secrecy, supplemented by glossy public relations and customer service blandishments.

The military are nothing if not plain spoken; they should be allowed to speak up a little more.

Three images remain of my time spent covering the Balkans since 1992. The first is of a bunch of shrieking lunatics frightful to behold, the Sarajevo Evil Horde. They do not have guns and they are not on the front line. The Evil Horde are the Sarajevo's football team's most devoted fans, yelping in delight at their first outing to the city's stadium in over two years, and watching as the band of the Coldstream Guards marches onto the pitch, a stunning image. The second is of Lieutenant-Colonel Bob Stewart expressing with total honesty his reaction to a dreadful massacre. And the third image is of a young corporal pinned down by fire on the road to Tuzla saying, 'I'm buggered if I know which lot are shooting at us!'

6

Reporting Conflict:
Who Calls the Shots?

IAN STEWART

We [journalists] do the same in war as we do in peacetime.
Robin Lustig of BBC radio[1]

INTRODUCTION: FROM PEACE TO WAR

In early September 1995, as defeat became inevitable, General Ratko Mladic, the Bosnian Serb commander, posted a last desperate warning, directed towards the United Nations Protection Force (UNPROFOR) in general and the United States component of that force in particular. His forces, he cautioned, would continue to resist UN intervention actively, threatening to 'make it like Vietnam'.[2] As history proved, it was an empty threat, but a threat that raises issues that lie at the heart of any discussion on the media presentation of war and conflict.

'Vietnam' remains the key word in understanding the attitude that governments of liberal democracies have towards the media coverage of war and conflict. In essence, Vietnam signifies the inability of the government of the most powerful country in the world to control the presentation of conflict in its own media, and the damaging effect that unregulated media coverage of war has on public support for military action. Thus, Vietnam emphasises a necessarily difficult relationship between the government, its military and the media during conflict: the military intent on secrecy and control, the media committed to openness and the reporting of the full effects of war. Understandably, not only have United States governments been keen to avoid another Vietnam, other Western governments mindful of American experience have sought to learn the lessons of Vietnam, and to plan carefully for the impact that media coverage has on modern warfare.

So much constitutes a familiar conventional wisdom. However, the cultural prominence of Vietnam highlights the fact that the media coverage of Vietnam was exceptional. The media coverage of modern war is, in reality, far from the tense power play between military and media that the legacy of Vietnam suggests. Indeed the purpose of this chapter is to ask whether the governmental machinery in war in fact too easily manages the British media. Although much of this management is desirable and reasonable, there are dangers in a largely uncritical media. Perhaps the biggest risk is that an uncritical media means a poorly informed public. In turn, such a public's support for military action can only be based on the manipulation of images and the repetition of sound bites, not upon considered judgement. The former kind of support may be useful, even necessary to stimulate in the short term, but in the long term only the latter sort of support can provide the backing that military action needs.

To understand how the media coverage of war is determined, we should turn away briefly from the presentation of conflict. We should examine the practical arrangements that in peacetime underpin the relationship between the Ministry of Defence and the media. This is a neglected area.[3] The tendency hitherto has been to emphasise the negotiation of the military–media relationship in wartime. This is an important omission: it is these peacetime arrangements and mechanisms that transfer the relationship from peacetime to wartime. The working relationships between government, the military and the mainstream media that are observed, developed and nurtured every day of the week are immensely revealing. Set against a background of legal guidelines, it is a relationship of mutual accommodation and benefit, a relationship made real in a set of working practices and expectations. It is also a relationship in which government is the major partner with the key power to shape the agenda of defence reporting.

Thus, the central claim of this chapter is to argue that much of the debate surrounding the media coverage of war is aimed at the wrong target. In the British context, successive governments and their armed forces have exerted, and will continue to exert, almost total control over the media coverage of conflict. The real aim of studying the media coverage of war might be to use our discussion to question the fundamental mechanisms underlying the political process and its expression in the press.

To support these claims, I will examine the mechanisms that connect the media to the governmental and legislative process in this country and which shape the character of the media in British civic life. First, I will sketch the legal framework in which media coverage of defence matters

65

exists, using the case of the BBC to illustrate how these limitations placed on coverage do not necessarily undermine the authority of the reporting. I will then examine the journalist's reliance on sources and the practice of 'balance'. I will argue that these working practices are a means by which the reporting of defence matters can be all too easily managed by the governmental public relations machinery.

For the purposes of stimulating debate, I will put forward a deliberately contentious version of my central argument. I will, however, stop short of suggesting that the media are totally controlled. I do not wish to argue in favour of any version of a conspiracy theory. There are often instances where the views of the political elites are not those given most weight in the media coverage of a specific issue. In these cases the media fulfil an important democratic function in giving exposure to alternative and dissenting viewpoints. However, I do suggest that by and large the political elite can expect to have the strongest and loudest voices in any media debate. And specifically in the case of war it takes an exceptional set of political circumstances for those elites to lose the power of largely determining the character of media coverage.

Finally, I will conclude by raising what to my mind are serious problems of the present relationship, problems not only for a free press and the democracy it seeks to inform, but also problems for the military in doing their job properly. But first, in order to place our discussion in context, it is important to return briefly to the important cultural legacy of the media coverage of the Vietnam War.

THE VIETNAM SYNDROME [4]

Despite convincing scholarship that argues otherwise, there remains an accepted wisdom that television coverage in the United States was the instrumental factor in the US military's inability to prosecute the Vietnam War to a successful conclusion.[5] The negative tone of media coverage, it has been argued, dissolved the support for the War in the United States. Even more damaging, military commanders in theatre, increasingly aware of the coverage their actions might engender on the small screen, were inhibited militarily. This is the Vietnam syndrome, a cultural legacy that has coloured attitudes towards the media coverage of war ever since. However, Vietnam has proved politically and practically useful for both military and media alike. For the media, specifically television news reporting, the Vietnam syndrome frames news-reporters as truth-seekers – determined to tell it all and answerable to no one in their quest for independent, objective reports. Thus, one legacy of Vietnam has been to afford news-reporters a privileged status as bearers of the truth, however unpalatable that truth might be. This status afforded to the media has, in turn, provided the military with a rationale for controlling the media. From the military perspective, Vietnam provides a prima facie case that media coverage by its nature distorts and, ultimately, weakens military efforts.

In providing governments with an apparently indisputable rationale to curtail media coverage, while at the same time underlining the independence of the media, the Vietnam syndrome frames the military–media relationship as one of tension and irreconcilable differences.

IMPARTIAL JOURNALISM: THE CASE OF THE BBC

Are the British news media as independent and as willing and able to cross the establishment as the legacy of Vietnam might suggest the United States media were? I believe a brief examination of the key institutional mechanisms that ultimately define the military–media relationship, combined with an appreciation of the journalistic working practices in which that relationship is expressed, will suggest otherwise. However, to argue that mainstream journalism is neither independent nor objective does not necessarily imply that the quality or the authority of news reporting need suffer. The example of the BBC is instructive. The world over, the Corporation has a deserved reputation for the high quality of its news reporting and analysis. The BBC is not independent. Quite the contrary: the BBC is a state broadcaster funded publicly and ultimately regulated by the state through the parliamentary system, as the Corporation's Charter makes clear.[6] Furthermore, the BBC is Charter-bound to support the state in time of war. This commitment defines the bottom line in the relationship between the BBC and the government, and although the BBC has on occasion sought to assert independence, its claims have not been seriously entertained. In 1950, for example, the government, the military, the media represented by the BBC, and the Press Censorship Bureau, met to discuss contingency plans for the next war. The senior military negotiator is documented as responding to the BBC's Chairman's avowal not to accept censorship in a future conflict thus:

> May I suggest that we face facts, and that it really does not matter what you or anyone else lays down now; the truth surely is that if the Government of the day, in any future war decide to impose a policy of censorship, the BBC will surely have to accept their dictum, as will the Press Censorship Bureau.[7]

The BBC's ultimate accession to the wishes of Parliament has not meant that the BBC's credibility as a broadcaster has suffered. Furthermore, the BBC's standing as an impartial and unbiased broadcaster is politically useful. The use of the Empire Service as a medium of propaganda encouraging United States involvement in the Second World War was only possible because of the fine reputation that the Corporation carried.[8] Not all politicians, however, have recognised how useful this reputation of independence can be. During the Falklands War, Prime Minister Margaret Thatcher was reportedly upset that the BBC talked of 'British troops' (ironically the commercially funded ITN was using 'our troops'). In fact the BBC's veneer of detachment was politically useful and lent added weight to its reporting. The lesson was learnt however. When John Major was questioned in Parliament for his opinion on the BBC's use of the same terminology during the Gulf War, the Prime Minister simply complimented the BBC for its 'remarkable reporting and impartiality'.[9] This enviable reputation is intact today even when other British institutions are under increasing attack; the BBC's reputation for truthful, authoritative reporting throughout the world serves as the benchmark standard for other, newer, British services, as well as many foreign services.

How can this be so? If the BBC is not independent, how can it be impartial? The answer lies in the BBC's diligent application of the normal journalistic working practice of 'balancing a story'. It is through this practice that journalism attempts to be as fair to the fact as possible. However, there are limits placed upon journalists: the constraint of time, the demands of the institution they are reporting for and the legal framework. For defence correspondents, all these constraints apply in an even stronger form. However, one constraint in particular has an especially powerful effect: their reliance on elite sources.

SUCCESSFUL MEDIA WAR IS THE CONTINUATION OF NORMAL WORKING PRACTICES

The media may not always report the truth, but the media always reports the news. Getting at the news is about access, and getting at political news is about access to elite sources. Let us consider the institution that constitutes the defence journalist's prime and often sole source, the Ministry of Defence (MoD). A journalist who seeks to write on defence matters must have access to the MoD, and the MoD Public Information Organisation seeks to ensure that the Ministry influences information made public through the media. The MoD press desk in Whitehall answers queries from the media, sends out press releases, and briefs defence correspondents. It is here that issues of national importance are handled. At local level, units and stations have Public Information Officers (PIOs), usually military personnel performing a secondary duty, whose role is to work with the local media ensuring positive coverage.

The relationship, whether national or local, is mutually beneficial. The press is given privileged access to information and photograph opportunities; in turn, the media are expected to report responsibly and fairly, that is to say reflect the views of their source. This simple fact accounts for the relatively uncritical media coverage that the MoD generally receives. Although several key issues, notably sexism, racism and bullying, are given critical exposure in the media from time to time, the body of 'negative' coverage is of essentially trivial stories of sexual impropriety.[10] Although the cumulative effect of such stories over time ought not to be underestimated, it is nonetheless significant that the MoD's budget, the second largest in Whitehall, is rarely a subject for such media scrutiny.[11]

The reporting of national defence matters, in war and peacetime, is subject to a number of legal checks that delineate the boundaries of war correspondence. Britain has been legislating on this matter since 1904.[12] The government's power to enforce censorship on reporting has always been an effective mechanism, as are the more insidious mechanisms of the Official Secrets Act, libel law and the use of 'D' Notices to remove the possibility of certain issues being raised in the media.[13] But however useful legally enforceable censorship is in the short term, it is likely to prove unpopular when the conflict is not a threat to Britain's survival. It is more effective to build these limitations into the practical relationship between the MoD and the media.

The accommodation between the MoD and the media in peacetime is transferred to wartime by means of a set of guidelines and regulations that have been drawn up by the MoD in consultation, significantly, with the editors of the major news services.[14] The resulting document, *Proposed Working Arrangements with the Media in Times of Emergency, Tension, Conflict or War* (known as the *Green Book*), sets out the terms of the relationship between the press and the military. These arrangements are part of the wider *British Defence Doctrine* guidelines which makes quite clear the necessity for a good relationship between military and media:

> The Media Op[eration]s maxim is to release as much accurate information as possible, subject only to operational security and the safety of British and Allied lives. This requires close co-operation with the media at home and in theatre ... Statements and briefings by ministers, senior officials and military figures provide the basis

of information about the overall political situation and the strategic nature of operations ... Editors and other media representatives are also briefed in the United Kingdom and in theatre to ensure that they understand the background situation and the operational response.[15]

In essence, then, a transference of normal working relationship from peacetime to wartime takes place. The working arrangements for journalists as outlined in the *Green Book* also explain that sensitive material will be embargoed – a perfectly reasonable caveat. Of course responsible journalists can often be entrusted with sensitive information. For example, in the 1991 Gulf War the then Brigadier Patrick Cordingley was able to brief with confidence the pool journalists who accompanied his forces. In addition to the journalists' natural desire not to do anything that would endanger the lives of British troops, there is nothing particularly unusual about senior journalists receiving information with an embargo. Indeed it is often by observing such embargoes and respecting the wishes of their sources that journalists develop their sources, and, therefore, the quality of the final journalism.[16]

Moreover, we should not forget that on some matters such as casualties, the media can be as sensitive as the military. Martin Bell, then of the BBC, records being asked by a newsroom editor in London as he prepared to file a story from Bosnia, 'Is there *blood*? We don't want to see any blood, at least not before the nine pm watershed. It's in the guidelines you know.'[17]

BALANCE

As the preceding account has outlined, the best way to establish and maintain a mutually accommodating relationship between the military and the media is to build that relationship into daily business. In this section I want to expand that point further by arguing that, in the main, accepted journalistic working practices make for unchallenging and relatively uncritical war reportage.

Let us examine the key (Western) journalistic practice of 'balancing a story'. This practice is based on a desire to represent both sides of any argument fully. A fine sentiment perhaps. However, the issues surrounding conflict and potential conflict are never so clear-cut, nor confined to two sides. The arguments, the issues, the history, and perception of that history involved are always complex. The practice of balance simplifies complexities and tends to a presentation of conflict in stark black and

70

white terms. Moreover, the 'two sides' of the argument presented in the media tend to reflect their sources in the elite civic life, in the British case essentially those arguments that are presented in Parliament. There is good reason for reporting these views; they are after all the views of the elected representatives and lawmakers. However, the range of views reflected can be a narrow one. As Noam Chomsky warns, 'Controversy may rage as long as it adheres to the presuppositions that define the consensus of the elites.'[18] Arguments and positions outside that consensus are excluded or marginalised. The scant coverage afforded to peace movements in the periods leading up to and during both the Falklands War and the Gulf War is a good example. Jeffrey Walsh observed of the latter conflict that 'As a result of the political consensus to liberate Kuwait and defeat Saddam Hussein, opponents of the war soon became marginalised, and their activities either ignored or misrepresented.'[19]

However, we ought not to be too swift to lay blame for the lack of meaningful debate at the feet of the journalist alone. Journalism is only as good as its sources and can only reflect those sources. In time of a national crisis such as a war those sources are, in the main, the political elite whose views inform parliamentary debate. The opposition character of formal political debate in Britain defines the first balance. What then is a journalist to do when there is no opposition from the opposition? In the conflicts in the Falklands and the Gulf this has been the case. The 'Opposition', the other side of the argument, has amounted to no more than a few pious remarks that the situation might have been avoided, but now the crisis is upon us the armed forces have the full backing of Parliament. At a stroke, any other points of view are seen as outside the main argument. The Opposition system even isolates members of its own party who oppose the war. Such mavericks, though they might get some media exposure, are framed in general as irrelevant to the main issues.

The key, then, to a successful media war from the perspective of the government is to ensure that there is a firm consensus across the political elite. Such a consensus delineates the boundaries in which debate and discussion take place. A closer examination of the media coverage of Vietnam suggests that the 'divided' media coverage of that conflict reflected the divisions within the political elite from which the media took their lead, rather than the wilful independence of an uncontrollable media. As Daniel Hallin observed:

> Republicans in Washington were questioning the President's credibility on the war long before most television correspondents were. At least a year before Cronkite called the war a 'bloody stalemate' and urged negotiation, the Secretary of Defense had reached

essentially the same conclusion. The collapse of America's 'will' to fight in Vietnam resulted from political process of which the media were only one part.[20]

Mladic's failure to 'make it like Vietnam' rested on a number of reasons: it was after all a completely different conflict fought under very different conditions. However, one of the core reasons why he could not fight the media war on his terms was the broad consensus in favour of intervention that existed within political elites across the UN, a consensus not necessarily apparent among the publics of those countries.[21] For Mladic's threat to become reality depended on a divided political will in the UN players. An undivided political elite will find little difficulty in containing, if not controlling, the media war.

The British governmental machinery, also, was keen to promote consensus. For the Gulf War, a BBC journalist recorded that the Prime Minister's press officer 'had clearly taken a calculated decision to ensure that the Downing Street Press Office did all it could to maintain a strong public consensus in Britain for the allied action'.[22] The Labour Opposition played its part in holding the consensus in place. The Shadow Foreign Secretary Gerald Kaufman was highly active in holding together the consensus, so active indeed in pursuit of this goal that a senior member of the government was reported as saying that Kaufman 'deserved a medal for his efforts'.[23]

Given a united political elite and clear statement of policy, the military can enter the operational theatre confidant of media coverage that will reflect that unity.

In theatre, especially a tightly controlled battlefield, the military are the media's source. The information, 'the bang, bang', the interviews with the powerful, are all in the gift of the military. Holding the cards, the military are able to tighten even further the arrangements that exist between the media and themselves. Of course, the simplest and most effective regulation is pooling, a useful practical ploy for journalists that provides safety, organisation and a steady supply of copy. In return accredited journalists contract to observe certain codes and the impositions of limits on their reporting. Journalists may express their misgivings about such arrangements but history tells us that such regulations have applied to journalists in every conflict since the First World War. Indeed, the similarities between the accreditation forms used during the First World War and those currently attached to the *Green Book* are striking.[24]

Technology, too, seems to be against the journalist. The impact of transmission technologies that might have been thought to herald the dawn of a new era of media coverage can in practice form a powerful constraint.[25] The lack of time to reflect, check and contextualise is bound to push the journalists evermore towards the accepted wisdom of their elite sources. There were over 1,000 journalists accredited to the Coalition forces in the Gulf War, but all were served by essentially the same source. Philip M. Taylor has described the result memorably as 'monopoly in the guise of pluralism'.[26] John Pilger's condemnation of 'ruling by pooling' as the 'the military's ability to distort and the media's malleability' is a criticism shared by many journalists.[27] However, it is no surprise that Pilger's critical commentary on the Gulf War was written in London.

CONCLUSION

Daniel Hallin has written that 'The behaviour of the media ... is intimately related to the unity and clarity of the government itself, as well as to the degree of consensus in the society at large.'[28] In stark contrast to the low public esteem which many sections of the news media enjoy, the status of the war correspondent has probably never been higher. Although perhaps it is significant that Martin Bell MP, whose journalism earned him a reputation for authority and impartiality, has suggested that objectivity in journalism is neither possible, nor indeed desirable. However, what is desirable is a relationship between the media and the defence community that is both responsible and demanding. Responsible journalism ought to demand more of both the defence community and the elite sources that are the media's access to material. In turn the defence community, by informing their public through the media, should demand more from the public in terms of understanding the responsibilities of supporting military action.

The reporting of war is a crucial component of a healthy liberal democracy. War reporting is not, however, and should not be, unbiased or unregulated: the lives of soldiers, airmen and sailors are too valuable to be gambled with for the sake of providing television audiences with exciting pictures. However, the limitations necessarily imposed on reporters in theatre need not apply before the theatre is entered. Especially in the crucial period leading up to military engagement, the media must be allowed to take the responsibility to report all shades of opinion, however unpalatable these viewpoints might be to their erstwhile prime sources. The fourth estate has a responsibility to acquaint the public with the ramifications of the war it is being asked to support.

On the other hand, the public, too, has responsibilities to shoulder: in lending support to war it should be made fully aware of the demands being placed on the armed forces acting in its name. The danger of unrepresentative and overly negative media coverage is well known; however, there is danger, too, in media coverage that is overly positive. Keen to avoid the issue of casualties, the Coalition forces' emphasis on hi-tech weaponry resulted in the Gulf War being portrayed as a near bloodless war fought almost exclusively on computer screens. Although a successful exercise in media management, the legacy of the media war in the Gulf might prove in the long term to be as militarily inhibiting as that in Vietnam. The Gulf War has created a popular and unrealistic expectation that future wars should be won quickly with few casualties (on either side). Distorted media coverage is in neither the public's nor the military's interest.

In conclusion, the key component in ensuring that a successful media war is waged alongside the conventional war is the existence of widespread support for the validity of the political goal the military action seeks. If the legacy of Vietnam reminds United States administrations of this fact, the Suez Crisis of 1956 does similarly in the British context. Although Prime Minister Anthony Eden's government benefited from press support from a sizeable portion of Fleet Street, other sections of the press reflected opposing views. This only happened because those newspapers had access to a section of the political elite able to express those views publicly. In short, this was another example of a divided political elite finding expression in divided press coverage.[29] However, a united political elite should not be seen as the ultimate goal of media relations in wartime. The target must surely be an informed and responsible public; in short, a popular consensus.

In the meantime, the importance of the media cannot be overstated. As the political situation in the Gulf in early 1998 teetered briefly on the brink of conflict between Iraq and forces led by the United States, the *Guardian*'s 'Austin' encapsulated this well in his front-page cartoon: an American general briefing on his battle plan tells his audience 'synchronise your watches with peak viewing time'.[30]

NOTES

1. Speaking at the Global Media conference held at the International Maritime Organisation, London, December 1997.
2. Channel 4 News interview, Tuesday 5 September 1995.
3. There are a few notable exceptions to this trend. A. Hooper, *The Military and the Media* (Aldershot: Gower, 1982), for example, looks at the peacetime arrangements and even goes as far as to look at fictional and dramatic representation of the armed forces on television. Notable, too, is the Glasgow

University Media Group, *War and Peace News* (Milton Keynes: Open University Press, 1985).

4. The Vietnam syndrome that President George Bush was so glad to 'kick once and for all' is, of course, more than a phenomenon of the media coverage of the War. Vietnam has had far deeper ramifications, a satisfactory examination of which goes far beyond the scope of this paper. However, the presentation of the conflict in the media was, and remains, a key element in understanding the attitudes towards the cultural legacy of the Vietnam War.
5. See D. C. Hallin, *The Uncensored War: The Media and Vietnam* (London: University of California Press, 1986).
6. The current BBC Royal Charter was issued in 1996 and runs for ten years.
7. Draft letter dated 18 January 1950 in Public Records Office, Kew (PRO), file INF 12/522.
8. See N. J. Cull, *Selling War: The British Propaganda Campaign Against American 'Neutrality' in World War II* (Oxford: Oxford University Press, Oxford, 1995).
9. Quoted in N. Jones, *Sound Bites and Spin Doctors: How Politicians Manipulate the Media and Vice Versa* (London: Cassell, 1995), p. 92.
10. Significantly, the main sources for these and many other 'scurrilous' stories are court-martial proceedings. By maintaining that certain sexual improprieties, including adultery, are a contravention of military law, the armed forces thus provide a forum where the indiscretions of private lives are discussed in public. Consequently, journalists can obviate the need to depend on the usual MoD sources and simply report the proceedings in full and free of 'spin'.
11. Kate Adie makes the same point in Chapter 5 of this book.
12. T. Rose, *Aspects of Political Censorship 1914–1918* (Hull: University of Hull Press, 1995), p. 11.
13. For a full discussion of these mechanisms and the potential scope of their power, see D. Leigh, *The Frontiers of Secrecy* (London: Junction Books, 1980).
14. The British have always included representatives from both the media and the government. The Joint Committee of the Admiralty, War Office and Press Representatives for the Informal Censorship of Naval and Military Information first sat in 1911 and was formalised in late 1912. See PRO file CAB 5/3.
15. *British Defence Doctrine, Joint Warfare Publication 0-01* (London: Ministry of Defence, 1996), pp. 4–17 and 7–11.
16. This is what the Glasgow University Media Group call 'ordinary journalism': the routine use of press briefings that allows political authorities to assume a consensus among most journalists on the range of views which are to be featured in any 'serious' fashion.
17. M. Bell, *In Harms Way* (London: Penguin, 1995), p. 213 (italics in original).
18. N. Chomksy, *Necessary Illusions* (London: Pluto Press, 1989), p. 48.
19. J. Walsh, 'Vic Williams, Conscientious Objector and the Peace Movement', in J. Walsh (ed.), *The Gulf War Did Not Happen* (Aldershot: Arena, 1995), p. 88.
20. D. C. Hallin, p. 213.
21. I am aware of course that this is a sweeping statement: in reality that consensus was severely tested and strained in places.

22. N. Jones, p. 92.
23. The government member was Gillian Shepherd. Nicholas Jones describes how Kaufman carefully orchestrated the media presentation of official Labour Party policy which publicly dissociated itself from the anti-war wing of the party. See N. Jones, p. 24.
24. See PRO file INF 4/1B.
25. For an appraisal of the impact of transmission technologies on war reporting, see J. Allen, 'From Morse to Modem', in I. Stewart and S. L. Carruthers (eds), *War, Culture and the Media* (Trowbridge: Flicks Books, 1996), pp. 148–64.
26. P. M. Taylor, *War and the Media: Propaganda and Persuasion in the Gulf War* (Manchester: Manchester University Press, 1992), p. 268.
27. J. Pilger, 'The Sins of Omission', originally published in the *Guardian*, reprinted in J. Pilger, *Distant Voices* (London: Vintage, 1992), p. 127.
28. D. C. Hallin, p. 213.
29. T. Shaw, 'Government Manipulation of the Press During the Suez Crisis', *Contemporary Record*, 8, 2 (Autumn 1994), pp. 274–88.
30. *Guardian*, 2 February 1998.

7

Stereotypes and Other Types: The Portrayal of the Army in British Television Drama

EDWARD BRAUN

At intervals over the past 20 years writers have been drawn frequently to military conflict as the focus for television drama, and the continuing success in the 1990s of ITV's series *Soldier, Soldier* in the key nine o'clock slot is proof of the Army's appeal to a broad viewing public. However, in seeking to reconcile the demands of authenticity with those of dramatic complexity, the writer is confronted with a particular problem when portraying the soldier. The problem is illustrated in Charles Wood's stage play *H*, set in the Indian Mutiny of 1857, in which Captain Jones Parry says:

> You have no ease if you
> cannot Order.
> There is nothing can help
> the mind in Disorder,
> like an Order,
> it helps the orderer
> much as it helps the ordered,
> Doubts do slip away.[1]

Good order and discipline are indispensable to effective military conduct; for their maintenance they require the training and regimentation of the individual, and it is to this end that the seemingly gratuitous sadism of the NCOs on the barrack square and the assault course is directed. From here, it is no great step to the stereotype – a concept seemingly irreconcilable with the complexity of characterisation that we normally associate with serious drama. Often, television drama, whether benign or hostile in intent, has done no more than represent the military as a series of variations on familiar themes. There have, however, been occasions when it has attempted to engage with the mind of the soldier in a far more problematic manner.

In a country such as Britain, which since the termination of national service in 1963 has maintained a wholly professional standing Army and a small volunteer reserve, there is little direct insight into the nature of military life; the populace at large may be inclined to regard it as remote from everyday experience, arcane in its ceremonies, and inherently inhuman in its ultimate function. Yet, as Val Taylor suggests in her recent comparison of Universal Pictures' feature film *Born on the Fourth of July* (1989) and BBC's drama documentary *Tumbledown* (1988), there may be a far more direct and troubling kinship between the soldier and the society whose interests he is employed to protect:

> The stereotype of the soldier stands at the confluence of the many discourses of a patriarchal system, embodying simultaneously the apparent moral contradictions of the hero and the killer; the archetypal repository of 'masculinity' – strong, courageous, macho, aggressive, physically and sexually dominant, traits which are held naturally to accrue to the male in a patriarchy. By dint of his role within the workings of the discourses of patriotism and nationalism, the soldier reflects and validates the conservative Establishment it is his function to protect and preserve; but he also constitutes a potential disruptive threat to it, by the very nature of the actions it employs him to undertake in combat and their moral ambiguity. He is both insider and outsider at once, and this is most fully apparent when he is known to have 'seen action'.[2]

Charles Wood, the author of *Tumbledown*, would argue that the roots of this relationship are embedded deeply in the philosophy of our traditional schools. Speaking on BBC television's *Bookmark* programme in 1988, he said:

> We fondly imagine that we are not a militarist society, but ever since Doctor Arnold got to work on his educational system we have been a *military* society, in that public schools have provided us with leaders in civilian and colonial and military life for a very long time. And public schools in one sense prepare young men for heroism.

It is, of course, a widely held view, and one well illustrated by R. C. Sherriff in *Journey's End*, his grimly realistic depiction of the First World War which ran for two years in the West End in 1928, and was revived on BBC television in 1988 (director, Michael Simpson). The action takes place during the German offensive on the Western Front at St Quentin in March 1918, and in Act Two the 18-year-old subaltern Raleigh, fresh from public school, is being gently introduced to the realities of life in the trenches by the former schoolmaster, Lieutenant 'Uncle' Osborne. The talk turns to rugby football, and Osborne modestly confesses to having played for the Harlequins and 'for the English team on one great occasion'. Their conversation moves from sport to warfare in an exchange which suggests that the same sense of fair play governs both:

> RALEIGH: How topping – to have played for England!
> OSBORNE: It *was* rather fun.
> RALEIGH (*after a pause*): The Germans are really quite decent, aren't they? I mean, outside the newspapers?
> OSBORNE: Yes. (*Pause*) I remember up at Wypers we had a man shot when he was out on patrol. Just at dawn. We couldn't get him in that night. He lay out there groaning all day. Next night three of our men crawled out to get him in. It was so near the German trenches that they could have shot our fellows one by one. But when our men began dragging the wounded man back over the rough ground, a big German officer stood up in their trenches and called out: 'Carry him!' – and our fellows stood up and carried the man back, and the German officer fired some lights for them to see by.
> RALEIGH: How topping!
> OSBORNE: Next day we blew each other's trenches to blazes.
> RALEIGH: It all seems rather – *silly*, doesn't it?
> OSBORNE: It does, rather.[3]

In his autobiography published in 1968, Sherriff, who as an Army captain had himself been wounded in France, wrote that his soldiers 'were simple unquestioning men who fought the war because it seemed the only right and proper thing to do. Somebody had to fight it, and they had accepted the misery and suffering without complaint.'[4]

It is illuminating to compare *Journey's End* with Charles Wood's film for television *A Breed of Heroes*,[5] described in the *Radio Times* as 'This impressionistic account of life as a member of the British forces in Northern Ireland ... early in 1971, their peace-keeping role gradually disappearing in an ugly war'. In a recent essay, Derek Paget contrasts Northern Ireland with the Falklands War which, like Grenada in 1983 and Panama in 1989, was an archetypal 'post-modern conflict, in which the image *preceded* the facts'. Typically, post-modern wars

> [t]ake place in countries 'remote' from home both literally and metaphorically; they last a very short time and end in 'victory'; they

involve opposition to political systems readily constructed as unacceptable by home public opinion ... they are unlikely to provoke much opposition from the rest of the world.[6]

In Northern Ireland, however, 'the war stands in antithetical relationship to the post-modern war in almost every respect: unsuccessful, costly, apparently interminable, and difficult to "sell" to the home public'.[7]

In an adaptation that remains close to the spirit of Judd's text, Charles Wood and his director, Diarmuid Lawrence, depict the early experiences of a company of Assault Commandos in west Belfast, harassed mainly by women and children and threatened by never-seen snipers. It is a situation far removed from the uncomplicated values and fair play of *Journey's End* and the contrast is reflected in the more problematic portrayal of the ill-matched group of officers, occupying vulnerable quarters in a bottling factory on the Falls Road. In a scene that contrasts with the induction of Lieutenant Raleigh, his counterpart Lieutenant Charles Thoroughgood, late of Oxford and Sandhurst, is interviewed on arrival by his commanding officer, Lieutenant-Colonel Gowrie. After the briefest of pleasantries, the exchange is curt and one-sided:

> GOWRIE: Let me come to the point, Charles – stones now, guns later; what ought we to do?
> THOROUGHGOOD: (*Pause*) Shoot them?
> GOWRIE: Did you enjoy Oxford? Every young soldier in this Battalion is a good Christian. I shall not interfere with your long-haired Oxford beliefs, but your soldiers are not fools. They have an ethic to combat communism, and need it – what do you have?
> THOROUGHGOOD: I hope ... I, I ...
> GOWRIE: I hope so too, Charles, because you're an atheist.
> THOROUGHGOOD: No.
> GOWRIE: (*consulting Charles's confidential report from Sandhurst*) Says here you are.
> THOROUGHGOOD: No, it says I'm an agnostic.
> GOWRIE: Same difference. Friend of yours gets his face blown away – hope it never happens – but you have to bury him without God's help. Could you, and look your Ackies[8] in their eyes again? Your friend, lowered into his grave minus his face, and you an atheist. (*Pause*) Lost for words. You will crack, Charles.[9]

Then, after enquiring affably whether Charles is 'dining in', Gowrie concludes the interview with the advice, 'As to your problem, see the Padre', leaving the bemused subaltern to retreat in confusion. Unsurprisingly, by the end of the film, as IRA activity mounts and battalion HQ is bombed, Charles has raised enough money from feeding lurid copy to a bullet-shy journalist to buy himself out of the Army.

Charles Wood is a rarity amongst British dramatists, demonstrating in his work an understanding of soldiering that stretches back over more than 30 years to his earliest plays, the *Cockade* trilogy, which drew on his own five years' experience as a trooper in the 17th/21st Lancers. In his preface to the published text of *Tumbledown* he writes:

> Honour and duty are admirable qualities: that they are often spoken of against a background of brutality and savagery does nothing to detract from their intrinsic worth. To be a soldier, if the undertaking is fully considered and understood, is a noble vocation. A soldier offers his life and often it is taken. Nobody is astonished when it is, nor should they be.[10]

It is a view that few of Wood's contemporaries would endorse. Peter Nichols, his long-time friend and literary sparring partner, wrote to him after reading the script of *Tumbledown*:

> The trouble for me is that, feeling as I do about war, I can't really sympathise ... Of course you've never said simple things about war, which is why you can write so much about it and I can't. You believe we can't understand war without understanding the warmakers and this springs in you from an admiration for their discipline and a love of their ethic ... I wish I weren't so worried about your love for these men and their larks.[11]

Edward Bond, a confirmed pacifist and impassioned denunciator of all manifestations of violence, has even less time than Nichols for 'these men and their larks':

> The Army's a sort of parodied version of civil society – it's without all the face-saving rituals and without all the social excuses and just the naked barbarism. It's a very corrupt form of society and a very foolish and vicious form which is an amalgam of sentimental sloppy reverence for dead idols combined with a real viciousness. Those two things go together to make up the disciplined British Army, or, indeed, any Army. There's no such thing as a good Army – it's like saying there's a gentle devil.[12]

Not all writers share Bond's undifferentiated spleen. In BBC1's controversial four-part series *Days of Hope* (1975), while Jim Allen and his director Ken Loach endorse Bond's view that there's no such thing as a good Army (and certainly no good officers or regular NCOs), the private soldier, though commonly drunken and licentious, may through the experience of war become humane, and even revolutionary. Thus, in the opening part set in 1916 Ben Matthews, a naïve farmer's son stirred by the jingoism of a recruiting meeting, enlists under-age and is eventually posted to Ireland to fight against the resurgent nationalists. When his platoon is forcibly billeted on a farm, the men sexually taunt the farmer's teenage daughter and force her to sing for them. Their obscene banter is gradually stilled by her plangent rendering of 'Glory-o to the Bold Fenian Men': they hear her out in respectful silence and leave her unmolested. The following day, a local boy lures one of their comrades into a booby-trap which blows him to pieces, but when Ben catches him he cannot bring himself to harm him, instead handing him over to the platoon.

At the beginning of Part Two, set in a Durham mining village during the miners' strike of 1921, we see Ben's reaction to his experiences in Ireland. He deserts from an Army convoy and finds refuge in the family of Joel Barnett, one of the local strike leaders. While the two men roam the woods, searching for food and trying to fathom revolutionary politics, the Army comes in search of Ben at Joel's house. In the course of their search they come across some Marxist pamphlets and an officer is summoned. As troops stand guard outside to hold back the angry crowd of miners and their wives, he interrogates the Barnetts' teenage daughter, Jenny, first fondling her breast and then answering her defiance by slapping her repeatedly in order to discover Ben's whereabouts. Again, a contrast is carefully established between the overbearing upper-class lieutenant with his polished Sam Browne belt and the luckless pink-cheeked boy soldiers in ill-fitting uniforms who have to suffer the taunts of the hostile crowd outside. Thus, the depiction of the military hierarchy conforms precisely to Allen and Loach's class analysis of British society in the 1916–26 period.

Days of Hope provoked a furious and long-running controversy, directed largely at the representation in Part One of the Army's brutal treatment of a group of conscientious objectors, including Ben's Quaker socialist brother-in-law, Philip Hargreaves. Many of the letters to the *Radio Times* were from angry veterans protesting at the perceived slurs on British military tradition and heroism, although just as many were outraged by alleged errors in minor details of drill or uniform (some misremembered).[13] It was a debate that was rerun with equal vehemence when Alan Bleasdale's *The Monocled Mutineer* was shown on BBC1 11 years later.[14] The series was adapted from the book of the same name by William Allison and John Fairley, which gives a necessarily speculative account of the extraordinary life and death of Private Percy Toplis and of his involvement in the mutiny at the Etaples base camp in September 1917.[15] When the book was first published in 1978, it prompted questions in Parliament about the events of the mutiny, which led to the discovery that all records of the Etaples board of enquiry had long since been destroyed. However, it was Bleasdale's 'costume drama with something to say about the times we live in',[16] loudly promoted in advance by the BBC, that revived the ancient debate about historical 'truth' and drove Tory columnists to new extremes of apoplexy in their denunciations of the Corporation's 'left-wing' bias.

In the first episode of the series, *The Making of a Hero*, Bleasdale's 'dashing rogue', played by Paul McGann, is seen as an RAMC stretcher-bearer on the Western Front in 1915. Forced to witness the gruesomely bungled execution of a young officer convicted of cowardice in battle, Toplis appropriates his identity and equips himself with an officer's uniform, a monocle and a Distinguished Conduct Medal. Thus transformed, he assumes the appropriate upper-class accent, learnt earlier as a juvenile offender in Lincoln gaol from 'a toff doing three years for fraud', and effortlessly sustains the masquerade in an officers' brothel, where he is much preferred to the overweight regulars. Returning on leave to the Nottingham mining village of his adolescent misdemeanours and now 'promoted' to captain, he is fêted by the whole community and gleefully humiliates his former overseers when invited to put the Voluntary Training Corps through its drill paces on the local football pitch.

Through all his transformations in the course of *The Monocled Mutineer*, the figure of Percy Toplis remains for the viewer transparently himself, and pleasure is generated through authority's floundering attempts to keep pace with him. In depicting Toplis's effortless assumption of the officer role, Bleasdale and O'Brien (greatly aided by the charisma of Paul McGann) are demonstrating the degree to which deference is accorded to the outward trappings of authority. Hence, if the integrity of the military structure is to be preserved, it is essential that Toplis be hunted down and dispatched with maximum ignominy in order to prevent the myth taking root in the popular imagination. Whatever the precise facts of the case, the great popular success of the series suggests that all the attempts to suppress the story failed. Helped firstly by Allison and Fairley and then by Bleasdale, the Toplis myth has proved stubbornly enduring, helping to problematise further the history of the First World War and 'to overcome deference to [its] criminally incompetent militarism'.[17]

However, Toplis is not the only character in *The Monocled Mutineer* to have stimulated Bleasdale's creative imagination. Cast as one of the ring-leaders of the Etaples mutiny (which in reality he may or may not have been), Toplis confronts the camp commandant, Brigadier-General Andrew Thomson, Royal Engineers. Denied cavalry reinforcements until too late, Thomson is forced into humiliating negotiations with the mutineers and then obliged to retire from the Army ('I'm going to have an illness. So I've been told!').[18] Earlier, while Toplis and his victorious comrades enjoy a night on the town in Etaples, Thomson contemplates the ruins of his career in the company of his adjutant and a rapidly consumed bottle of whisky. He recalls an earlier occasion when, as commandant of the Royal Military Academy, Woolwich, in the long hot summer of 1911, he had generously authorised parades in shirt sleeves, sponsored end-of-term dances and encouraged the Academy's dramatic society – only to suffer a public reprimand from the Chief of the Imperial General Staff:

> I stood beside Sir John French, facing my cadets, their parents and friends, members of my own family, *while he attacked me for the lack of discipline at Woolwich.*
> (*He is now crying very quietly*)
> Had to take it like a man while he demanded a return to ... proper standards of dress ... more drill, less leave ... and an end to our 'hectic' social life. That's what he said. I stood by his side, facing front, and that's what he said. I left Woolwich shortly after.
> (*Long pause. We perhaps see a look of ill-disguised contempt on* GUINNESS's *face. We see the tears streaming down* THOMSON's *face*)
> ... And I returned to King's regulations, to the very letter of the law ...
> (*Stands up, moves towards the door with his drink*)
> ... no more small indulgences ... the bastards could parade in Hell without a shirt sleeve to be seen, for all I cared.[19]

In Timothy West's finely studied performance as Thomson we witness the collapse of a once humane and generous officer, broken by a custodian of military orthodoxy and now destroyed finally through rigidly upholding that same orthodoxy in the draconian training regime at Etaples. Whether the real-life Thomson would have possessed the articulacy and self-awareness to have so voiced his feelings is open to question; certainly, his aged governess remembered 'Old Chips', as he was known, as 'a very forbidding, even rather terrifying, and certainly not a very talkative man'.[20] But, with justifiable dramatic licence, Bleasdale first presents a seeming military archetype then gives a profoundly moving insight into the tragic collision between human imperfection and dehumanising conformism.

To repeat Derek Paget's definition, the Falklands/Malvinas Conflict in 1982 was the perfect 'post-modern' war, ideal for packaging and selling to a nation only too eager to endorse its prime minister's wrathful vengeance against the impudent Argies.[21] Conveniently remote in the South Atlantic, the reality of the fighting was carefully mediated through images approved by the Ministry of Defence and through the portentous delivery of the daily bulletins from its appointed spokesman, Ian MacDonald. Within months of the War's ending this uncomplicated authorised version of events was set to be confirmed in dramatic form when the BBC commissioned a script from Ian Curteis, veteran of 86 transmitted plays and series over 20 years. *The Falklands Play* was scheduled for transmission on 2 April 1987, the fifth anniversary of the Argentine invasion, but, after four drafts and demands for further changes from the new head of Drama, Peter Goodchild, Curteis's leaden, triumphalist script was shelved in July 1986 due, as the BBC implausibly claimed, to the imminence of the next general election (which eventually took place on 11 June 1987).[22]

When it was discovered in the autumn of 1987 that *Tumbledown* was being filmed on location in Wales the *Sunday Express* announced:

> Five months after dropping a TV play about the Falklands which treated Mrs Thatcher sympathetically the BBC is secretly filming a new play by a left-wing author opposed to the Task Force.[23]

Thus the tone was established for much of the debate that attended the BBC1 transmission on 31 May 1988 of this most contentious of all British films about war. In fact, the *Sunday Express* was not wrong in presuming Charles Wood's opposition to the war; in his own introduction to the published text he writes:

> As for my own feelings about the Falklands War, I feel intense guilt, for I hold it to be wrong that young men like Robert Lawrence were maimed and killed because our skills in avoiding wars are not nearly so good as our skills in promoting them.[24]

But where it *was* wrong was in presuming that this was what Wood's *script* was about. In fact, consistent with much of his earlier work, he was drawn not by the political or the strategic issues of war but by the mentality and experiences of the individual soldier, in this instance a 21-year-old Scots Guards officer, Lieutenant Robert Lawrence MC, who had the back of his head blown off by an Argentinian sniper's bullet during his platoon's assault on Mount Tumbledown in June 1982. A year before the *Sunday Express* 'revelation', apprehensive that the Curteis affair might lead to the cancellation of his own film, Wood had written a letter to the *Guardian*, making his position clear:

The screenplay, *Tumbledown*, was very carefully written with the full co-operation of Robert Lawrence and his family. I avoided any political stance, concentrating on the courage of Robert Lawrence in the Falklands, when recovering from his terrible wound and, not least, when recounting his feelings honestly and accurately.[25]

Immediately following the film's transmission John Keegan, Defence Editor of the *Daily Telegraph*, was scathing in his criticism of Robert Lawrence's own published allegations,[26] and expressed doubts about the BBC's motives in making *Tumbledown*, describing its producer, Richard Broke, as 'a compromised figure' for having earlier been a party to the falsification of history in *The Monocled Mutineer*. At the same time, however, he was careful to exculpate Charles Wood:

He is neither 'pro' nor 'anti' war. As an ex-soldier, he knows that soldiers do not think in those terms. Their emotions about fighting are both total and complex and almost inexpressible to anyone who does not belong to their brotherhood. If he had a model for *Tumbledown*, it may well have been the brilliant film *Platoon*, about the Vietnam war, which also tantalised civilians by the ambiguity of its morality.[27]

Reminiscent of the furore provoked by *The Monocled Mutineer*, in which some military historians questioned the very presence of Percy Toplis at Etaples in 1917, it was again the factual accuracy of *Tumbledown* that most concerned its critics, much being made in the press of the BBC's last-minute decision, following the threat of legal action, to cut 12 seconds from the final assault sequence in order to remove the suggestion of cowardice under fire on the part of a young lieutenant. Equally objectionable was the claim, amply documented in the Lawrences' own account, that the Scots Guards, a 'family regiment', had neglected to look after one of their own. However, one retired general expressed a more robustly pragmatic view in writing to the *Daily Telegraph*:

We have to shove them [the wounded] into the back of our minds. Soldiers are creatures of the present. They cannot always be reminded of the consequences of war ... There is no such thing as a returning hero, only a returning soldier.[28]

It was precisely this rough imperative that Robert Lawrence encountered and which his whole conditioning left him completely unprepared to handle. As Wood writes in his preface:

The central character is a soldier and hero of Empire – just when we thought it was safe to come out. As Robert says often, what he did down there in the Falklands has made him an outsider, a freak even, as surely as it has crippled him. Brought up in a service family, he was unlikely to question the notions of duty and honour absorbed at home and, later, at Fettes, nor would he meet many dissenters or pay them any regard.[29]

But at no point in the film is the viewer allowed the familiar and reassuring image of 'the hero of Empire'. One is confronted with the contradictory facets of Robert's character; they challenge resolution through the variety of points of view, the disjunctive time-sequence, the juxtaposition of reality and fantasy, collision montage, contrasting film grading, and intertextual references.

Thus, the opening pre-credit sequence, with its stirring Waltonesque music, undulating Cotswolds landscape, dry-stone walls, nestling villages and dappled sunlight on country roads and an F-111 swooping overhead, introduces us to two debonair young men in their racing-green Panther sports car. So reassuringly familiar is the imagery, so traditional the typeface of the title, that we could well be in Curteis country. But as they drive into the courtyard of the spacious home of the Stubbs family we briefly glimpse two women's faces, pale with apprehension, and the music is drowned out by heavy rock from the car radio. With difficulty, the black-leather-jacketed Robert levers himself from the car and looks up at the sky through black sunglasses. At once, the picture quality is grainy and unsteady and we are with Robert in the Falklands three years earlier as he is helicoptered from the battlefield, the back of his skull shattered. When the action cuts back to 'the present' of 1985, Robert and his fellow officer, Hugh Mackessac, are recounting the story of Robert's rescue to an avid George Stubbs while his wife, Helen, looks on in stony incomprehension of 'these men and their larks'. Abruptly again, we are back in time, this time to April 1982 and the Ceremony of the Keys at the Tower of London with Robert and the guard in red ceremonial dress and bearskins. As the bugler sounds the last post, the film cuts to Robert's idealised self-image, shot in blue tinted black-and-white, of himself poised heroically on the prow of a landing craft. To a drumbeat we hear the song: 'I will go, I will go/When the fighting is over/To the land of ...'. Then back to the conclusion of the ceremony. Next, on a television screen in close-up we see the departure of the men of The Parachute Regiment and the Royal Marine Commandos for the Falklands, to the mingled contempt and envy of Robert: 'Bloody Paras ... Look at that one, beret over his eyes. A real Tom that one, the maroon machine.'

We then alternate rapidly between lunch with the Stubbs, Robert with his languid upper-class brother officers in the officers' mess, Robert stricken on Mount Tumbledown, and Robert happily running through Chelsea at the head of his platoon. The character that emerges is in no sense endearing, with his affected drawl, the macho horseplay with his skinhead soldiers, his aggressively fast sports car. In the climactic Tumbledown sequence at the close of the film, Lawrence's terrible injury is seen in part to be the consequence of his own rash heroics as, with a cry of 'Isn't this fun?' and brandishing a rifle in each hand, he foolishly offers himself as an easy target against the skyline. But Wood has carefully reserved this scene until the end, by which time the viewer has come to respect Lawrence's bloody-minded refusal to be categorised as 'invalided out'. Both Val Taylor[30] and Derek Paget discern in the casting of Colin Firth as Robert Lawrence a deliberate intertextual allusion to the 'romantic soldier-heroes of 1940s cinema', and most particularly to Kenneth More's portrayal of Douglas Bader in *Reach for the Sky*. Paget writes:

> For Douglas Bader, the Second World War fighter 'ace' with the artificial legs, substitute Robert Lawrence, the Falklands War 'hero' with half his brain blown away; but for Bader's 'Old Britishness', read Lawrence's 'New Britishness'. *Tumbledown* offers the trope of the Wounded Hero re-written for our times. Lawrence's post-imperial significance (and his post-modern strength as a character in a play) is that his 'sacrifice' was *not* subsumed in Baderian stiff-upper-lip heroics; on the contrary, he caused a radical rereading of Old Britishness by screaming and shouting his refusal of the old role. Behind the various objections to *Tumbledown* lurked the dislike of *any* kind of opposition from within the Establishment itself. The post-modern hero disrupted the upper-class spectacle; this Falklands Actor would not stick to the script, and threatened to upstage the triumphalists.[31]

Significantly, in his *Daily Telegraph* critique of the Lawrences' book and *Tumbledown*, John Keegan does not question the authenticity of such a type, but argues, in terms that might apply equally to Wood and Eyre's film:

> In his book, Robert Lawrence reveals attitudes that should have been extirpated in his training as an officer. Even making allowance for all that has happened to him, he shows a self-centredness, coarseness of language and manners and contempt for the values of others which an officer is taught to overcome. As it happens, he passed

through Sandhurst when its course had been reduced to six months. Friends of the Army warned of the consequences. Tumbledown may be one of them.[32]

A less engaged viewer of *Tumbledown* might well question whether a reformed and satisfactorily regimented officer would have emerged even from a full 12 months' training at the Royal Military Academy. Unlike Keegan, such a viewer might conclude that Lawrence's character, precisely by virtue of his contradictions, reveals a disturbing congruence with the system of values that made him, embracing both the Army and the society of which it is an integral part.

At the conclusion of his preface Wood writes:

> I wrote *Tumbledown* after listening to [Robert Lawrence], at first uneasily fascinated. It was as if I had been given the chance to talk to a surviving Nolan after his forlorn and frantic ride across the front of the advancing Light Brigade, the opportunity to be around at the beginning of a myth. Lowell Thomas must have licked his lips in the same way when he set about inventing Lawrence of Arabia.[33]

But he resisted the enticing symmetry of the myth and presented instead the untidy reality. In an age of media constructs and spin-doctoring the need is not for myths but for what David Hare has described as 'images which are not official, not approved; that break what Orwell called "the Geneva conventions of the mind"'.[34] There could be no more precise definition of what Charles Wood and Richard Eyre achieved with *Tumbledown*, or of what must be attempted by any dramatic representation of our problematic relationship with those we pay to protect us.

NOTES

A version of this chapter was first given as a paper at the conference on 'The Media and International Security' at RMA Sandhurst in September 1995. This version has been published previously in T. Howard and J. Stokes (eds), *Acts of War – The Representation of Military Conflict on the British Stage and Television Since 1945* (Aldershot: Scolar Press, 1996). Thanks are given to Ashgate Publishing Limited for granting permission for its inclusion here.

1. C. Wood, *H* (London: Methuen, 1970), p. 50.
2. V. Taylor, 'Playing Soldiers: The Politics of Casting in *Tumbledown* and *Born on the Fourth of July*', in G. Holderness (ed.), *The Politics of Theatre and Drama* (Basingstoke: Macmillan, 1992), p. 183.
3. R. C. Sherriff, *Journey's End* (London: Heinemann, 1958), pp. 38–9.
4. R. C. Sherriff, *No Leading Lady* (London: Victor Gollancz, 1968), p. 72.

5. Directed by Diarmuid Lawrence. Transmitted on BBC1, 4 September 1994.
6. D. Paget, 'Oh What a Lovely Post-Modern War: Drama and the Falklands', in G. Holderness, pp. 157–8.
7. Ibid., p. 159.
8. 'Ackie': a soldier in the (fictional) 'No. 1 Army Assault Commando (Airborne)'.
9. Text unpublished.
10. C. Wood, *Tumbledown* (London: Penguin Books, 1987), p. xii.
11. Ibid., p. xiii.
12. Interview with Edward Bond, 6 November 1973, in *Theatre Papers*, Second Series, 1, '*Bingo* and *The Bundle*', Dartington College of Art, 1978.
13. See *Radio Times*, 4–10 October 1975.
14. The series was transmitted in four parts, 31 August–21 September 1986, director, Jim O'Brien. For a discussion of the issues raised by the series see Julian Petley, 'Over the Top', *Sight and Sound*, 56, 2 (Spring 1987), pp. 126–31; 'Special Roundup: Cries of Rage about Toplis', *New Statesman*, 26 September 1986, pp. 16–17.
15. W. Allison and J. Fairley, *The Monocled Mutineer* (London: Quartet, 1978).
16. Alan Bleasdale, quoted in *Radio Times*, 30 August–5 September 1986, p. 73.
17. Letter from David Watkins, *Radio Times*, 27 September–3 October 1986, p. 96.
18. A. Bleasdale, *The Monocled Mutineer* (London: Century Hutchinson, 1986), p. 115.
19. Ibid, pp. 106–7.
20. W. Allison and J. Fairley, p. 43.
21. See D. Paget (note 6 above).
22. See I. Curteis, *The Falklands Play* (London: Hutchinson, 1987); G. Reeves, '*Tumbledown* (Charles Wood) and *The Falklands Play* (Ian Curteis): The Falklands Faction', in G. Brandt (ed.), *British Television Drama in the 1980s* (Cambridge: Cambridge University Press, 1993).
23. *Sunday Express*, 4 October 1987.
24. C. Wood, p. xv.
25. Letter from Charles Wood, *Guardian*, 4 October 1986.
26. J. Lawrence and R. Lawrence, *When the Fighting is Over* (London: Bloomsbury, 1988).
27. J. Keegan, 'When Truth Becomes the First Casualty of War', *Daily Telegraph*, 1 June 1988.
28. *Daily Telegraph*, 4 June 1988, quoted in G. Reeves, p. 148.
29. C. Wood, p. xii.
30. V. Taylor, pp. 187ff.
31. D. Paget, p. 169.
32. J. Keegan (see note 27).
33. C. Wood, p. xv.
34. D. Hare, *Writing Left-Handed* (London: Faber & Faber, 1991), p. 36.

8

Media Perceptions of Other Forces: Iraq and the 1991 Gulf War

SEAN McKNIGHT

THE DEBATE OVER IRAQ

The role of the Western media is an aspect of the 1990–91 Gulf Crisis and War that has generated fierce debate. It is widely accepted that the media are an increasingly powerful presence on the world scene, and the Gulf War underlined their importance. The US administration – mindful of the 'lessons' of Vietnam[1] – saw winning the public-relations war as an essential preliminary to taking military action against Iraq. Lieutenant-General Thomas W. Kelly, Pentagon Director of Operations, whose adept handling of the press ensured he gave most of the daily Pentagon briefings personally during the crisis, succinctly expressed the administration's concern to retain public support in arguing that, 'Anybody who doesn't recognise that the support of the American people is a critical element of combat power is pretty dumb.'[2]

Since the defeat of Iraq, the apparent ability of television to transmit news in 'real time', and the vivid imagery of war appearing nightly on television screens throughout the world, has reinforced a commonly held perception that the media constitute a fourth estate.[3] A cynic might observe that the Gulf War appeared to be a wonderful advertisement for the power of television. CNN's new status and fame, in particular, resulted directly from its coverage of the conflict.

The war also stimulated debate among journalists and academics studying the media. Much of this has focused on how the media influence policy, but the war has thrown up a much more contentious debate – particularly in the United States – which concentrates on the alleged manipulation of the media by Western governments and criticises the quality of much of the reporting from the Gulf. The purpose of this chapter is not to directly address these issues, important though they are, but to examine the impression of Iraqi military strength given in the American and British media, and the reasons why such an inaccurate picture received wide currency.

This chapter does not intend to investigate the errors the media made in reporting on specific operational and tactical matters. Despite the resources the media possess for gathering information, journalists are unlikely to have access to tactical details. As Nik Gowing has put it, 'journalists don't have independent means of verifying where the Republican Guard are',[4] and, as a result, they are open to being manipulated for operational reasons. This may outrage liberal defenders of a free press, but it would clearly be absurd for the military to facilitate the media operating as in effect 'Iraqi intelligence officers'.[5] The purpose of this chapter is rather a general evaluation of the military capabilities of the Iraqi state as they were propagated in the media.

THE PERILS OF PREDICTION

The origins of this chapter can be traced back to a major academic conference on the Gulf War held at Keele University in Britain in September 1992; numerous learned papers were given at this conference, but on one topic there was a puzzling silence – nobody seemed particularly interested in why Iraqi military capabilities had been so poorly understood in the West. Many defence experts in the West had exaggerated Iraqi military capabilities in the months leading up to the liberation of Kuwait, and some of the participants at the conference had been spectacularly inaccurate in their predictions of events in the Gulf, something to which they seemed indifferent or oblivious.

Prediction is a risky business – as any betting man will tell you – and one study of a sample of Gulf War predictions published in American newspapers found that 90 per cent of them had proved to be incorrect.[6] The present author is only too aware of the dangers of prediction, having concluded that Saddam was 'just sabre rattling' in late July 1990. However, the reasons why Iraq was so poorly understood are important, and exploring this, rather than pointing to individuals who made mistakes, ought to be a matter for scholarly questioning.

Unlike the academic community, one group that is extremely critical and self-critical about its coverage of the war is the Western media. Many journalists, particularly in the USA, have expressed their concern that Coalition governments were allowed excessive freedom in managing the news. Indeed, the American Society of Newspaper Editors made two protests against the Pentagon ground rules for media coverage of the war prior to the Coalition ground offensive. Those who believed that the US government manipulated the news had their fears confirmed by the post-war public pronouncements of some of President George Bush's cabinet. Secretary of State James Baker, for instance, told the press:

> The Gulf War was quite a victory. But who would not be moved by the sight of that poor demoralised rabble – outwitted, outflanked, outmanoeuvred by the US military. But I think the press will bounce back.[7]

Some writers have seen the media's role in the Gulf as reflecting the Western, and particularly the United States, dominance of the inter-national media. This interpretation paints the media as either dupes of the Bush administration, or knowing accomplices in furthering the violent birth of the US-dominated 'new world order'.[8] This *angst* in part explains the refusal of US journalists to co-operate with their government in covering Haiti prior to the 'peaceful' US invasion of 1995, and the generally poor level of relations between the US government and its media since the Gulf War.

The debate in Britain is far more genteel, which in part reflects the greater cynicism of British journalists, who expect governments to be secretive and manipulative and do not believe – in contrast to their American colleagues – that they have a special constitutional status.[9] However, the lack of passion in the debate in Britain also reflects the success with which the Ministry of Defence enabled journalists to get newsworthy items expeditiously to editors: as Peter Preston, then editor of the *Guardian*, told the British International Press Institute shortly after the war, 'We did not miss deadlines.'[10]

Issues such as freedom of the press are central concerns for media academics and journalists, and it is understandable that the reasons why Iraq was underestimated as a potential aggressor, and overestimated as a military threat, are peripheral to their examination of the media coverage of the war. However, the exaggeration of Iraqi strength has not – in contrast to other types of analysis of the Gulf War – been totally ignored in these debates. It is in the writings of those most critical of the Western media that the clearest explanation for the failure to understand Iraq is outlined. According to many of these critics of Western policy, the USA either failed to warn Iraq against invading Kuwait or tacitly (or even overtly) encouraged it to use force.[11] This analysis is supported by many in the Arab world who see the Iraqis as victims of a US plot designed to legitimise a Western destruction of an over-mighty Arab state.[12] Some even

93

argue that the United States enticed Saddam Hussein into invading Kuwait, and then deliberately misled the media about Iraqi military might.

Noam Chomsky, one of the more pointed critics of the government–media relationship, describes how an exaggerated image of Iraqi military strength was created by 'Pentagon disinformation ... about colossal fortifications, artillery powerful beyond our imagining, vast stocks of chemical and biological weapons at the ready, and so on'.[13] In this view, the purpose of the elaborate deception of the media was 'to help justify the carpet and terror bombing of both military and civilian "assets" of this Third World country'.[14] Without any other explanation, this rather conspiratorial view of the reasons for exaggerating Iraqi military strength may become widely accepted, and it has already been so in some circles.

PESSIMISTS AND OPTIMISTS

The impression given of Iraqi military capabilities in the Anglo-American media before February 1991 can be divided into two broad 'schools'. First, there were those who might be labelled as 'pessimists', suggesting that the Iraqi military were so capable that they would inflict major casualties upon the Coalition, and even if they were ultimately defeated would succeed in forcing upon their enemy a ground campaign of several months. Slightly greater credence was given to the 'optimists' who predicted a Coalition victory, but even the 'optimists' believed that the Coalition would pay a relatively high price for its victory, and that it was likely that this might leave Saddam as the 'moral' victor.[15] Neither in the press nor on television were there many who predicted a rapid and overwhelming Coalition victory, and even these 'hyper-optimists' tended rather to hedge their bets.

The 'pessimist' assessment of Iraqi strength was partly a consequence of the speed with which Iraq went from being relatively un-newsworthy to the lead news item. The media required information following Iraq's invasion of Kuwait; and 'hard' data, such as that provided by the International Institute for Strategic Studies' authoritative yearbook *Military Balance* was often consulted by journalists needing to acquire rapidly some knowledge of the Iraqi military.[16] The size and equipment of the Iraqi military – hitherto in the public domain but attracting little interest – did suggest they were a force to be reckoned with.

Western political leaders were later reported to be shocked 'by the enormous size of the Iraqi military establishment'.[17] However, not only did the raw data suggest Iraq had very capable armed forces, but also this emerging picture was stoked up by the tendency to accept Iraqi claims at face value. Even prior to the Iraqi invasion of Kuwait, Saddam's threats to 'scorch half of Israel'[18] were given wide credence in the media. The *Washington Post* on 5 July 1990 represented Saddam's threat to Israel as an 'airborne version of Hitler's ovens'. In the USA several papers printed articles critical of previous American policy towards Iraq, but these were often chiefly critical of Western complicity in 'arming the monster': although there was a debate in the media concerning policy towards Iraq, its military strength was accepted as given.

Following the invasion of Kuwait, the potential strength of the Iraqi armed forces became a matter of great importance to Western armed forces, governments and the media. Typical of many of the early assessments of the potential enemy in the Gulf was that of the *New York Times*, whose front page of 13 August 1990 commented that, 'For 10 years, as Iraq developed a vast army, chemical weapons, nuclear ambitions and a long record of brutality, the Reagan and Bush administrations quietly courted President Saddam Hussein.' In the days following the Iraqi invasion little was written about the prospects for liberating Kuwait. More commonly expressed were the fears that even United States military intervention could not prevent a successful Iraqi invasion of Saudi Arabia. This early pessimism in evaluating the Iraqi threat can be clearly seen in an article in the *Sunday Times* on 5 August 1990, which is worth close examination. 'One Man's Army Against the World' describes a powerful military machine, commanded by a leader who was certainly ruthless and most likely insane. The Iraqi armed forces enjoyed the advantage of 'formidable size' and 'formidable firepower'. Even more significant was the experience of Saddam's soldiers: 'There is no country in the world that can field a military force with such extensive combat experience.' So formidable was Iraqi military strength, the article speculated that if the USA deployed forces into the area it could leave them facing 'main battle tanks skilfully used and the prospect of defeat on the ground'. Also, 'Pentagon experts' were cited as believing that the Iraqis could occupy Dhahran and the Saudi oilfields, pre-empting any US attempt to intervene. The most dire scenario focused on Iraq's ability to use chemical weapons, warning that, 'In the wrong hands the effects of chemicals can be as devastating as a nuclear bomb, and there is little doubt that, if facing defeat, Saddam would order his troops to use chemical weapons.'

This analysis of Iraqi military strength was typical of much of what was both written and said in August 1990. The 'pessimist' perspective can be characterised by its focus on the magnitude of the Iraqi forces; the equipment – frequently described as 'high-tech' – at their disposal; the experience of combat Iraq gained in the eight-year war with Iran, which ensured that its military were 'battle-hardened'; the importance of the

'Elite' Republican Guard; and Saddam's 'doomsday' weapons, of which chemical weapons were the prime example.

Expectations that the crisis might escalate during summer 1990 proved false, allowing the USA and its allies to build up their forces in Saudi Arabia. The Coalition military build-up signalled that the USA was very likely to take forceful action: this, given the American experience of foreign adventures since 1960, was by no means certain in early August 1990. The physical manifestations of Western military strength in the Gulf began to put the Iraqi military into a more realistic perspective. The media had time to reflect and research, and the Western military presence in the Gulf gave them something other than Iraqi numbers to report upon. As a result the balance of reporting shifted towards the 'optimist' school of thought even before the end of August 1990.

A more realistic appraisal did not mean Iraqi military weakness was being accurately assessed in the media. For instance, the *Sunday Times* 'Insight Team' on 19 August 1990 illustrated the rapid shift towards 'optimism' when it announced that 'instead of the "battle hardened" [Iraqi] troops of a fortnight ago, more realistic assessments rate them little better than a good 3rd World Army with a few fine units': a more accurate judgement, but still too generous. However, like the rest of the media, the *Sunday Times* occasionally reverted to pessimism. A few weeks before the final Coalition land offensive, its 20 January 1991 headline proclaimed 'Allies Face Long and Bloody War'. One of the clearest examples of the persistence with which some of the pessimists clung to their views is that provided by Paul Rogers, Professor of Peace Studies at Bradford University, writing in the *Guardian* four weeks after the air war began. Rogers wrote that 'even the most optimistic military pundit has to accept that it is not going according to plan'; despite the generally more realistic analysis of Iraqi strength prior to the Coalition ground offensive he claimed that 'Coalition forces have seriously under-estimated Iraqi capabilities', and concluded with a prediction that 'We will be lucky if the war is over within six months.'

The 'optimistic' analysis of Iraqi strength as formidable, but capable of being defeated, lacked the dramatic impact of the 'pessimists', and was characterised by a general ambivalence as to the likely outcome of a Coalition resort to war. *Newsweek* on 4 February 1991, while reporting upon Coalition dominance in the air war, pointed out that there was 'room for a lot of interpretation' in assessing the impact of the bombing. Despite expecting a Coalition ground offensive that would liberate Kuwait, the 'optimists' in the media expected the war to be bloody, and regarded the lowest official estimates of likely Coalition casualties (3–5,000 killed and wounded) as being too low.[19] A similar caution characterised television news. Normally the 'good' news of the Coalition dominance of the air would be followed by warnings that any ground conflict would be far from one-sided. Hopes that Coalition losses would be small were seen as dependent upon the air campaign sufficing to force an Iraqi withdrawal, and Yehoshua Saguy (former head of Israeli military intelligence) reflected the prevalent mood of caution when he warned that, 'Soon will come the moment of truth when the Americans must decide if they are ready to pay the price of ground fighting.'[20]

The *Daily Telegraph*, perhaps the leading British newspaper in commenting on matters military, took a very similar line, and although it rightly described the Iraqi army as having 'little flair for high-manoeuvre warfare', it also evaluated 250,000 troops of the Iraqi Army as, 'of a standard approaching that of the American, British and French forces'. Although the *Daily Telegraph* was one of the few newspapers to argue that the menace of Iraqi chemical weapons had been exaggerated, on 12 January 1991 it warned that 'Saddam is almost certain to use them before air attacks destroy his stocks', and feared that Scud missiles carrying chemical warheads would be used to attack Coalition rear areas. Indeed, throughout the air war against Iraq there was a stream of cautionary stories in the Western media; reports that bomb damage assessments suggested that Iraqi forces were bloodied but unbowed;[21] claims that chemical weapons had been supplied to Iraqi forces in Kuwait;[22] and claims that the Pentagon felt its commanders in the theatre were being dangerously optimistic. Indeed, the media regarded the confidence of Coalition commanders in the Gulf as dangerously bullish, and preferred the more cautious attitude of officials in Washington and London.

It is true to say that in the months prior to the Coalition victory in the Gulf, all the military weaknesses of the Iraqis were discussed in the media. However, only a very selective recollection of what was written and said could sustain the thesis that the Iraqi armed forces were accurately assessed. In any event, only a sustained effort could have reversed the impression of Iraqi strength created by reporting in early August.[23] There was only a small minority of 'hyper-optimists' who correctly predicted that Iraq would be rapidly defeated at relatively low human cost to the Coalition. In an article written on 12 January 1991, the *Daily Telegraph* Defence Editor, John Keegan, who is also a notable military historian, suggested the war would be won quickly, and at modest cost in Coalition lives because 'in human terms, [the Iraqi Army] is not up to fighting a Western regular army in any circumstances'. Writing in the *Sunday Times* another historian, Professor Norman Stone, also predicted a rapid Coalition victory. But these 'hyper-optimists' were insufficient in number to counteract the overall belief that the Coalition would suffer heavy casualties, perhaps unacceptably heavy, in defeating the Iraqis.

VALLEYS, PEAKS AND CONSUMERS

It is important to remember that the 'product' of the media is not consumed in the same way as academic historians conduct their research. One alarmist article about Iraqi chemical weapons was not necessarily cancelled out by one thoughtful critique of the fundamental flaws in the command and control system of the Iraqi Army. How people absorb the news depends upon many factors unconnected with the merits of the analysis, not least of which is the 'entertainment value'. The information derived from the media is a sharply contoured landscape in which the spectacular 'peaks' receive far more attention than the deep dull 'valleys'. An excellent example of this is an article written in late August for *The Times* by Michael Evans which thoughtfully discusses the problems of a strategy of containment (the 'valley'), but is headlined 'Desert Shield Could be Bush's Vietnam' (the 'peak'). Evans' article suggested that taking the offensive might be preferable to containment, but the headline powerfully attached to the prospect of war in the Gulf a long, bloody and ultimately futile American conflict of the past. A newspaper or television channel that attempted just to educate its customers, rather than entertain them, would quickly discover its ratings declining, and the Western media – especially in the USA – are exceptionally competitive. Dramatic images, crisp sound bites and sensational stories, as well as relaying of information, are the stuff of journalism – a process that has been described as the 'bias of newsworthiness'.[24] When a crisis is of short duration the newness of the news can be entertaining in its own right. However, the crisis in the Gulf lasted for months, and in such circumstances aspects of the situation with 'star' potential were likely to become more prominent. It is the nature of the print and electronic media to emphasise the spectacular, which more often than not is the spectacularly disastrous. This may seem frightfully obvious, but most of the reasons for Iraqi military weakness were complex and tended to lurk in the deep dull valleys rather than the peaks. Consequently, just measuring the volume of media coverage that exaggerated Iraqi military potency understates the impact of the coverage on public perceptions.

Most television stations and some newspapers attempt to cover the news in a balanced fashion: in some cases balance is a legal requirement and in others it is seen as an ethical obligation. The balanced approach to news makes it difficult to present an emphatic case, and, particularly with television news, a perspective favouring one side is frequently followed by a contrary item. This pattern was often followed when examining military matters in the Gulf, items on Coalition military strength being followed by a contrary piece on the Iraqi forces. Coverage that had (rightly) suggested the Coalition would inflict an emphatic military defeat upon Iraq, if left 'unbalanced', would have been assailed as dangerously one-sided. Such overt presentational impartiality is more important to serious journalists than cynics might believe, since 'impartiality legitimises journalistic authority'.[25]

One of the unlikely stars of the media war was the Scud missile, which 'became an image early on because they were fired and they provided good pictures as well'.[26] Frequent media exposure gave this ageing and inaccurate missile a political significance that its relative military ineffectiveness did not justify. Scud newsworthiness can be seen from the frequency it appeared in the press; for instance, in *The Times* from 18 January to 26 January 1991, six of the eight daily front pages carried Scud stories, and four times the Scud was a lead story. The Scud was introduced to the public as a devastating weapon at the start of the crisis, a star billing it retained after Iraq's defeat. The front page of the *Sunday Times* on 19 August 1990 makes it clear that Scud stories did attract the reading public, by the way it directed readers to its 'Focus Special': 'Iraq moves deadly Scud missiles into Kuwait, threatening US troops'. In January 1991 Anthony Cordesman, American Broadcasting Corporation's (ABC's) resident expert for the duration of the crisis, described the Iraqi Scud as 'a horrifying killing machine' which despite the hyperbole was an effective television sound bite.[27] On television, pictures of Scud launches and the air-raid sirens sounding over Dhahran at night regularly filled a space on the prime-time news. The transformation of this obsolete 1950s missile into a 'high-tech' threat for the 1990s was completed by ill-informed discussion of its possible role as a delivery system for chemical weapons.[28] That Scuds were portrayed as a chemical threat is demonstrated by two leading British tabloids, *Today* and the *Sun*, both of which reported inaccurately that the first Scuds launched at Israel had carried chemical warheads. Television reports of the same incident also suggested a chemical attack – 'one of television's worst nights'[29] – and even when reports warned not to exaggerate the importance of pictures of Israelis putting on gas masks, the image was of imminent apocalypse. The speculation that the Scud could carry a chemical warhead was a 'peak' (reinforced by a library shot of a Scud launch), but the contrary view required some understanding of the complexities of chemical warfare and delivery technology, making it a 'valley' which made little impact on the general public.

Similarly, Iraq's chemical, biological and nuclear weapon capability received star billing in the media. These 'weapons of mass destruction' had previously demonstrated their newsworthiness during the 1980–88 Iran–Iraq War. The *New York Times*, for instance, featured 95 main stories on chemical weapons during that war, in comparison to 58 stories on foreign policy and only six on Saddam.[30] Probably the one specific event of the Iran–Iraq War which was widely remembered in the West was the Iraqi chemical attack on the town of Halabja. This memory was reinforced by television regularly showing pictures of the attack in the months prior to the Coalition offensive. The 'lessons' of Halabja were that chemical attack could kill thousands of Coalition troops; but it was never pointed out that Halabja was an Iraqi town, that the victims were unprepared civilians, and that in 1988 Iraq – unlike in 1991 – could use a wide variety of systems to deliver chemical munitions. Chemical weapons were frequently described as the 'poor man's atomic bomb', and virtually nobody, on television or in print, either questioned whether these weapons did have an impact similar to nuclear weapons, or challenged the view that Iraq was likely to resort to them. The Iraqi programme to develop biological and nuclear weapons received less attention in the media, but nonetheless discussion about these mysterious weapon programmes proved to be newsworthy, and after the war provided thriller writers with some interesting plot lines. Headlines in *The Times* on 19 August 1990 such as 'Iraq's Nuclear Capability Greater Than We Thought' were sufficiently ambiguous to make the possibility of an Iraqi nuclear weapon a subject for anxious debate.

Other 'star' stories strengthened the expectation that Iraqi forces would at the very least fight well enough to cause significant Coalition casualties. Special Forces are newsworthy, and the 'Elite' Iraqi Republican Guard were given a very generous press. Similarly, the 'Saddam Line' could be talked up as 'elaborate fortifications', and the supposed Iraqi plan to flood moats with burning oil was suitably dramatic and enabled newspapers to produce some fascinating diagrams. Finally, there was the menace of deliberate or accidental damage to the environment; 'experts' were quoted predicting that oil fires would create a phenomenon similar to a 'nuclear winter'. Even though reports were sceptical of these threats to the environment, just raising the possibility of such a disaster strengthened expectations that the clash of arms in Kuwait would be catastrophic. Discussion of such frightening scenarios would have needed to be substantially outweighed by contrary reports if the image of disaster to come was to have been dispelled.

Often the more subtle nuances of spoken commentary, and lengthy articles, about Iraq were overwhelmed by visual images; maps and pictures could have a dramatic impact on the way a situation was perceived. Typical of this was the large photograph placed by the *Sunday Times* at the head of its 'Gulf 4-Page Special' for 12 August 1990, showing troops in chemical warfare gear: a dehumanised, sinister and powerful image. Modern computer-generated graphics make it relatively simple for newspapers and television to create effective but simplistic images; more complex issues like the quality of a tank, the attitude and skills of its crew or an army's ability to wage manoeuvre warfare cannot be conveyed in such a powerful visual form.

Clearly, powerful visual images are going to be generated by modern warfare. Even though it was later believed that Iraqi casualties were lower than initially estimated, images such as the pictures of the Mutla Ridge tended to endure. In particular, live television reports can unintentionally have a profound impact. CNN's Charles Jaco managed to stir public fears about chemical weapons while reporting live on a Scud attack: he smelt an odd odour – it was methane from the oil tank farm across the street – screamed 'gas' and dived for his gas mask.[31]

Finally, the sensationalisation of news contributed to the exaggeration of Iraqi military capabilities. Sensationalism is central to the appeal of the popular press, but it is not confined to this section of the media. At its worst, media sensationalism was dishonest, as the commander of British 7th Armoured Brigade discovered when his warning that some casualties were inevitable was turned into headlines such as 'Prepare For A Bloodbath'. Such headlines might initially appear in the popular press, but once published their impact can be magnified by repetition, even if the repetition is wrapped up as condemnation of irresponsible reporting. In this instance the sensationalism was deliberate, one of the reporters even warning the brigadier, 'we have really made a bit of a saga out of casualties'.[32]

The image of the Iraqi military portrayed in the media was in part a consequence of the nature of the media, in terms of the way an audience 'consumes' media output, and how information is presented. Not only did readers and watchers remember 'peaks' that suggested the Iraqi military would inflict heavy casualties on the Coalition forces, but also the media often presented information that strengthened this impression. The requirement for 'stars', and interest-boosting sensationalism also influenced the nature of the coverage.

JOURNALISTS AND SOURCES

Journalists covering the Gulf War were not just conduits for information, but had arrived at their own conclusions, and the vast majority expected the war to be much less one-sided than it was. At the start of the crisis journalists were caught 'on the hop' by events – there had been a feeling that 'we can forget about the Middle East for a bit'[33] – and initially they were rather uncritical in their search for information. This information vacuum created an environment in which 'rumours become fact and fact becomes exaggerated'.[34] As a result, much of the reporting on occupied Kuwait was somewhat hysterical, and journalists were not giving considered opinions, but instead tended to relay what information they had been able to obtain.[35]

To the unexpected nature of the crisis can be joined the relative ignorance of most of the journalists concerning military matters. Some reporters were able to use their previous experience, or fall back on their own academic expertise,[36] and a small minority – such as John Keegan – are reputable military historians. However, few journalists have any specialist knowledge of military matters or have experienced military service. The *Washington Post* features writer, Henry Allen, who was a Vietnam veteran, said the briefings at Riyadh 'are making reporters look like fools, nitpickers, and egomaniacs, like dilettantes who have spent exactly none of their lives on the end of a gun or even a shovel'.[37]

Relative ignorance of the region, and the military, made journalists even more dependent on their sources for obtaining information and developing interpretations. For journalists covering the Gulf this meant official sources, both formal and informal, 'independent' experts and the personal contacts. Illustrating the importance of official sources, much of the authoritative reporting on the Middle East crisis came from the Washington 'newsbeats' where there was an unrivalled concentration of official sources.[38] It is clear that 'reporters overwhelmingly turn to officials as sources for political stories and for framing the policy content of stories'; this is a firmly established finding of media research, and it is accentuated in matters of national security.[39] This relationship between officialdom and the media potentially supports the thesis that journalists were manipulated into exaggerating Iraqi military strength because that is what Western governments wanted.

However, accepting that official sources are very important to the media does not automatically imply that reporters are either the partners in crime, or unwitting dupes, of the governing elites. Indeed, the intertwining of government establishments and the media often makes the media more powerful critics of policy. The idea that there is one monolithic government line is also a rather naïve one, since governing elites are frequently divided, and critical coverage of policy in the USA tends to peak when powerful elements in Congress express contrary views to those of the administration. Even where there is relative political unanimity in the governing elite this does not rule out knowledgeable individuals, who do not always sing from the same songsheet.

The media are also not solely dependent on official sources, and alternative perspectives are often sought from non-government experts. Journalists had over six months from August 1990 to consult experts, and develop their own understanding of events in the Gulf. American newspapers and television channels made particular use of retired officers who not only understood the military, but were able get favourable access to the armed forces. Newsweek hired Colonel David H. Hackworth, the most decorated veteran of the Vietnam War, who 'moved from division to division like a wraith, relying on a network of officer cronies to float through the controls'.[40] Indeed, some experts missed out the 'middleman' journalist, and expounded their views directly on television or in print.

Yet, many of the experts used by the media can hardly be described as independent. Some had important links with their governments, and others had interests in the Middle East. Often an expert's loyalties were ambiguous as 'in their spare time, experts are establishing their credentials as experts by advising or taking the counsel of the same government officials that journalists seek out in the first place'.[41] In particular, in the USA it is not uncommon for academics to hope to move into a powerful position in public service. Even those whose advice cannot be seen to be tainted by close connections with officialdom or the military were affected by the pressure not to behave 'irresponsibly'.

It is important, however, not to assume that a previous career even in the armed forces meant it was impossible to be critical of the government. *Newsweek*'s Colonel Hackworth, for instance, was highly critical of his ex-colleagues in the military: 'I was very unhappy with the military's paranoia and their thought police who control the Press ... I had more guns pointed at me by Americans and Saudis who were into controlling the Press than in all my years of actual combat.'[42]

The pressure to behave 'responsibly' was also an important factor influencing most journalists as well as the experts. This was particularly so for American journalists, who faced extra pressure to behave patriotically because of the widespread belief that media coverage had lost the Vietnam War. This 'responsible' behaviour was one aspect of the media's performance that was criticised following the Gulf War. Indeed, in the Gulf, journalists who 'played by the rules', at times co-operated with the military to police their colleagues who refused to accept the restraints of the media pools system.[43]

Finally, the journalists deployed to the Gulf were unusually open to manipulation by the military. The military were able to control access to newsworthy stories to an extent not possible back home. The simple

103

matter of getting copy back home quickly enough to still be news relied upon military co-operation. The US Marines in the Gulf gave the media better access than the Army, and were much more helpful in getting news despatched expeditiously; as a result they received far greater attention in the media than their numbers warranted.[44] The media were also dependent on the military for more basic needs such as transport, food and safety. The *Independent*'s Robert Fisk echoes the fears of many in the media at the 'cozy' relationship developed with the military in the Gulf:

> Most of the journalists with the military now wear uniforms. They rely on the soldiers around them for advice and protection. They are dependent on the troops and their officers for communications, perhaps for their lives. And there is thus a profound desire to fit in and a frequent absence of critical faculties.[45]

CONSPIRACY OR UNCERTAINTY?

Although it is excessively paranoid to see the media as merely servants of US government policy in the Gulf, clearly they could be manipulated. It is therefore not unrealistic to suggest that the media were encouraged to exaggerate Iraqi military strength to justify the deployment of over-whelming force. Less vitriolic critics of 'media manipulation' – such as Nik Gowing – suspected that the military 'had to portray the worst case scenario and the worst threat as much as a political tool to get the maximum level of force commitment'; however he also recognised that 'it is legitimate in a war which is being very rapidly assembled to paint the worst case scenario because if we don't then you obviously stand under resourced'.[46]

Unfortunately for the conspiracy theorists, exaggerating Iraqi military strength caused the Coalition as many problems as it solved. Fear of high casualties in the USA – a fear Saddam Hussein remarked upon to April Glaspie, the US Ambassador to Iraq – was likely to erode public support for the military option. The frequency with which the ghost of the Vietnam War was invoked made it clear that the USA feared military failure. In both the USA and Britain, there was a correlation between authoritative public predictions of high Coalition casualties and opposi-tion to using force. Indeed, Iraqi military strength was most often referred to by those arguing against Coalition offensive military action.

It is also rather bizarre to assume that Western governments had a co-herent, consistent and accurate understanding of Iraq. These governments were being presented with very contradictory analyses during the crisis;

after the war those that predicted correctly basked in the glory, but the less successful stayed quiet or rewrote history. That the British government received very accurate predictions from the computer models used by the Centre for Defence Analysis (CDA)[47] is a matter of public record, but other computer models proved much less optimistic: one computer 'game' before the war wiped out a British tank regiment in half an hour. Similarly, in the USA the government received very different estimates of Iraqi strength from intelligence agencies and think-tanks.

Uncertainty concerning Iraqi military capabilities inside the US administration is revealed by the arguments in October 1990 about the timing of an offensive. The political leadership – concerned that time was on Iraq's side – strongly preferred an early offensive. However, the military insisted that American strength needed to be doubled in the Gulf before any offensive was launched. The US government believed Iraq might put up a formidable resistance, and was forced to accept the political risks of delay. Those who believe the media were manipulated into exaggerating Iraqi military strength have failed to consider that their governments might have honestly believed that Iraq would be a formidable enemy on the battlefield.

The source of many of the direst warnings about Iraqi military strength make it unlikely that this was government 'spin-doctoring'. It was the experts who were most obviously independent of governments who were 'pessimists'; those more likely to toe the official line, such as ex-military personnel, were often 'optimists'. Similarly, 'unilateral' reporters in the Gulf did not on the whole assess Iraqi military weakness accurately. The *Independent*'s Robert Fisk clearly demonstrated that he was not expecting the clash of arms to be totally one-sided when he reported in the newspaper on 23 January 1991:

> Journalists officially accredited ... are not brought to this particular forward location ... and when you drive into this swamp of mud and water, it is not difficult to see why. For the gathering of allied armies here ... bears little relation to those comfortable, efficient scenarios outlined by American and British commanders in Riyadh. The mass of [Coalition] troops and armour gathered here for the offensive have had to fight their way through a logistic nightmare, which at times left armoured units unable to find their headquarters.

The only group which might have had a significant 'optimistic' influence on the media was the senior officers of the Coalition forces in Saudi Arabia. However, their optimistic bomb-damage assessments once the air war started were questioned both by the media and by officials back home.

Finally, there is little evidence of overt governmental control over the media. Only five items were referred to Washington for official arbitration about whether they should be published and only one of these was actually altered.[48] In Britain it was reported on television that in all likelihood there would be an outflanking movement to the west of the main Iraqi defences in Kuwait, but the government did not interfere; it seems there was discussion about squashing this sort of speculation, but the decision to let it be indicates that the media were allowed considerable freedom.[49]

THE WEST AND IRAQ

It is easy to forget that Iraq prior to 1990 was only infrequently big news. During the war with Iran, 'hardly any American news stories were datelined Iraq',[50] and it seemed 'Iraq did not fit into a journalistic map of a Near East dominated by Israel ... and by Egypt'.[51] Although 4,214 stories and editorials relating to Iraq were published by the *New York Times* and *Washington Post* between 2 August and 8 November 1990, under 200 appeared in the same two newspapers throughout the 1980s.[52] The *New York Times* back in 1981 suggested, 'chances are Iraq's president, Saddam Hussein, is less a holy warrior than a cautious optimist', a judgement that sums up the general Western attitude to Iraq just prior to its invasion of Kuwait. Reporters attempting to inform themselves about Iraq in August 1990 discovered that there was little authoritative information available. Despite the length and severity of the Iran–Iraq War, there were few serious accounts available. Most of the academics who did study Iraq before 1990 rarely focused on military matters, and on the whole they had a 'cautious but optimistic' assessment of Iraq's likely intentions once it succeeded in ending the war with Iran.[53]

In early 1990, Western governments, particularly the United States, took a similarly optimistic perspective of Iraq. This was partly because the collapse of the USA's close relationship with the Shah's Iran in 1979 left it with little option but to hope Iraq would act as the protector of the Gulf from the new revolutionary Iranian government. Iraq's invasion of Kuwait shattered American hopes that it might be possible to 'do business' with Iraq. It is always hard to think clearly in a crisis, and the Bush administration was not helped by contradictory assessments of American intelligence agencies. The CIA, for instance, told the President the day before Iraq invaded Kuwait that the problem would be resolved peacefully. These intelligence problems resulted partly from the dependence on electronic means of gathering data, and cuts in human intelligence assets.[54] American analysts detected movements, and counted numbers, but did not understand the nature of the Iraqi Ba'athist state and its armed forces.

Just like those working in the media, the US government found itself attempting to assess an Iraqi state of which it had little understanding. There was a plenitude of information about Iraq produced by Iraq itself, but interpreting this data was similar to the problems faced at the time by those attempting to understand the old Soviet Union from its official statistics. The judgement, 'People in general, even habitual followers of foreign affairs, had no ready-made framework from which to derive a reaction',[55] ought to be extended to Western governments reacting to the Iraqi invasion of Kuwait. Facing a disaster to their Middle East policy, and without much information or comprehension, it is understandable that in August 1990 the US administration believed Iraq was a formidable military power. Not every member of the Coalition believed Iraq's armed forces were so formidable. Some French sources took a 'hyper-optimist' line, and Egyptian military and official sources were very accurate in their predictions of a dismal Iraqi military performance. These nations had previously maintained close military links with Iraq, and their views should have been taken seriously. However, the United States may not have seen either of these countries as reliable sources, and in any event other states that also had close contacts regarded the Iraqi military more highly. For instance, the Soviet Union – which had worked closely with the Iraqi armed forces – assessed Iraqi military capabilities highly, with predictions in the Soviet military press that the USA was heading for military disaster.

Critics of manipulation of the media also totally ignore the fact that the country which was most overtly attempting to manipulate the media was Iraq itself. Saddam repeatedly boasted of his military might, and warned of the awful consequences of using force against Iraq. In August 1990 he proclaimed, 'The Iraqi people are capable of fighting to the victorious end which God wants ... the blood of our martyrs will burn you'.[56] As late as January 1991 he broadcast on Baghdad radio warning the Coalition, 'The unjust people will be defeated after shedding their foul blood and the severed members of the bodies of their supporters will be left as food for birds of prey.' Most of the extreme threats coming out of Iraq were eventually partly refuted in the Western media, but it was rare either in print or on television for Saddam's unpleasant military bombast to be fully exposed for what it was.

With such wide variations in official assessments of the Iraqi military – which overwhelmingly supported the expectation that the Coalition faced a serious enemy – it is understandable that experts generally erred on the side of caution. Those in, or close to, Western military establishments, who on the whole were more realistic in their predictions, did not want to be seen to encourage a complacent attitude, and their desire to avoid false optimism was very strong.[57] Similarly, politicians avoided an upbeat line on Coalition military prospects because this was politically dangerous and they were well aware that the price for their policies might be the lives of fellow citizens. Caution in such matters is natural for those operating in the public domain, and it seems bizarre to conclude that this caution reflects a comprehensive conspiracy to fool the media.

THE ACADEMIC PERSPECTIVE

Without a pre-existing body of information and understanding of Iraq's military potential, those best placed to produce an assessment of Iraq should have been those academics who were to some extent removed from the pressures that affect politicians, journalists and those connected with the military.[58] The academic world ought to have been able to correct the image of Iraqi strength derived from the raw data and the powerful imagery. However, academic analysis failed to fill the 'understanding vacuum' and many of both governmental and media errors resulted from the failure of most academic experts to assess Iraq's armed forces accurately.

Predictions for likely Coalition casualties produced by 'think-tanks' on both sides of the Atlantic were wildly pessimistic. In the United States, the overtly anti-war Center for Defense Information predicted US casualties of 45,000; the Brookings Institute estimated there would be 15,000 American dead; and the Center for Strategic and International Studies cautiously suggested American casualties would run into thousands. In London, the International Institute for Strategic Studies (IISS) expected significant Coalition losses, and anticipated that Iraq would resort to chemical warfare. Indeed the IISS's Donald Kerr warned in August 1990, 'it is important that no-one be suckered into a land war [against Iraq]. It would be Vietnam without the trees and with sand.'[59]

In contrast to the self-critical debate of the media and academics studying the media, there has been no attempt by the academic world to understand its own failure to evaluate properly the Iraqi armed forces during the crisis in the Gulf. Indeed, one British university department, which collectively and repeatedly misunderstood the nature of the Iraqi armed forces, has publicly boasted of how frequent appearances on television boosted its profile. Nevertheless, the record of academic failure was remarkable. The military analyst Anthony Cordesman, whose *The*

Lessons of Modern Warfare: The Iran Iraq War is one of the better informed works on the 1980–88 War, predicted heavy casualties for the Coalition in 1990, and claimed the Iraqis would resort to large-scale chemical attacks.[60] The view that Iraq would inflict substantial casualties upon the Coalition was a judgement upon which – unusually – academics from both ends of the political spectrum agreed. Right-wing expert Dr Edward Luttwak claimed the US military were obsessed by 'fanciful tactics, flashy weapons and promising gadgets that seem fine in peace-time exercises but fail in combat';[61] while Professor Paul Wilkinson warned that the conflict with Iraq would be 'one of the most lethal wars since 1945 … [with] a high possibility of weapons of mass destruction being used'.[62] Academics working in 'peace studies' in particular echoed the view of dire consequences for the Coalition, as well as the Iraqis, resulting from any war. Very few academics took a position that was neither 'optimistic' nor 'pessimistic'; and on the whole opinion veered to the latter position rather than the former. The academic world did not challenge the image of the Iraqi military emerging in the media in August 1990: it actually strengthened this image.

This failure reflects a general reluctance among Arabists in the academic world to highlight the weaknesses of Middle Eastern states. In particular, 'progressive' states, among which Iraq was numbered before 1991, were rarely analysed critically. Critics of Iraq, such as Kanan Makiya (author of *Republic of Fear*), were treated by most experts in the West as anti-Iraqi propagandists until Saddam invaded Kuwait. A refusal to recognise the repressive totalitarian nature of the Iraqi regime made it harder to appreciate the weaknesses of the Iraqi military, as these weaknesses were in part a product of the nature of the regime.

A more general problem is the low regard in which the academic world holds the study of things military. There are few British and American universities which make a serious effort to study war, and the bias is towards the 'higher' strategic aspects of the subject. The study of anything beneath this strategic level is often dismissed as the province of military pornographers, rivet counters, retired officers, and odd-balls. John Keegan, who was one of the few experts publicly to predict the likely course of the conflict accurately, has an interest in the operational and tactical levels of warfare, but academics that focus on this aspect of warfare are a relatively rare breed.

This lack of expertise does matter: the results of battles actually do change things. Battles in the Gulf War were decided by factors such as the differing capabilities of T-55 and Abrams or Challenger tanks, Iraqi combat skills, the military doctrines adopted by both sides, and the fighting spirit of the troops at the 'sharp end'. Most of this information was in the public domain prior to 1990; even the most totalitarian of states could not conceal what was happening on the battlefield during the eight-year long Iran–Iraq War, during which the Iraqi military were never able to use their weaponry to its full potential. In particular, despite a huge numerical advantage in the air, the Iraqi airforce underperformed throughout the war. Above all, the things that enable armed forces to function, all-arms co-operation, leadership and fighting spirit, were for various reasons manifestly absent or weak in Iraq.

CONCLUSION

The Western media exaggerated the military strength of Iraq, a tendency which was given added impetus by the nature of both television and print journalism. In doing this, the media were neither the dupes nor the accomplices of government: they were initially reacting to a newsworthy event on which there was apparently a paucity of information. As the crisis matured, a more measured media judgement of the Iraqi threat emerged, reflecting the understanding of the Iraqi forces held by Western governments, armed forces and other experts. But this measured judgement was still incorrect, and in any event it would have required an immense effort to make the 'hyper-optimist' position into a widely accepted perspective. Once the media occupied the Iraqi information vacuum, those who might have altered the early assessments of Iraqi military strength if anything strengthened the initial error. Members of the US administration were 'optimists', because they too failed to appreciate Iraqi military weaknesses; the timing and nature of the Coalition offensive reflected the official belief that the Iraqi armed forces were stronger than they actually were. That this assessment was an honest error rather than part of a cunning plan to deceive the public is given greater credence by similar, if not worse, misunderstanding of the Iraqi armed forces by the Western academic world.

The media, academia and officialdom all failed to evaluate the Iraqi armed forces realistically. Of the three, it is the academic world which ought to be held most culpable for this failure, but it is also the least likely area from which a conspiracy to deceive the public could emerge. This collective failure does matter, and not just for those interested in the scholarly analysis of things military. For the West the delay in launching an offensive was risky, and, if Kuwait had been liberated earlier, without the massive deployment of force, greater political damage would have been inflicted upon Saddam Hussein's regime. From a humanitarian perspective a better understanding of the Iraqi military might have moderated the pounding the Coalition inflicted upon Iraq. It is even possible that exaggerating Iraqi military strength encouraged Saddam to risk an armed confrontation with the Coalition. Finally, it needs to be recognised that where there is an 'information vacuum' the media will fill it when a story becomes news, and that this enhances the media's power to form opinions. If unchecked, this process makes it harder to develop well-considered policy.

NOTES

1. It continues to be widely believed, especially in the US military, that the media lost the USA the Vietnam War despite extensive academic research which confutes this view.
2. Quoted by W. L. Bennett, 'The News About Foreign Policy', in W. L. Bennett and D. L. Paletz (eds), *Taken By Storm* (Chicago, IL, and London: University of Chicago Press, 1994), p. 17.
3. In the mid-1990s the old British Army Staff College at Camberley recognised the power of the modern media, substantially expanding the time spent on its various courses dealing with the media and the armed forces. The importance of the media continued to be emphasised in the Joint Services Command and Staff College which replaced Camberley and the other service colleges in 1998.
4. Author's interview in 1995 with Nik Gowing, then Diplomatic Editor for Channel 4 News.
5. Ibid.
6. D. A. Charters, 'Apocalypse Soon: The Failure of Predictive Strategic Analysis in the Gulf Crisis', unpublished research monograph, Centre for Conflict Studies, University of New Brunswick, 1994, p. 3. I am grateful to Dr Charters for providing me with a copy of this paper.
7. Quoted in D. L. Paletz, 'Just Deserts?', in W. L. Bennett and D. L. Paletz (eds), pp. 282–3.
8. The contributors to H. Mowlana, G. Gerbner and H. I. Schiller (eds), *Triumph of the Image: The Media's War in the Persian Gulf – a Global Perspective* (Boulder, CO, and Oxford: Westview Press, 1992) tend to construe Western governments and the Western-owned media as partners in a conspiracy to manage information on the Gulf War.
9. These views were expressed to the author in the course of an interview with Mike Evans, *The Times* Defence Correspondent, 1995.
10. Quoted in J. J. Fialka, *Hotel Warriors* (Washington, DC: Woodrow Wilson Center Press, 1992), p. 10.
11. M. Morgan, J. Lewis and S. Jhally, 'More Viewing, Less Knowledge', in H. Mowlana, G. Gerbner and H. I. Schiller (eds), pp. 219 and 224.
12. On a visit to the Gulf region in 1998 the author was told by an educated ex-officer that Saddam was a Zionist agent acting against the interests of the Arab nation as a whole.
13. N. Chomsky, 'The Media and the War: What War?', in H. Mowlana, G. Gerbner and H. I. Schiller (eds), p. 52.

14. A. G. Frank, 'A Third World War: A Political Economy of the Gulf and the New World Order', in H. Mowlana, G. Gerbner and H. I. Schiller (eds), p. 10.
15. Although Saddam's claim to be the real victor of the war was given greater credence with the length of his survival in power, such a claim clearly was not based on any aspect of the Iraqi military performance of 1991 – indeed, it is clear that even zero Coalition casualties would not have prevented Saddam making this claim.
16. Most journalists covering this story were not defence specialists such as John Keegan of the *Daily Telegraph* or ABC's Anthony Cordesman. Michael Evans of *The Times*, who was interviewed by the author in 1995, regarded the annual IISS *Military Balance* as an essential source of information.
17. M. Evans in *The Times*, 12 February 1991.
18. Quoted by A. M. Rosenthall in *New York Times*, 5 April 1990.
19. J. Zaller, 'Elite Leadership of Mass Opinion', in W. L. Bennett and D. L. Paletz (eds), pp. 198–9.
20. Quoted in *Newsweek*, 4 February 1991.
21. For instance, in *Newsweek*, 4 February 1991.
22. Quoted in *The Times*, 21 February 1991.
23. For comparison, Nik Gowing in his paper, 'Real-Time Television Coverage of Armed Conflicts and Diplomatic Crises: Does it Pressure or Distort Foreign Policy Decisions?', working paper 94-1, Joan Shorenstein Barone Center on the Press, Politics and Public Policy (Cambridge, MA: Harvard University, 1994), makes it clear just how hard it was to shake the initial impressions created by reports on the conflict in Bosnia.
24. D. A. Charters, p. 12.
25. T. E. Cook, 'Domesticating A Crisis', in W. L. Bennett and D. L. Paletz (eds), p. 108.
26. Interview with Nik Gowing (see note 4).
27. Quoted in J. R. Macarthur, *Second Front* (New York: Hill & Wang, 1992), p. 111.
28. It seems that surface-to-surface missiles in general have had their 'profile' raised by the Gulf War. It is not uncommon in academic conferences for missiles to be bracketed with 'other weapons of mass destruction'.
29. Interview with Nik Gowing (see note 4).
30. G. E. Lang and K. Lang 'The Press as Prologue', in W. L. Bennett and D. L. Paletz (eds), p. 47.
31. Cited in J. J. Fialka, p. 64.
32. P. Cordingley, 'Future Commanders Be Warned!', *Despatches*, 3 (Autumn 1992), pp. 16–17 (see also Chapter 12 below).
33. Author's interview with Edward Mortimer of the *Financial Times* in 1995.
34. Interview with Nik Gowing (see note 4).
35. There is certainly a strong case that journalists were manipulated by governments to ensure that Iraqi actions were painted in the very worst light, but this does not mean the same can be assumed about assessments of the Iraqi military.
36. Some reporters actively pursue explicitly academic projects: for instance Channel 4's Nik Gowing took a sabbatical at the Harvard School of Government, and the *Financial Times'* Edward Mortimer has had a spell at the IISS.

37. Quoted J. J. Fialka, p. 62.
38. T. E. Cook, in W. L. Bennett and D. L. Paletz (eds), p. 112.
39. W. L. Bennett, in W. L. Bennett and D. L. Paletz (eds), pp. 23–4.
40. J. J. Fialka, p. 62.
41. Ibid., p. 29.
42. Quoted by M. Getler in H. Smith (ed.), *The Media and the Gulf War* (Washington, DC: Seven Locks Press, 1992), p. 166.
43. R. Fisk, in H. Smith (ed.), p. 146.
44. J. J. Fialka, pp. 7–8.
45. R. Fisk, in H. Smith (ed.), p. 146.
46. Interview with Nik Gowing (see note 4).
47. Featured in the Channel 4 'Equinox' series programme 'Technology and the Gulf War', 1992.
48. Louis A. 'Pete' Williams, 'Statement Before the US Senate Committee on Government Affairs', in H. Smith (ed.), p. 33.
49. Interview with Nik Gowing (see note 4).
50. G. E. Lang and K. Lang, in W. L. Bennett and D. L. Paletz (eds), p. 51.
51. Ibid., p. 59.
52. W. A. Dorman and S. Livingston, in W. L. Bennett and D. L. Paletz (eds), p. 67.
53. P. Robbins, 'Iraq in the Gulf War', in H. Maull and O. Pick (eds), *The Gulf War* (London: Pinter Publishers, 1989), p. 57.
54. Norman Friedman, *Desert Victory: The War for Kuwait* (Annapolis, MD: US Naval Press, 1991), p. 8, suggests that the absence of any American human intelligence sources in Iraq left an information vacuum that was filled by the media.
55. G. E. Lang and K. Lang, in W. L. Bennett and D. L. Paletz (eds), p. 43.
56. Quoted in J. Pimlott and S. Badsey (eds), *The Gulf War Assessed* (London: Arms & Armour, 1992), p. 173.
57. As the author found, as part of a team from the Royal Military Academy, Sandhurst, War Studies Department, briefing British 7th Armoured Brigade in 1990. When challenged by the chemical warfare officer of 40 Field Artillery Regiment, it was not easy to persist in maintaining that Iraq was unlikely to use chemical weapons, and that they would be very ineffective if it did.
58. Academics who expressed views in the media have been treated as quasi-journalists in this chapter. This section is primarily focused on academic research which was not intended for a wider public: work produced within the protection of an 'ivory tower' is produced to a different format, and in a different environment.
59. Quoted in *Daily Telegraph*, 8 August 1990.
60. Cordesman was ABC's resident military historian for the crisis, but this prediction was given at a briefing attended by Edward Mortimer of *Financial Times* (see interview by the author, note 34).
61. E. Luttwak, 'Blood for Oil', *Independent*, 27 August 1990.
62. Quoted in P. Towle, 'Pundits and Patriots', occasional paper 50, Institute for European Defence and Strategic Studies, 1991, p. 11.

Part Three:
The Military Experience of the Media

9

Mixing with the Media

BRIGADIER A. M. A. DUNCAN

These newspaper scribblers have the impudence of Satan. They come into camp, poke about amongst the lazy shirks, pick up their camp rumours and publish them as facts. They are a pest, and I would treat them as spies, which in truth they are. If I killed them all, there would be news from Hell before breakfast.

Major-General William T. Sherman
during the American Civil War

The relationship between the military and the media in time of conflict has never been one of the easiest of associations. The military would wish to conduct their operations in a manner that offers the very best conditions for the security of themselves, their equipment and their aims. The media, on the other hand, consider that they have a duty to inform the public of events as and when they unfold, with no restrictions imposed upon them. On the surface it would appear that these two views are diametrically opposed and have little chance of any mutual reconciliation. In 1970 the ITN journalist, Alastair Burnett, stated, 'I come from a school of journalists that believes that it is natural that there should be a conflict between the armed services and journalism or the media ... it is natural that a state of war exists between us'.[1] Indeed, Brigadier Christopher Elliott contends in the article from which this is quoted that relations between military and media are inevitably condemned to antagonism and difficulties.

More recently however, views on this seemingly intractable problem have hinted at a solution. Dr Stephen Badsey concluded in 1994:

Nor are the two sides doomed to face each other with hostility. In the absence of any coherent theory of military media relations, in

117

modern conditions the problems faced by the military in dealing with the media may best be viewed as similar to the problems of alliance warfare, in which the allies have similar but not identical objectives, and in which tolerance and understanding is required from all.[2]

Similarly, in an address to the Higher Command and Staff Course, Martin Bell stated that, 'The Army and media are partners in the same enterprise.'[3]

There is increasing evidence that this element of mutual dependence does exist in military–media relationships, despite differences in culture and interest which might otherwise divide them. However, that is not to say that relations are anywhere near perfect: far from it. Antagonism exists on both sides and there is still much distrust and suspicion. At the same time, the deployment of soldiers onto any operation remains big news throughout the world, as witnessed by the huge media coverage given to the recent campaigns in the Gulf, Bosnia, Somalia and Haiti.

The aim of this chapter is to examine the effect of the media on the planning and conduct of campaigns in order to provide guidelines for the operational military commander. It concentrates on the media requirement for campaigns in which United Kingdom armed forces may deploy independently or as a member of a joint, combined alliance or coalition, for high or low-intensity operations, including those with the United Nations. Although examples are drawn mainly from recent Army experiences and work, it is intended that the principles are equally applicable to the three services. The guidelines offered are directed specifically towards those who may command at the operational level. However, many of the principles will *per se* remain applicable at the tactical level.

Since the Gulf War there has been considerable discussion of the dynamic relationship between the military and the media, but most of the consequent military studies have focused on the procedural aspects of handling the media in time of conflict. There is still some improvement to be made to the military's attitude and overall approach to the whole issue of military–media relations. First, because recent rapid advances in technology have changed the type and quality of news reporting by the media. Secondly, because since the end of the Cold War many states have embarked on high-profile operations with the United Nations, a trend which seems likely to continue for the foreseeable future. Thirdly, because combined joint operations will become the norm as opposed to the exception. And finally, because there is little doctrinal guidance for senior commanders on how to manage and control what has been described as 'a media flank in all operations which stretches back to the United

Kingdom and home base – to leave this flank unguarded is a huge danger'.[4]

Of the many forms of media it is perhaps in television that the most dramatic technical advances have occurred in the last few years:

> We are in the 'Decade of the Dish'. While the military arsenal contains the latest stealth and smart technology, the television journalist's arsenal contains a lap-top computer, a Marisat telephone, and a portable 'up link' satellite dish the size of a large umbrella.[5]

The war correspondent has little need to rely on the military for transmission of his copy which can be with his television company's base and on the air within minutes. Even in 1991, during the Gulf War, the media were operating with astonishing speed:

> One did not realise, at first, just how powerful the system was. A story could be filmed, edited and transmitted in about three hours. More importantly, live links could be quite easily hooked up. The latest, up to the minute news could be broadcast direct to the families at home. All from the middle of nowhere.[6]

By 1993 the media had become even faster in their reporting; in the summer of that year Captain Peter Bullock released a press statement from the British Public Information Centre in Vitez, Central Bosnia, 40 minutes after a British soldier had been shot and wounded. Forty minutes *later* the news was transmitted across the world on satellite television.

Today, real-time television pictures can be transmitted down a telephone quickly and simply. This ever-increasing rate of response has a number of ramifications. First, the journalist is more independent, has his own discrete communications and thus has less need to comply with any military media plan. Secondly, the quality of reporting and any analysis is by necessity shallower because of the limited time available if the reporter is to get his scoop in on time; there is therefore scope for gross, albeit inadvertent, distortions of the truth. Philip Jacobsen stated:

> Bosnia is an example ... if a soldier is killed on camera, [the story] will almost certainly run. Remember that newspapers come out once a day; the next they are used to wrap chips. This immediacy, spurred by the competition from TV, makes it essential to file the story first, and then consider and negotiate later.[7]

The operational commander must be prepared to deal firmly with such situations and be ready to correct any distortions of the truth quickly and

119

positively. Thirdly, the proliferation of communications for the media has led to greater numbers of correspondents covering each conflict, precipitating an even greater control problem for the military. At the height of the Gulf War, there were over 1,500 media personnel in theatre: 'the pace of technology means that in future the media will not be controllable. They will become a parallel operation, with a degree of co-operation with the military.'[8] Military commanders must make thorough and timely arrangements to control the media in order to avoid the danger of being swamped. Direct control may well be difficult, and in this case the commander must anticipate with a subtle plan to 'shape the media battlefield'. Large international media organisations such as CNN may well have media teams deployed on each side of a conflict. Narrow national interests will not apply and the media will be transmitting the bigger picture to the world and the protagonists: 'CNN will in effect be operating as intelligence briefers, forward air controllers etc – for both sides.'[9] This can be of considerable benefit to the operational commander, as he may well be able to extract useful intelligence from any footage screened, including, for example, estimates of bomb damage and the morale of the enemy. Finally, this speed of reporting will place the media inside the operational commander's decision cycle. With military reporting slowed by a hierarchical chain of command the comparative swiftness of the media's communications may mean that information will be broadcast to the world before the military or politicians have received notification from troops deployed in theatre. Operational commanders have the right to expect the very best of modern communications, but they must also make every effort to organise their commands to overcome procedural reporting problems and get the best out of the in-place C^3 (Command, Control and Communications) systems.

There are also inherent problems if the report is not going out in real time; in particular, the news editor may adjust the reporter's copy to fit the time and format available. Clearly, the editor has no first-hand or in-depth knowledge of the full facts surrounding the copy he has received. He may therefore put an inaccurate slant on the story. Mark Damazer has summed up the problem succinctly: 'Editors are not ex-correspondents. Correspondents never move on to be editors – this causes problems.'[10] To counter this, the Ministry of Defence (MoD) must be prepared to step in robustly, in parallel with any action taken by commanders in theatre, in order to set the record straight. Millions of pounds are spent each year on commercial advertising; a tangible recognition that the media have a considerable capability to influence and persuade. The military must utilise this potential and commanders should grasp the opportunity as and when it occurs to use the media to advertise their Public Information plans.

The experiences of commanders in previous conflicts offer us some useful pointers for the future. In the Falklands Campaign, both military and media entered the conflict with preconceptions, some of which were confirmed and others contradicted. The circumstances of the war were somewhat unique; there were only British media involved with the Task Force or on the Falkland Islands after fighting started and, of course, there were no problems with the host country. The tactical commander had few difficulties, as the then commanding officer of 2nd Battalion, The Parachute Regiment commented: 'At no time did the media influence any decision that I made.' [11] Conversely, the other half of the partnership was not quite so content. In her book, Valerie Adams describes much of the evidence given by the media to the House of Commons Defence Committee after the conflict as 'a catalogue of complaints about inadequate facilities, inconsistent censorship and downright obstruction by the Royal Navy and the MoD public relations officers accompanying the task force'. [12] And at a higher level of command, Rear-Admiral Woodward, the Operation 'Corporate' Task Force Commander commented somewhat ruefully in his memoirs: 'I had never dealt with this phenomenon before, thus I was unsure how to handle them and what to tell them ... the result was a minor catastrophe in the eyes of the Foreign Office, and on downwards. And upwards for that matter.' [13] Suffice it to say that the learning curves for both media and military during the Falklands War were almost vertical. After the conflict the suggestions on media–military relations in the formal report of the Defence Committee of the House of Commons formed much of the basis for the MoD *Green Book*, [14] which will be examined later in more detail.

By the time of the Gulf War many of the problems encountered in the Falklands had been identified and addressed. The outline contingency plans were a great help to the military Public Information staffs:

> When the press made their inevitable demands and tried to pin us down on all the familiar issues such as media parties, pooling, censorship, communications, briefing, escorts, etc, we were able to point them towards existing plans which had been based on dialogue and they quickly discovered that there was a firm foundation on which renewed crisis-led dialogue could take place. [15]

Senior commanders were again much in demand both for the planning of the media campaign and to speak to correspondents. The extent and amount of work involved was graphically illustrated by Brigadier Patrick Cordingley: 'very soon media was not third on my list of priorities but first on the agenda of the daily conference'. [16] It is interesting that while the well practised and qualified pool of TAPIOs (Territorial Army Pool of Information Officers) did invaluable and essential backup work, commanders preferred to employ highly qualified and experienced regular officers to front up to the media. For their part the correspondents preferred to deal with a regular officer. Major-General Rupert Smith used Colonel John King, an experienced and able ex-commanding officer of a mechanised infantry battalion, as his 'Chief of External Relations'. Similarly, Brigadier Patrick Cordingley chose an experienced man: 'and I took one of my most experienced and competent majors from his unit and promoted him temporary lieutenant colonel, putting him in charge of the P Info activities'.[17]

The British Forces Commander in the Gulf War, Lieutenant-General Sir Peter de la Billière, spent a great deal of his day working with and briefing the media. By the time that hostilities had commenced he had some 90 people spread throughout the British Forces, whose sole task was to, in his words, 'establish a positive and constructive relationship with the media'.[18] Operational commanders should not underestimate the considerable influence that the demands of the media will make on their style of command, and more importantly, on the amount of time that dealing with the media will consume out of each working day. Rear-Admiral Christopher Craig, the Task Force Commander in the Gulf War estimates: 'I reckon I gave something like ten per cent of my entire waking, breathing, consciousness to something to do with media relations. I had it right, but I could still perhaps have done more.'[19] Lieutenant-General de la Billière concurred with Rear-Admiral Craig's views: 'I used to spend an average of two hours a day on media matters and nothing else.'[20] Major-General Cordingley revealed that as the Commander of 7th Armoured Brigade in the Gulf War in the early days of deployment 50 per cent of the daily conference was taken up with press issues.[21] Thus the operational commander will have to designate resources to deal with the media and find a senior and trusted commander who can take some, but not all, of the load of dealing with them off his shoulders. More importantly, he will have to allocate a hefty chunk of his own time to those media problems, briefs and meetings where his personal contribution is essential. In short, considerable resources will be needed for the protection of 'the media flank'. As Lieutenant-Colonel Stech of the US Army commented, 'Paying attention to the media is of paramount importance, for a combat commander anything else would be irresponsible.'[22]

In more recent operational deployments the media have been seen as a positive aid to the work of the military. In Bosnia the BBC filmed some crucial negotiations during the early days of the British deployment:

The media in Bosnia sometimes served the useful purpose of being present to record agreements – there were sometimes no other records. Being held accountable in the forum of world opinion can occasionally be a powerful means of persuasion and agreements made on camera are more difficult to break.[23]

Indeed Lieutenant-Colonel Bob Stewart described the media on peace-keeping operations as 'a very useful adjunct to our armoury – and there are no Rules of Engagement we have to comply with before using them'.[24] British military–media relations in Bosnia have been particularly cordial, perhaps because of the unique nature of the United Nations humanitarian task and the fact that the troops deployed were and are seen far more as part of the United Nations rather than directly belonging to, or being responsible to, any one particular nationality. That is not to say, however, that success cannot be capitalised upon for the future. As Martin Bell stated, 'I believe the Army today reflects society as it has never done before – it is doing the will of the people as it conducts operations in Bosnia. As it does this it is also forging a new and unique relationship with the press which is quite different from the past.'[25] Commanders must learn to foster and promote this relationship as it can make a considerable contribution to operational success.

Whilst relations in Bosnia may have been cordial at the tactical level there were still problems at higher levels of command. Operation 'Irma', the British government's initiative for the evacuation of seriously wounded civilians from Sarajevo, caused an uproar throughout the rest of Bosnia and Croatia creating enormous problems for the British soldiers deployed on the ground.[26] The media carried the story on the television and in the press for a number of days, but the British government, through their actions, had broken the principle of impartiality towards the warring factions in Bosnia. The media cannot be blamed, they were merely the conduit for the news. This crisis represents a prime example of what can happen if communication between the operation commander in theatre and the politicians at the home base breaks down; both need to ensure they have good communications, understand each other's problems and are working in concert. If not, the media will quickly use such an opportunity to drive a wedge between them.

Despite what may be seen as an overall improvement in recent military–media relations there have been some reverses. In the United States deployment to Haiti for Operation 'Restore Democracy', several hundred journalists, including eight separate CNN teams, preceded the deployment of the soldiers. President Bill Clinton asked for a voluntary embargo on news coverage while the troops deployed and published a seven-point set of guidelines he wished the media to follow. The press corps refused to accede to his requests. As Nik Gowing commented:

> For the first time in a contemporary conflict, the [US] administration was playing its media negotiating hand from weakness. It was discovering its virtual impotence in the new age of satellite and information technology. Unlike in Saudi Arabia or Grenada, US forces did not command 'the theatre'. They were powerless to control the movements of cameras or transmissions from satellite dishes, except by polite persuasion.[27]

This unfortunate setback for the Americans demonstrated the ramification of their commanders not fully appreciating the importance of 'the media flank' until only two days before the launch of the operation. The neglect of the media plan by the United States forces is all the more surprising when contrasted with their excellent PSYOPS (psychological operations) plan for Haiti, which commenced at D-Day minus 180 days.

What guidelines does the operational commander currently have to help him in his handling of the media? Dr Stephen Badsey has suggested that 'Commanders' plans for media at the moment are largely a matter of personal style.'[28] There is a British *Army Manual of Public Relations*[29] which is still extant, but it was produced in 1967 and could politely be described as somewhat antiquated; there were few satellite dishes around in 1967. Only two pages are devoted to public relations on operations. In fairness 'public relations' is generally taken as being the everyday public relationship between the Army and the rest of society and is thus not directed towards the relationship with the media in time of conflict. The recently published *ADP1: Operations* gives a clearer recognition of the need for a commander to take the media into consideration in his plans: 'The influence of the media has become a major factor affecting operational judgements and therefore demands close and careful attention by the operational commander himself.'[30] It defines relations with the media as follows: 'Public information concerns that information which is released or published for the primary purpose of keeping the public informed, thereby gaining their understanding and support.'[31] This definition is somewhat restricted and passive and it should be expanded to include the following more positive objectives:

- To fulfil the constitutional and legal obligations of the Army that the British Public should be kept informed of Army activities undertaken on their behalf.
- To attempt to gain, maintain or increase public support, both at home and in a wider context, for Army actions in theatre.

• To maintain the morale of the forces in theatre.

The public can be divided into the four categories of British, international, host nation and enemy, which may overlap or be omitted according to the nature of the operation.[32] Each of these publics will have separate media demands and requirements as part of the overall plan. In the case of the first three categories the commander will strive to foster and maintain a positive relationship. In the case of the enemy public some actions may well fall within the province of PSYOPS rather than Public Information. The activities of PSYOPS and Public Information must be separated but they will have to be co-ordinated in order to ensure they do not conflict with one another. Given the influence of the media and the way in which they impact on the commander at the operational level, there should be an obligatory requirement for a 'media line of operations' within a campaign plan. This will be particularly pertinent when troops are deployed on Operations Other Than War (OOTW). Current British doctrine for OOTW[33] regards the principle of consent as a key to success. A clear media plan will help to maintain consent in accordance with the public information objectives outlined above.

In any future coalition involving Britain, the United States may well be the senior member. The United States Army's latest equivalent of *ADP1: Operations* is *Field Manual 100-5 Operations (FM 100-5)*. This doctrinal manual also recognises the importance of the media on operations and makes significant comments. In the introduction it states:

> Dramatic visual presentations can rapidly influence public – and therefore political – opinion so that the political underpinnings of war and operations other than war may suddenly change with no prior indication in the field.

And, perhaps more significantly for the operational commander:

> The higher the echelon of command the more likely the impact of media coverage. Strategic direction and, therefore, the range of operations and their duration, may be dramatically affected.[34]

Media impact is further considered in the section of *FM 100-5* which deals with force projection considerations. There is a vital sentence: 'The importance of understanding the immediacy of the impact of raw television coverage is not so that commanders can control it, but so they can anticipate adjustments to their operations and plans.'[35] This emphasis within a key doctrinal pamphlet for the United States Army reflects further acknowledgement of the importance of the 'media flank' and the need for a commander at the operational level to understand the capabilities of the media and the effect they can have on operations.

As stated above, subsequent to the analysis of the problems encountered between military and media in the Falklands, the MoD published a document originally entitled *Proposed Working Arrangements with the Media in Times of Emergency, Tension, Conflict or War*, known more colloquially as the *Green Book*. This has been amended over the years to reflect the development of the relationship between the military and the media. However, no specific provision has yet been made for Operations Other Than War. The public information plans for both Operation 'Haven' in Northern Iraq in 1991, and Operation 'Grapple' under United Nations command in Bosnia in 1992, had to be improvised. The *Green Book* aims to identify what editors can expect from the MoD and what the MoD seeks from the media. Within that overall aim the book has two objectives: the first to propose procedures which the MoD will adopt in dealing with the media and the second to cover the practical arrangements for media representatives who will accompany the armed forces. It should be noted that the *Green Book* is a British publication aimed specifically at British media, although some reference is made to combined warfare. Subjects covered are the arrangements for registration, accreditation, pooling, facilities, casualty reporting and what is politely referred to as 'security vetting', but which means, in effect, how a voluntary censorship system might work. In the current version there is an important responsibility for the operational commander to note: 'Security vetting will be exercised in theatre. It will be an operational function of the UK force commander and will be conducted by operational officers, separate from the PR function.'[36] In short, the *Green Book* is a document which describes procedures, but it has been generally well received by both media and the military and it will be a key part of any media plan for the operational commander.

There is now no requirement for the media to rely on the military for the transmission of copy to the home base. Technology enables the 'dish' to send copy around the world. The military may therefore no longer apply 'security vetting' by denial of access to military communications. This has been partially recognised in the latest version of the *Green Book*, where as part of the working arrangements the military expect the media to sacrifice some of their rights in return for food, transport, and information within the war zone. In the past, where access has been denied to communication systems, such as in Grenada in 1983, enormous ill will was created. But the media still have their own priorities of deadlines, newsworthiness and profit which will make them reluctant to comply with the wishes of the military. More importantly, the very question of any form of censorship other than self-censorship is a contentious subject. Censorship carries with it overtones of oppression and denial of freedom. It is, for example, completely forbidden under German law. How then would security vetting apply in a coalition which had Germany as a partner? Tom Pocock has put forward a simple formula which relies more on common sense than constitutional law: 'If your story is going to risk one human life, it should not be written.'[37] Martin Bell has suggested that journalists can exercise a form of self-censorship,[38] and this would perhaps work, but only with those journalists who are viewed as the more 'responsible'.

Under the conditions of the *Green Book* accredited journalists surrender, albeit reluctantly, their right to pass copy back without any control.[39] When the ground war started in the Gulf a news blackout was imposed. The media received it badly:

> It was outrageous because essentially what they were saying was we do not trust you to reveal sensitive information when speaking on air ... it was not a fair form of censorship ... they lurched from trusting us to not trusting us just because the ground war had started and that seemed illogical.[40]

It was all the more invidious when Sandy Gall, an ITN reporter who was not accredited, popped up on the lunchtime news on the first day of the land war with a world exclusive. That said, there appears to be a consensus among the British media that they were fairly treated by those who had to vet their copy. Stewart Purvis, Editor-in-Chief of ITN's operations wrote after the Gulf War:

> I said that we would be watchful in case the military tried to withhold or censor information not for reasons of operational security but for other reasons – for instance, to cover up a serious military mistake, or to hide bad news for the sake of morale. The correspondents returning from the Gulf report that this did not happen.[41]

The key to any censorship is therefore trust between media and military: an undertaking by the military not to impose unnecessary restrictions and by the media an acceptance of military judgement where controls are imposed. Building that trust will be a major task for the operational commander and he must exercise the right of censorship with care. Guidelines for those in the force who may have to censor must be entirely clear and unambiguous.

The pool system is an essential feature of the *Green Book*, whereby correspondents can be grouped into manageable teams. In the Gulf War these teams lived cheek by jowl with the military: a particularly successful arrangement. That is, of course, if a place in a pool can be found. Ian Cobain (who did not get a place in a pool) was not impressed: 'In short, the pools were not the place to be if you were looking for a good story, or if you simply wished to provide honest images of the war.'[42] Conversely, Stewart Purvis was quite happy with the arrangements for the ITN correspondents: 'the British television news pools system did enable us to report a war in the most advanced and effective way ever, using a system the military could cope with, under guidelines which both sides could live with'.[43] Despite the problems, the pool system represents an acceptable procedure on which commanders should continue to build trust between military and media in an atmosphere of mutual co-operation. It has one important unstated bonus for the military; by assigning correspondents permanently to front-line units an inbuilt element of censorship also develops. It would be a somewhat foolish correspondent who deliberately filed copy which compromised his own safety.

Non-accredited media have the potential to cause the most problems in theatre. Although non-accredited correspondents do not receive the privileges of those who are accredited, they are still expected to comply with the 17 categories as published in the *Green Book* and which form the 'ground rules' for what correspondents may and may not report. In the Gulf a French photographer, Isabelle Ellson, who chose not to follow these rules was denied access to further briefings and information. Dr Stephen Badsey divided non-accredited correspondents into those who cannot get accredited through no fault of their own due to sheer numbers, and those who deliberately reject access to British and other facilities in order to remain independent. Both groups will be a problem and will have to be accommodated. There is a suspicion that such journalists would not cause quite such a problem if the threat to correspondents in theatre were high. As David Beresford of the *Guardian* noted about the Gulf War: 'If the conflict had been less one-sided there can be little doubt there would have been many casualties in the media.'[44] Non-accredited correspondents will require careful consideration in any media plan if they are not to be alienated.

One of the areas in which the press have considerable effect is in the reporting of casualties. The majority of the world's media now understand the basic requirement not to name a casualty, in accordance with *Green Book* guidelines, until the next of kin have been informed. The difficulty is in judging the effect of casualties, as invariably vividly portrayed in the media, on the public opinion of the home base. It is not easy to generalise as to how the operational commander should handle this problem because each conflict is unique. However, there are a number of indicators which should be considered as a start point. The first is whether the conflict is deemed to be a war of national survival, in which case the public is more tolerant of casualties. Similarly, if the war is seen to be just, it stiffens tolerance, and a short or highly successful war will perhaps by nature tend to result in fewer casualties. But these factors also need to take national public opinions into account. The United States of America pulled out of Somalia in the wake of public furore after pictures of six dead US Rangers had been broadcast on national television in October 1993. Conversely, France had nearly 40 soldiers killed in Bosnia 1992–94 with no apparent change in French public opinion towards the use of her troops. Media illustration of what could be seen as unacceptable casualties caused on the enemy can have its problems too, as witnessed by the graphic pictures of the carnage on the Basra road in the Gulf War and the subsequent public outcry. The issue of casualties is problematic for a commander: detailed policy and arrangements for casualties should be prepared and planned in advance within the overall media plan.

The *Green Book* details the precise conditions for media briefing: attributable, unattributable, background and not for use. While British journalists may be clear on the meaning of these terms, media in a multi-national or United Nations environment may not have the same inter-pretation. What is apparent is that good briefing is an essential element of any Public Information work and commanders should grasp the oppor-tunity to put the military view. Major-General Patrick Brady of the US Army has said:

> War story information often comes from isolated and insulated soldiers and civilians who are frequently in no position to know the big picture ... The people deserve more than this. Commanders can broaden their view and should be allowed to do so.[45]

However, there has been, and will continue to be, much confusion over the precise meaning of the briefing terms. Major-General Brady has a clear line, strongly supported from personal experience by the present author:

> However the encounter may be labelled – background or off the record – one immutable basic fundamental rule is; if you do not want to see or hear it do not say it. Once the words pass your lips you cannot get them back.[46]

For commanders and those who brief on future operations the message is quite clear.

129

Despite the potential areas of friction the *Green Book*, with some modifications, forms a useful set of guidelines from which to move forward. Although it is essentially a document which covers the relationships between British media correspondents and British armed forces, it does have wider application to combined operations. The United Kingdom is the framework country for the NATO Allied Command Europe (ACE) Rapid Reaction Corps (the ARRC), and this is perhaps a good market-place in which to take the initial move of promoting wider use of the *Green Book* within NATO countries.

Despite a greater awareness of the media within the British Army there still remains prejudice and preconceptions about the press, journalists and reporters. There is an almost inbred fear that the media are out to do the military down. The British armed forces are extremely sensitive to any criticism, as Lieutenant-Colonel Bob Stewart, the commanding officer of the first battle group deployed into Bosnia commented:

> In the military, we tend to think that even the slightest criticism made by the media is a disaster. Ninety-five per cent of an article can be glowing and yet we torture ourselves over the five per cent of criticism. That is madness of course and yet we still do it. I am afraid we have to get a little bit used to the rough and the smooth.[47]

Brigadier (later Major-General) Patrick Cordingley shared these views: 'but for every adverse story there were hundreds that were positive'.[48] The message for operational commanders is to relax a little and accept that soldiers can generally be relied upon to do the right thing. Public Information staffs have at last recognised that soldiers are capable of talking to the media. For Operation 'Grapple' in Bosnia each soldier was issued with a small, one-page guide to dealing with the media: six do's, seven don'ts.[49] With small modification it would be applicable to any operation in any theatre, but sadly it was overclassified, with 'RESTRICTED' writ large at top and bottom. Soldiers are trusted to carry weapons with live rounds, and are then expected to follow quite complex rules of engagement. A private soldier is expected to care and maintain an armoured vehicle worth millions of pounds, but he is not, in fact, trusted to make a simple statement to the press. Soldiers are invariably the Army's best advertisements in broadcasting the media message on operations. Outside the military some have more robust views on the ability of the soldier and there is a widespread belief that properly trained and motivated regular volunteer soldiers are much less open to critical media coverage of their activities.

But the zealot can also play a part in complicating matters. The most recent draft copy of a tactical *aide mémoire* for section commanders included 'media plan' as a fixed and formal co-ordinating instruction for every phase of war: an unnecessary detail for a corporal. What is required is the issue to all soldiers of a simple and straightforward media guide, similar to the one issued for Operation 'Grapple'. This will be an essential element of a commander's media plan. Training and mutual education of both media and military must also be the way forward, although here there are signs of improvement; in 1994 the Army Command and Staff Course at the Army Staff College, Camberley, held its first formal media study day. The Higher Command and Staff Course has a similar media package.

In planning for operations the media plan is an essential factor. Lieutenant-General de la Billière stated:

> A commander has got to spend a great deal of time concerning himself about media affairs, not on a damage limiting scenario, but on a proactive, how best can I use the media in the operation I am planning? You make your military plan and then decide where the media are going to fit in.[50]

And from the present author's time as a battalion commanding officer on Operation 'Grapple':

> The media plan was a factor in most operations. I had to think how will this operation go down, what will people think? The media plan was the way that we were going to present this, not that it changed anything I did, but it was important that the operation was presented in the best possible light ... it took time and experience to work out ... We aimed to develop a co-ordinated media plan to match the operational plan. The two ran in parallel.[51]

The media plan is thus an essential part of the overall operational plan. The estimate for this plan can be constructed simply from the published generic estimate process outlined in *ADP2: Command*,[52] with, as always, the application of common sense to match the circumstances. For example, it has been suggested that:

> In planning any military operation it should be possible to estimate where the threshold of media attention might lie by including such factors as the size, level of combat intensity and geographical location of the operation.[53]

Commanders will be well aware that every deployment of British troops onto operations will continue to attract intense media interest.

131

In conclusion, relations between military and media are not doomed to antagonism and failure, although there will always be potential sources of friction. Operational commanders need to appreciate that there is a 'media flank' to their operations, which must be both controlled and protected. The military must also learn to understand the effect that modern technology has had on the ability of the media to report on, and at times distort, the battlefield, while appreciating that the media will need special measures to ensure that they and the military can both operate in harmony, and achieve their separate aims. The *Green Book* has useful procedural guidelines on which to build, although commanders must be aware that despite plans and delegation, a considerable amount of their personal effort must be with the 'media flank'. Prejudice from both sides can be broken down through more positive and tolerant attitudes, while harnessing the unique power of the media to reflect the aims of the media plan. As Brady has said:

> The battlefield is information, and the target is public support ... use the facilities of the commercial media as often as they can be useful in getting the truth to the people. Journalists will say that war is too important to be left to generals. Reporting of war is too important to be left to reporters. Soldiers need to get involved in this.[54]

Finally, the suggestions in this paper are offered as guidelines which are not meant to be prescriptive. These guidelines are intended to be practical and useful, as opposed to right or wrong; they should be adapted and amended as appropriate to fit the circumstances. But, in 'mixing with the media', the last word remains with Lieutenant-General de la Billière: 'I would say that all Commanders must learn to live with the media, be trained to handle them and the pressures they bring, and give it the necessary priority in their plans.'[55] It is all a question of the 'necessary priority'.

NOTES

The original version of this paper was written while the author was attending Higher Command and Staff Course Number 4 (HCSC 4), February 1995, held at the Army Staff College, Camberley. A subsequent version was published in *Despatches: The Journal of the Territorial Army Pool of Public Information Officers*.

1. Quoted in C. Elliott, 'The Impact of the Media on Modern Warfare',

Despatches: The Journal of the Pool of Territorial Army Public Information Officers, 4 (Autumn 1993), pp. 21–33 (hereafter *Despatches*).

2. S. Badsey, 'Modern Military Operations and the Media', *The Occasional*, paper number 8 (Camberley: Strategic and Combat Studies Institute, 1994), p. 26.

3. Martin Bell, in an address to HCSC 4, 2 February 1995.

4. Dr Stephen Badsey, in an address to HCSC 4, 1 February 1995.

5. N. Gowing, 'Real-Time Television Coverage of Armed Conflicts and Diplomatic Crises: Does it Pressure or Distort Foreign Policy Decisions?', working paper 94-1, Joan Shorenstein Barone Center on the Press, Politics and Public Policy (Cambridge, MA: Harvard University, 1994), p. 3.

6. R. de Norman, 'To War with the Press: Some Recollections of the Media in the Gulf', *Army Quarterly and Defence Journal*, 121, 4 (October 1991), p. 433.

7. Philip Jacobsen in an address to HCSC 6, 10 February 1993.

8. Ibid.

9. Colonel David McDine, former Senior British Army TAPIO (Territorial Army Pool of Public Information Officers), in a discussion with Major Richard Robinson, Army Command and Staff Course 28, Camberley, 13 June 1994.

10. Mark Damazer, Editor BBC News Programmes, in an address to HCSC 8, 2 February 1995.

11. Brigadier (then Lieutenant-Colonel) David Chaundler, in a presentation on Operation 'Corporate' to Army Command and Staff Course 28, Camberley, 22 April 1994.

12. V. Adams, *The Media and the Falklands Campaign* (London: Macmillan, 1986), p. 7.

13. Admiral Sandy Woodward and Patrick Robinson, *One Hundred Days* (London: HarperCollins, 1992), p. 109.

14. Ministry of Defence, *Proposed Working Arrangements with the Media in Times of Emergency, Tension, Conflict or War* (*Green Book*), including amendments up to 26 July 1994.

15. H. Colver, 'To End on the Winning Side', *Despatches*, 2 (Autumn 1992), p. 9.

16. P. Cordingley, 'Future Commanders – Be Warned', *Despatches*, 3 (Autumn 1992), p. 15 (a version of which is reprinted as Chapter 12 of this book).

17. Ibid., p. 16.

18. P. de la Billière, 'The Gulf Conflict: Planning and Execution', *Journal of the Royal United Services Institute for Defence Studies* (Winter 1991), pp. 7–12.

19. From a series of interviews conducted as part of a research project at the Army Staff College, Camberley by Major Nigel Watts in 1994.

20. P. de la Billière, p. 11.

21. P. Cordingley, p. 16.

22. F. J. Stech, 'Winning CNN Wars', *Parameters* (Autumn 1994), p. 47.

23. B. Stewart, *Broken Lives – A Personal View of the Bosnia Conflict* (London: HarperCollins, 1993), p. 180.

24. Ibid., p. 323.

25. Martin Bell, in an address to Army Command and Staff Course 28, Camberley, 9 February 1994.

26. N. Gowing, pp. 80–2, covers the full ramifications of Operation 'IRMA'.

27. N. Gowing, 'Real Time Television Wins a War', *Independent*, 27 September 1994.
28. Dr Stephen Badsey, in an address to HCSC 8, 1 February 1995.
29. *The Army Manual of Public Relations*, Army Code 70430 (London: HMSO, 1967).
30. *Army Doctrine Publication Volume 1: Operations*, Army Code 71565 (London: HMSO, 1994), (hereafter *ADP1: Operations*).
31. Ibid.
32. This is taken from a suggested revised/improved version of Public Information as defined in *ADP1: Operations* circulated in an unpublished discussion paper by Dr Stephen Badsey.
33. This was first set out in *The Army Field Manual Volume 5: Operations other than War, Part 2, Wider Peacekeeping*, Army Code 71359(A) (London: HMSO, 1994). In 1997 the *Wider Peacekeeping* manual was superseded by *Peace Support Operations*, but the principle of consent remains unchanged in the doctrine.
34. *Field Manual 100-5 Operations* (Washington, DC: Headquarters Department of United States Army, 1993).
35. Ibid., pp. 3–7.
36. *Green Book*, p. 15.
37. T. Pocock, 'If it is Going to Risk One Human Life ...', *Despatches*, 2 (Autumn 1991), p. 34.
38. Martin Bell, in an address to HCSC 8, 2 February 1995.
39. *Green Book*, p. 8.
40. A. Thomson, *Smokescreen – The Media: The Censors: The Gulf* (Tunbridge Wells: Laburnham & Spellmount, 1992), p. 32.
41. S. Purvis, 'The Media and the Gulf War', *Royal Society of Arts Journal*, CXXXIX, 5423, (November 1991), p. 3.
42. I. Cobain, quoted by the Newspaper Society in a letter to Hugh Colver, 29 May 1991.
43. S. Purvis, p. 3.
44. D. Beresford, quoted by Colin Brown in *Independent*, 28 May 1991.
45. Major-General P. Brady (former United States Army Chief of Public Affairs), *ARMY, The Journal of the United States Army*, 40 (September 1990), p. 83.
46. Ibid., p. 11.
47. B. Stewart, p. 324.
48. P. Cordingley, p. 15.
49. 'Aide Memoire: Operation GRAPPLE and Operation HANWOOD', Army Code 71537 (Rev) 2/93, HQDT/18/35/98, p. 28-1.
50. P. de la Billière, p. 11.
51. Taken from the Watts study (see note 19).
52. *Army Doctrine Publication 2: Command*, Army Code 71565 Part 2 (London: HMSO, 1994), Annex D to Chapter 8.
53. S. Badsey, p. 23.
54. P. Brady, p. 85.
55. P. de la Billière, *Storm Command* (London: HarperCollins, 1992), p. 63.

10

Lessons Learned: A Personal View of Military–Media Relations on Peacekeeping Operations

COLONEL G. R. COWARD

INTRODUCTION

The guns in and around Sarajevo are silent; violent death is now a consequence of a traffic accident or criminal activity rather than war and genocide. UNPROFOR, the United Nations Protection Force, has gone, replaced by NATO in the form of IFOR (the Implementation Force) and then SFOR (the Stabilisation Force). Elections have been held and a joint presidency formed; democracy is making a faltering start. Living conditions are slowly improving; cafés and bars now operate above ground, and even, during the warmer weather, on the pavements of that once vibrant, cosmopolitan city. The building and glass trades cannot meet demand and the people are no longer fearful of entering the Markala market-place, although most continue to harbour much of the hatred and suspicion bred by over three years of war. There remains at least one daily Sarajevo activity which is a legacy from those bitter days of conflict: the daily press briefing, back now where it started in 1992 at the Holiday Inn on what was once Sniper's Alley. The organisation is slick, professional and expensive. The US Army major with a master's degree in journalism who runs the place is proud to show anyone around; he almost seems to have time on his hands. NATO has learned from the UN's mistakes, as, in this day and age, media relations are vital business for the military on operations, especially those of a peacekeeping nature.

My own experience of military–media operations in Bosnia is restricted to an eight-month UN tour from the close of 1994 to August 1995. I held the post of UN Military Spokesman, initially under

Lieutenant-General Mike (later General Sir Michael) Rose, and then under Lieutenant-General Rupert Smith. I arrived at a relatively low point in UN–media relations, although these had not really been particularly cordial since the original Srebrenica crisis of April 1993. Rose enjoyed a brief media honeymoon during early 1994, but, following the Bosnian Serb attacks on the Gorazde safe area in April and the Bihac safe area in November, attitudes gradually hardened and the relationship became adversarial, particularly with the United States media. There was a distinct lack of trust between Public Information (P INFO) staffs and the media representatives in Sarajevo. Not only did the Sarajevo press corps consider that the UN was failing to meet its mandate, but they had also begun to look upon the organisation as the fourth party to the war, constantly feeding them propaganda and lies. Of course the truth was different. UNPROFOR had a thoroughly contradictory mandate covered by a plethora of confusing United Nations Security Council resolutions and lacked the necessary resources to meet all but the basic humanitarian aspects of the mission: defence of the five safe areas garrisoned by inadequate UN units really was impossible. But the media based in Sarajevo vented their frustration with the international community on the local messenger, the UN spokesmen. In particular, press briefings were a scrum, and one or two of my predecessors found the pressures too great and moved on quite quickly. During the short 1994–95 cease-fire brokered by ex-President Carter, and the change of command between Rose and Smith, we endeavoured to improve the media–military relationship, at pains to ensure a neutral delivery of balanced information. And then the war started up again before the snow had begun to thaw.

The remainder of my tour as a military spokesman passed by in a blur. Not long after the Bosnians launched their winter assault on Mount Vlasic, the 1,600 kilometre confrontation line lit up almost everywhere; sniping and then shelling had returned to the streets of Sarajevo. As BBC reporter Martin Bell said, 'there was no peace to keep'. Calls for restraint went unheeded and, as the Balkan spring warmed, so did the war. After Lieutenant-General Smith's ultimatum of 26 May 1995 over the use of heavy weapons from the weapons collection points around Sarajevo, the Pale ammunition compound was bombed by NATO, at UNPROFOR's request. Over 70 Bosnians were killed in the Bosnian Serb shelling of Tuzla and, after a second air strike, hoards of UN peacekeepers around Sarajevo and Gorazde were taken hostage by the Bosnian Serbs. Once the hostages were returned via Serbia, General Mladic focused on Srebrenica and Zepa: thousands were expelled or taken prisoner, or so we thought. In reality, thousands were murdered in the killing fields of eastern Bosnia. I left, but the war went on to reach its crescendo in the autumn after NATO air strikes had crippled Bosnian Serb C³ (Command, Control and Communications) and the Croats had stormed east from Knin.

I returned to Bosnia in June 1996, as part of IFOR, in command of an aviation regiment, primarily supporting the British-led Multinational Division (Southwest) (MND (SW)), but also providing the aircraft for Lieutenant-General Mike (later General Sir Michael) Walker, who was commanding the Allied Command Europe Rapid Reaction Corps (ARRC). I was therefore able to find plenty of excuses to revisit Sarajevo. I also had an almost unrivalled opportunity to look closely at many of the battle areas around Bosnia that I had tried to explain (rather poorly it turns out) at the press briefings in Sarajevo the previous year. Of course, the most striking contrast to my previous tour in Bosnia was how much difference a peace agreement, the deployed might of IFOR and the active ground involvement of the United States made. IFOR had a purpose and a direction that the UN lacked the previous year: there was a series of agreed objectives and an explicit end state. The media operations organisation of the ARRC was also impressive; well organised, well resourced, well trained and well manned, a single focus in Sarajevo; a far cry from the UN hand-to-mouth operation to which I belonged. That is not meant as a criticism of the UNPROFOR Public Information staff, for the environment had become entirely different. I do not believe that matters could have been much different under the circumstances, but the comparison is necessary, however unfair it may be to those concerned.

This short chapter attempts to draw together some of the key lessons learned during my short time in the peacekeeping media relations field and to examine how far these may or may not have been assimilated by the NATO peacekeepers in Bosnia. My perspective is perforce a military one, but owes much to the influences of Alexander Ivanko (my civilian counterpart in Sarajevo), to Colonel (now Brigadier) Alaistair Duncan (author of Chapter 9, 'Mixing with the Media') and to Dr Stephen Badsey, whose paper, *Modern Military Operations and the Media*[1] was the only reference I managed to read prior to taking up the appointment.

INFORMATION STRATEGY

My principal criticism of the UN information organisation on joining it was the lack of any coherent, strategic information guidance, or indeed an information plan. In Zagreb, before moving down to Sarajevo, I sought a copy of the information plan or any lines to take on specific issues. It was explained that there was no strategy or plan as such, merely public pronouncements by senior UN officials such as the Secretary-General, the

Special Representative of the Secretary-General, and the various spokes-men within the mission. It was also not policy to issue lines to take, as these too came from public pronouncements of these same UN officials. I was counselled to scan the wires regularly to ensure that I kept in step with whatever was emanating from New York and Zagreb. It seemed like a scene from the BBC television comedy series *Yes Minister!*

Although there was no formal strategy or plan, the military force commander had issued a guidance note to military Public Information officers which gave us a number of objectives, target audiences and a mission:

> To provide the international and local media with timely, accurate and detailed information in order to exploit every opportunity for presenting the activities of UNPROFOR in a positive light, thus furthering the opportunities for promoting peace in Bosnia Herzegovina in a proactive way.

This was all good stuff, but no strategy. We in Sarajevo had a view of how to proceed, but without an agreed strategic plan this was quite often at variance with the pronouncements of Zagreb and New York. The media very quickly found any slight differences and attempted to drive the equivalent of a squadron of Challenger tanks between us.

In spite of this lack of strategy, information was one of the key activities in UNPROFOR in 1995. Lieutenant-General Rose had seen the need to bring the information department into his immediate circle and, when I arrived, I worked from the General's outer office alongside his Military Assistant. My civilian counterpart or I were included in all visits and negotiations, albeit in a non-speaking role; the profile was being raised to reflect the importance of this aspect of peacekeeping. Lieutenant-General Smith tended to keep the media at arm's length, and so an even greater burden fell on the spokesmen's shoulders; but, as a corollary, information was the first subject covered at any briefing session and a special information policy meeting was held every day, chaired by the General and attended by the Head of Civil Affairs and the spokesmen.

By contrast, during the latter half of 1996, IFOR not only had a very detailed operational plan which was inextricably linked to the Dayton Agreement, but also woven throughout it was a coherent information strategy which quite clearly differentiated between the local and international communities. Every operation order included a media line, which was communicated up and down the chain of command. There was little scope for misunderstanding: IFOR could speak with one voice. Moreover, Media Operations retained their place at the forefront of commanders' minds, with special early-morning strategy sessions and full coverage during daily conference calls. Lieutenant-General Walker, the ARRC Commander (COMARRC) had even managed to recruit a senior media strategist who was there in the background, thinking through the possible impact of each of the potential issues: war criminals, elections, training and equipment, and so on.

MANNING

Back in 1994, BBC journalists Nik Gowing and Kate Adie were both highly critical of the British Army's use of relatively low-grade officers in Media Operations in Bosnia, especially those from the Territorial Army Pool of Public Information Officers (TAPIOs). They were not alone in believing that we did not put sufficient priority on the appointment of suitably qualified and experienced officers for Public Information posts. The TAPIOs have since been reorganised, and renamed the Media Operations Group (Volunteer). In truth, peacetime appointments to Public Information in divisions and districts did not have the necessary tariff or cachet to attract officers of above-average quality; some did the job extremely well, but this was more likely to be by luck than judgement. The same initially applied to our forces in Bosnia; some individuals were a great success, others not so. Eventually, after a few high-profile gaffes, it was decided at the highest level to select specially the individuals for key Media Operations appointments such as spokesmen. Since then, we seem to have got it about right at this level. However, Media Operations organisation has to fight within a diminishing pool for high-quality junior staff on Peace Support Operations, and this pool is increasingly augmented by the Territorial Army. The Territorials involved in Media Operations are no different from any other military unit, having a broad cross section of ability within their ranks, but at least they all have a modicum of relevant media and/or military experience. Sadly, it would seem that Mr Gowing and Ms Adie have had the misfortune to come across most from the lower end of the spectrum. Their underlying point though is a valid one; we must find the right people for the higher-profile Media Operations jobs which involve direct dealing with the international media. For that we must write explicit job specifications which call for a preponderance of regular combat and combat support arm officers and then aim early enough to identify the right individuals. I suspect that a few of the Territorials are not suitable for this front-of-house task, but there are plenty of posts within the mobile news teams and in staff planning to make best use of their talents.

139

At the operational level there has been much discussion on the right mix of civilian and military personnel, as well as the need for overall strategy and co-ordination. When Lieutenant-General Smith arrived in Bosnia he was keen to employ an information 'supremo' above the two spokesmen (one civilian and one military), who would develop strategy, issue lines to take and co-ordinate all aspects of an information plan; able to provide in-depth background briefings to senior journalists, without formally being a spokesman. Eventually a UN Civil Affairs Officer was recruited for the post, but, before he could have an impact on matters, he was moved on. Although I initially resented having another civilian placed between the commander and myself, it made eminent sense to have this level of co-ordination, freeing the spokesmen to deal almost exclusively with the media. Finding the right individual to fill the post was the problem, but it can be done, as NATO has proved with the appointment of a one-star (brigadier-equivalent) US ex-journalist to provide information strategy advice to COMARRC. In addition, the ARRC had a full colonel non-spokesman, who stood above and behind the two main spokesmen, to plan and co-ordinate all aspects of the information plan, which also included PSYOPS (psychological operations) of a benign nature aimed at the local community.

The search for the right people to man information departments goes on, and it would seem that the vogue in Sarajevo has been to recruit journalists. As I departed from Bosnia in December 1996, two relatively prominent journalists were recruited to fill information posts in the UN and OSCE.

TRAINING

In my own case, there was little time for specific training prior to deployment, although dealing with the media had been part of the curriculum at the Army Staff College and I could recall the essence of what we had been taught. Nonetheless, I sought out the television interview-training officer who gave me a short refresher. After debriefing those first faltering attempts, I am relieved to learn that I apparently improved on the job. The major deficiency in my training was an in-depth appreciation of the media themselves and exactly how the various elements work and what their objectives and pressures are. While the front end of television and radio news may not hold too much mystery to us, the working of a news room, the power of the editor and the role of wire services both written and visual, probably do. The significant differences between United States and British media organisations are also worth noting, as is the kind of technology that is now in use. I was relatively lucky joining a mission during a temporary cessation of hostilities; there was time to pick up this sort of depth of knowledge from my civilian professional colleagues and the members of the media themselves; others had not had this luxury. I note that even recent spokesmen have also lacked this kind of background media knowledge.

In addition to the training of Media Operations staff, the remainder of the force requires an element of media relations training. This has long been a part of British Army pre-deployment training at its bases in Warminster, and Sennelager in Germany. Everyone receives a one-hour awareness package, which provides an overview of media interest in the operation, highlights a few pitfalls and puts across the essential do's and don'ts. Currently these are:

Do

- Always be polite;
- Always report press presence;
- Talk only about matters of fact within your area of responsibility;
- Refer all other questions to the Public Information staff;
- Think before you speak;
- Try to be helpful;
- Be honest, positive, professional and remain calm.

Don't

- Give any formal interviews without prior clearance from Public Information staff;
- Discuss NATO operations, plans or procedures;
- Give any information about local forces, which might be of use to their opponents;
- Your thoughts and opinions are your own – never give them to the media;
- Mislead or take sides;
- Let the media pressurise you into saying things you would rather not say or should not discuss;
- Carry the press in the vehicle unless properly authorised.

All commanders down to sergeant receive an additional package, which includes a little more depth and specific media training, including hostile media interview-training. Prior to my most recent deployment, I was co-opted to provide an element of local colour and recent experience. The same officer who gave me my interview training covered this aspect, and an ITN journalist conducted most of the one-to-one interviews. The scenario was realistic and specific: the forthcoming elections in Bosnia, which were not going quite to plan and therefore had considerable potential for humiliation and haranguing. A few of the more senior officers of the divisional headquarters were involved in a series of relatively hostile press conferences which came quite close to reality, and it gave them much needed confidence to tackle the real thing on arrival in Bosnia. As it turned out, none of the press briefings in Banja Luka ever reached that level of hostility and the election passed off without major incident.

MEDIA

If all peacekeeping operations – or Peace Support Operations as they are now known – are a moderately strong magnet for the media, those in crisis have an electro-magnetic attraction. During my experience, the mission was more often in crisis than not, and the number of media representatives in Sarajevo burgeoned to 300 or 400 with support staff representing almost every nation in the world. When the local media were added, our relatively meagre facilities were soon overloaded and press briefings became a scrum. The demand at times was insatiable: on one day I conducted 18 television interviews, and countless telephone interviews to radio, television and newspapers around the world – at one o'clock in the morning I unplugged the telephones! During the Srebrenica crisis, one Dutch television station booked me for their evening news every night for ten days.

The most demanding elements of the media are without doubt the wire services, who are constantly on the look out for up-to-date information. Reuters, AP and AFP were all present in Sarajevo, and were under pressure to file up to half-a-dozen times a day, more if there was something particularly interesting going on; most of our business was conducted on the telephone. Television also has a number of equivalent companies, and thankfully for much of my time a pool system operated, which meant that we would only be needed to provide one interview which would be shared among all companies: I hate to think what it would have been like without this! Radio was also present, dominated by the BBC. The major British and American broadsheet newspapers, as well as *Time* and *Newsweek*, tended to maintain journalists in the city, often only stringers. It is through these media that complex issues are best put across: they have the space to cover them properly, while a television interview lasting one minute and 40 seconds does not. During crises, all major British, German, French and American television networks, as well as CNN and BSkyB, were present in the city. However, when any of them lacked a physical presence, these organisations were able to make Bosnia the lead story by using the wire service copy, coupled with television pool footage, and even a telephone interview with either a UN spokesman or Sarajevo-based stringer. As there was always a satellite uplink in the city provided by the European Broadcasting Union, this could then be varied by a live two-way interview later in the day. Of course, when a company had its own crew in town and sole or preferential use of satellite uplink, the response to a changing situation was often almost immediately relayed around the world; what Nik Gowing has described as 'the tyranny of real time'. However, television is not just news, and the current affairs programmes of the networks also offer the opportunity to put across complex, in-depth issues, although the peacekeeper who thinks there is no risk in this is a fool.

Our stated policy was to deal with all forms of media equally. To quote the UN Guidance: 'Treat all accredited media representatives equally, regardless of the relative importance or nationality.' This we endeavoured to do, although we were constantly criticised by the wire, radio and print journalists for favouring television. An element of this may be true, but the reality was that we never refused a bona fide request for information, worked on a first-come first-served basis, and a television interview, especially a live one, was more time consuming than a brief conversation on the telephone. Sadly, we also were unable to provide a 24-hour service due to lack of manpower, and, in retrospect, both this and the criticism over favouring television could have been alleviated by more staff.

The NATO Press and Information Centre at the Holiday Inn in Sarajevo is the tangible evidence that the importance of proper staffing and the need to be able to deal with peak demand has been thoroughly understood in this context. From only one English-speaking military spokesman in my day, IFOR enjoyed the services of up to five. I cannot be sure that they offered a 24-hour service, but it was certainly more than the maximum of 14 hours that the United Nations provided.

RELATIONSHIPS AND IMPARTIALITY

The need for fairness and equality in dealing with the media is paramount, and perhaps one of the most important lessons of my time in this field was the fundamental need to establish relationships with the media that are built on trust and mutual respect. Very few of the journalists that I came across were the 'reptiles' popular folklore would have us believe, although it would be naïve to think that the organisations for which they work are not motivated by a need to turn a profit. Media space (air time or column inches) has to be filled: the more exclusive and controversial the better. Even those that had effectively taken the side of the Bosnian Muslims with whom they shared Sarajevo tried very hard to maintain an element of objectivity and, more often than not, gave the UN the benefit of the doubt. Most recent writing on this subject since Brigadier Elliott's essay, 'The Impact of the Media on Modern Warfare',[2] which suggested that the media–military relationship was doomed to antagonism and mistrust, has emphasised that this is not necessarily so; in my experience, certainly not so on peacekeeping operations.

But there were charlatans too. From time to time there would be instances of journalists breaking confidences. One of my colleagues was quoted in an American newspaper after having briefed a reasonably famous journalist off the record; the quote was apparently too good to miss. On another occasion, after having attended an explicitly off-the-record dinner with the commanding general, one journalist asked me at the following day's on-the-record press briefing the very same question in an effort to gain the general's frank response from a quotable UN official. Luckily, the other journalists present that previous night not only resisted the temptation to do the same, but also supported my robust position against the individual concerned. Occasionally there were also instances of television companies being shoddy with their use of unqualified library footage or inaccurate stories. Usually a quick phone call was enough to put them right, but one company often quickly reverted to type as the pressure to fill a 24-hour news channel with interesting pictures grew too great.

The UN was also often accused by the international media of lacking impartiality: it was a foregone conclusion that the parties would take this position. On quite a few occasions there would be howls of derision from the press corps when we described Bosnian Serb activities in neutral terms while the press expected us to condemn them out of hand, as they would do in their copy later that day. At the same time, whenever we condemned the Bosnian Muslims for their treatment of the UN or UN peacekeepers, we were criticised for being too hard on them. Perhaps we were, but the UN expected a higher standard of behaviour from one of its members, particularly since we had their explicit consent for our involvement. Over time, and as the Bosnian Serbs incurred even greater international condemnation for their treatment of UN hostages and the Bosnian Muslims in the enclaves, we – and especially my civilian colleague, Alexander

Ivanko – were able to be much blunter in our condemnation of their activities, and this appeared to help our credibility with the press corps.

During my last tour to Bosnia I was heartened to see that the relationships between the Sarajevo press corps and the IFOR Media Operations staff appeared to be as close and as mutually productive as I think ours had been in the previous year. This was probably helped by the changed circumstances – the journalists had much less to be dissatisfied with in the NATO, post-Dayton era – but it was obvious that our military successors were keen to maintain their impartiality and credibility too. No doubt they still had a need to guard against the occasional unscrupulous journalist and shoddy report on television.

CONCLUSIONS

I suspect that NATO continued to learn new lessons and relearn a few old ones in the media-relations field each week in Bosnia. The main test is what we manage to retain and put in place in order to continue to improve our performance as Peacekeepers in this vitally important area. I fervently hope the UN has managed to draw some of these conclusions and develop suitable mechanisms for developing, resourcing and regenerating something like IFOR's strategy and media plan for future mandates, wherever they may be. But we certainly cannot be complacent, communications and the media are at the forefront of technological developments, and it will pay us to keep pace with them in an era of increasingly likely Peace Support Operations.

NOTES

1. S. Badsey, 'Modern Military Operations and the Media', *The Occasional*, paper number 8 (Camberley: Strategic and Combat Studies Institute, 1994).
2. C. Elliott, 'The Impact of the Media on Modern Warfare', *Despatches: The Journal of the Pool of Territorial Army Public Information Officers*, 4 (Autumn 1993), pp. 21–33.

11

The Media and the Minder:
The Royal Navy's Perspective

LIEUTENANT-COMMANDER D. J. PICKUP

WHAT IS THE 'MINDER'?

To the journalist the term 'minder' refers to a soul who deserves much sympathy and understanding – the official whose task it is to interpose himself between the media and the military – to act as a buffer. It seems to have a rather juvenile connotation, indeed the *Concise Oxford Dictionary* defines the term as 'one who attends to something ... particularly a child'. Some observers may not find this entirely inappropriate.

Officially, the description which should be used is that of 'media escort officer', although the official titles used to describe such people include Public Information Officers (PIOs), Public Affairs Officers (PAOs) or even simply Public Relations Officers (PROs). These terms, however, can be misleading and imply a task which is usually considered as having little operational significance. Indeed, until quite recently the whole issue of public relations was believed to require a small department often consisting of one person whose primary role in life was to keep the media off the backs of those with better things to do. The role of the unit PRO was primarily to be reactive, and only proactive if the issues concerned were so trivial as to be insignificant. Appointments usually reflected this attitude. Unless the command was of sufficient size and/or importance to warrant a significant degree of media interest, unit PRO tended to be a secondary task for junior officers, or those other officers whose normal duties afforded them such available time as to take on the onerous additional responsibilities of PRO. As such it held the equivalent status of mess wines member or children's party organiser. The exaggeration is slight. If the command took the job seriously the officer concerned might have been sent on a public relations course which, until the 1982

Falklands Conflict, was little more than a day-visit to the Public Relations section of the Ministry of Defence.[1] Even in large establishments the responsibilities of the officer required to deal with the press would be subsumed into the greater role of the community relations officer, which includes liaison with local authorities and institutions as well as normal Public Relations (PR) functions.

The duties of the PRO were generally undemanding and consisted of little more than providing biographies of the commanding officer and acting as escorts to the local press on annual open days or, in the case of the Royal Navy, visits to foreign ports. Problems involving operational matters or the reporting of accidents were normally referred to higher authority: at senior command or even Ministry of Defence level where the professionals were based.

However, the nature of the role of media liaison changes fundamentally when a nation's armed forces move away from the peacetime environment and into war. The nature of the media's interest in the armed forces changes also. The emphasis shifts from the banal to the dramatic. Stories of a human interest nature only lose their immediacy. They may be reported in due course, but their priority declines as the possibility of armed conflict increases and the threats to national interests and the lives of national citizens become greater. In such a context the nature of the PR role has also had to change to reflect different moods and perspectives.

During such a period, Public Relations decision-making passes from being a local to a national concern and, usually, the unit PROs find that the PR task is among the first to be removed, at least in any meaningful way.[2] As the procedures and the rules that govern PR increase in significance, politicians and senior military officers take a much greater interest in both the image and the message. Public Relations becomes too important to leave to unit PROs, and the professionals move in.

To do their job properly in wartime the media need to become as integrated with the military as possible. The reason is obvious: the most newsworthy stories will lie where the main action is and the military lie at the source of this action. Yet the military dare not allow the media a free range over the areas of action. The military desire and require as much control as possible. Only in exceptional circumstances can unit PROs be entrusted with this role of control; in any case their proper operational tasks now require, quite rightly, their undivided attention. Authority must find others who are trained and fitted to do the job. In the case of the United States a vast army of reservists is available.[3] In the case of the United Kingdom the Ministry of Defence will provide civilian information officers backed up by specially selected serving personnel. In addition, each service has a number of reserve officers it can call upon.

The Royal Naval Reserve Public Affairs Branch (PAB) consists of 40 naval officers, about half of whom are women, and five Royal Marines officers. Almost all have served on the active list. Those now working in the media industry are especially valuable. The Territorial Army's Pool of Public Information Officers (TAPIOs), recently renamed the Media Ops Group (V), can deploy some 70 people in a time of emergency, and 7644 Flight of the RAF Volunteer Reserve fulfils a similar function albeit with smaller numbers. Both the Army and RAF branches are made up of people with media connections.

Although each service has a slightly different recruitment policy, the general policy has been proven to be a significant improvement both in peacetime and, more pertinently, in war. The RNR (PAB) experience in conditions afloat and the operational context in which naval warfare takes place enable the Branch to offer a service experience to the media which, perhaps, the other two reserve branches cannot. But a lack of media expertise means that training has to be orientated mainly towards communication techniques.[4] The Army and RAF Public Information organisations, recruiting from the media professions, have the contacts within the media but, initially at least, may lack the operational experience. Whatever the background, however, the media has a growing respect for the professionalism of all three organisations which may be born out of an understandable scepticism for their civilian counterparts, some of whom have been perceived, certainly in the past, as little more than failed journalists who have little or no operational understanding of the armed forces they serve.[5]

This chapter will look at why the role of the minder was considered necessary and how it has developed over the last 20 years. It will draw largely on the experiences of two campaigns, the Falklands Conflict of 1982 and the Gulf War of 1991, and will be based mainly on the perspective of the Royal Navy. This is partly because of the background of the author, but mainly because it was the Royal Navy's relationship with the media during the former campaign which forced the Ministry of Defence to analyse its whole attitude to public relations in all its forms.

WHY IS THE MINDER NECESSARY?

The military mind is, understandably, only happy when it is in control of the entire situation in which it finds itself. In an operational sense this obviously means the battlefield, be it at sea, on land or in the air. Ultimate control implies victory. So, if the military finds an area of activity on the battlefield over which control is tenuous, it is conceived as a threat to the overall objective of victory. With control should be linked the word 'security'. In the sense of retaining confidence in the military situation, and the secrecy of how this situation was achieved, this has been the key to many military successes and lack of it the cause of a similar number of failures.

Any organisation which threatens security and over which the military can exercise little or no control constitutes a threat to this situation and has to be taken very seriously indeed. The initial reaction of the military is to ban it from any activity in which it might have an input into the outcome of the operation. If this is impossible for any reason then the best must be made of a bad job and the military must exercise as much control over the situation as it can, within the constraints of the legality of the action and the very nature of the society of which the armed forces are a part.

The media, in a free liberal democracy, may be seen to be that threat. In a totalitarian style of government, control is natural; the media is as much part of the system as the politicians and the soldiers. As such, the military do not feel threatened and will encourage the media to report what the military require it to report. In such a system the media will almost certainly comply. The threat that the media poses in a liberal democracy, however, is perceived as a serious one, even, perhaps especially, in peacetime. During such a period the popular media will seek to embarrass the armed forces as with all the institutions of state. Unfortunately, the eccentricities of the armed forces make them a particularly attractive and vulnerable target as they try to grapple with changing social conditions. In peacetime the military must come to terms with this situation and, using a professional and sophisticated public relations system, at worst limit the damage and, occasionally, make use of the press itself, something the services are gradually coming to understand.

In wartime, however, the situation is different and potentially much more damaging. Uncontrolled media loose on the battlefield may compromise more than the simple outcome of that particular engagement. They also may become a physical danger to themselves, a factor which the armed forces emphasise strongly as they try to persuade the media of the discipline required in objective war-reporting.[6] This situation can become more complex when the sophistication of the latest communications techniques are considered. Ironically, the media may have a greater access, through financial resources, than the military to the latest forms of communications such as satellite links. The introduction of the minder is an attempt to maintain some degree of control. It is borne out of experience,[7] and, to some extent, lack of trust.

The era of the mass media began in the last century with the invention of relatively rapid means of communication. Such devices as the telephone and telegraph allowed much faster news-gathering; and the construction of railways, roads and, later, the development of air travel allowed the news to be disseminated more quickly. Twentieth-century developments such as wireless telegraphy, television and computerised data links merely speeded up the processes further.

In the earlier era, however, control remained relatively easy. For one thing, many of the journalists and their masters were establishment products themselves, and had no wish to contribute to the decline of any aspect of that establishment. Furthermore, the means of communication were scarce and often confined to the military. Most journalists practised self-censorship to what might now be considered an alarming degree. Those who did not found themselves subject to local military censors and restricted access to those means of communication without which their jobs became impossible. To the problems of censorship and communications must also be added the attitude of the military which was suspicious of the journalist to the point of open hostility.[8]

The precedent for the need for control of the media in more contemporary times is the Vietnam War, in which the United States found itself losing a war arguably not only on the battlefield but also in the parlours of middle America. The First Amendment to the United States Constitution, which enshrines the freedom of information, was used by the media in Vietnam to report the American effort, warts and all. And there were some very big and ugly warts. Attempts by an increasingly frustrated and desperate government to persuade the media of the necessity for self-censorship and editorial discretion met with little constructive response.[9]

When the United Kingdom became involved in the Falklands Conflict in 1982 it had very little recent experience, and very little time, on which to base a comprehensible and logical media policy. Fortunately for the Ministry of Defence, the United Kingdom has no equivalent of the United States First Amendment. A further advantage lay in the geographical nature of the operation itself. The Falklands lay some 8,000 miles away and were inaccessible by any other means than the British Task Force which was hurriedly constituted to retake the islands from Argentinian control. In other words, the Ministry of Defence had not only the ability to censor but also a total control of communications.

In these circumstances it would seem that the military should have no difficulty in removing or at least limiting the influence of the media during the operation itself, especially when by far the majority of the British media and the British people were fully behind the Thatcher government's commitment to retake the islands. Yet, the way the media were handled caused so much resentment that the whole of the Ministry of Defence's media-handling, and, to some extent, Public Relations, policy had to be urgently rewritten following the campaign.

It was perceived from the very beginning that the Ministry of Defence was unable to provide facilities commensurate with the demands of a modern highly sophisticated media industry. It also refused to allow any non-British journalists to sail with the Task Force. There were many reasons for this, not the least of which was the Ministry of Defence itself. According to Robert Harris:

> It was the Ministry of Defence in London which was held to be chiefly responsible for the poor quality of the coverage and for several incidents which either bordered on, or manifestly were, the result of misinformation.[10]

Furthermore, the attitude of the armed forces in general and the Royal Navy in particular was negative. Captain Linley Middleton of HMS *Hermes*, according to Michael Nicholson, even told the ITN crew that 'We were an embarrassment to him.'[11] Middleton subsequently restricted the dissemination of information through the ship in case it reached the wrong people, a point to which this chapter will return in due course.

The combination of mistrust, outright hostility, lack of information and over-censorship produced an attitude in the embarked media that became more frustrating as the operation developed. Most criticism, however, was levelled at the Ministry of Defence civilian minders who had been allocated to the ships to act as a buffer between the servicemen and the journalists. There is some evidence to show that the policy had not been completely thought out. According to the University of Wales, Cardiff study by Mercer, Mungham and Williams:

> Each ship had been assigned at least one civilian information officer to look after the complement of journalists. The 'minders', as they became known, soon became caught in the cross-fire between journalists and the military. Indeed, they were often the cause of conflict. They were the focus of much criticism by the Task Force journalists, yet they had some things in common with their accusers. The minders had been despatched in much the same haste as the journalists; availability rather than suitability prompted some choices on both sides of the information fence. They too had mostly left without being briefed and little or no experience of life at sea. And, with one or two exceptions, they lacked seniority in their own hierarchies. These formidable disadvantages might have been offset

by strong personal qualities and clear, consistent policies; without such strengths the minders found it difficult to win the confidence of either their captains and therefore the journalists.[12]

Consequently, relationships which should have been built on a basis of co-operation and trust soon broke down. Harris, writing in 1983, criticised their lack of awareness of the media's role: 'They had absolutely no sense of urgency or news. They had no idea of deadlines or how to project a story to obtain the maximum impact.'[13] The study by Philip M. Taylor extended this view to cover how the minders dealt with a very sensitive subject: 'The vetting by minders also delayed texts and altered them, sometimes in trivial ways that infuriated the journalists.'[14]

The task of the minders was to escort correspondents, advise them on what they could report, check copy and ensure that it did not break any of the Ministry of Defence guidelines, have it cleared by an officer on board ship and then arrange for its transmission back to London. To accomplish these complex objectives it is obvious they needed the co-operation of many departments around the unit or ship. This needs the development of personal relationships and respect. Most of the Falklands minders were unable to foster respect, trust or anything approaching a good working relationship with either the ship or the press. This resulted in frustration for all concerned.

The analyses conducted following the Falklands Conflict concerning the media and their relations with the armed forces highlighted many issues, the problem of media escort being but one.[15] Each service believed it had suffered through adverse press coverage, although it was the Royal Navy which perceived it had come off worst. This, in retrospect, may have been an exaggeration, but certainly the Royal Navy did not help its own case by excessive secrecy and its natural mistrust of the media. All services are to some degree affected by this latter point, but navies, by the very nature of their main area of activity, far from the public gaze, perhaps became rather obsessed by this belief. The other two British services had certainly much more experience of the media, in many cases hostile. The Northern Ireland commitment had been a vast learning process for the Army, many of the lessons being learned the hard way.[16] The Royal Air Force has, from its inception, been adept at projecting a positive public relations image and has been able to use its general sympathy towards the media to counter some of the more contentious issues facing it, such as the problems associated with low flying. The Royal Navy's experiences were largely reactive in dealing with media coverage of accidents or particularly salacious courts martial, each of these tending to produce a rather jaundiced view of the media, and by the media. Even the more positive aspects of the Royal Navy's image, as portrayed in the brilliant *Sailor* fly-on-the-wall documentary series of the 1970s had been greeted with cynicism in many traditional naval areas.[17]

Captain Middleton's comments (see above) reflected much naval thinking, and this would remain so for a number of years to come.[18] However, another PR problem confronted the Royal Navy at the conclusion of the war. In 1981, the year before the Falklands Campaign, the Defence Secretary, John Nott, had produced a Defence Review entitled *The Way Forward*[19] in which the role of the surface ship, particularly in the NATO North Atlantic scenario, was seriously questioned. The strategic thinking behind this had led to much contentious debate on the future of the Royal Navy, and it must have been with some relief that the Argentinian invasion of the Falklands had offered senior naval officers and their champions in the defence establishment the opportunity to regenerate their arguments, notably on the place of the surface escort (destroyers and frigates) in late twentieth-century naval warfare.[20]

There is little doubt that the British liberation of the Falklands archipelago could not have been achieved without control of the surface of the sea and as such enhanced the justification of surface ships, at least in the force projection role. But instead of concentrating on this fact the media, according to the Royal Navy, had concentrated on the vulnerability of surface ships to air attack. Consequently, the public's mind had been filled with explanations of why Argentinian bombs did not explode and images of a burned out HMS *Sheffield* and an exploding HMS *Antelope*. These points were seized on by all those who had generally agreed with Defence Secretary Nott's arguments voiced a year earlier.

Although many in the Royal Navy would have wished to blame the media solely for this, it was realised by the Royal Navy's internal enquiry that it was largely the fault of the Royal Navy itself for failing to motivate people to explain to the media the true lessons (in their opinion) of the Falklands, and for failing to provide people who could devote themselves more fully and professionally to developing better relations with the media.

It was the system of providing minders that came in for particular criticism. As a number of the comments reproduced above reveal, the media were far from happy with the performance of the press escorts during the Falklands campaign. This view was echoed by many of the senior military officers who, on reflection, wished they could have had access to senior and competent military advisers who were familiar with the services and, preferably, had experience of the pressures of command.[21] As such they viewed the Israeli system of using youthful retired senior officers in this role with some envy. Israel, however, is a different country with different security priorities, and the example she provided was not entirely relevant to the British situation.

With a few exceptions the minders provided for the Falklands were members of the Government Information Service (GIS): for example, Ian McDonald, the Ministry of Defence spokesman in London for most of the conflict. GIS was a branch of the civil service which, like many others, had an individual career pattern which could move officers around not only within the Ministry of Defence but also other government departments. Their service experience, therefore, may have been limited to perhaps little more than occasional interest; or, in the case of older members, national service; or the knowledge picked up in a relatively short space of time at the Ministry of Defence. This was not what the senior commanders wanted.

The pattern of minder had to be changed and a way found for service experience to be used. Options were identified. Could a greater use be made of unit PROs? Perhaps non-combatant service officers might be considered, such as the service educational branches. Thirdly, an option concerning the use of reservists was discussed, and, fourthly, the possibility of producing better trained and informed civilian information officers was analysed. Each of these options had its advantages and disadvantages. In all but the larger organisations, unit PROs had other more pressing duties. Education officers were felt to lack operational experience and in any case their branches were being phased out, and the civilian option had been seen to be a failure in the Falklands.

The Royal Navy, in common with the other two services, opted for a solution involving the formation of a specialised and specific branch of the reserve forces.[22] As stated in the introduction to this chapter, the Royal Naval Reserve Public Affairs Branch (RNR PAB) was to differ from its two sister services in that its members were to be recruited primarily for their service experience rather than their expertise in media affairs. As such it reflected a view that both the Cardiff report and the House of Commons Defence Committee report emphasised in that the Royal Navy's requirement was somewhat different from the other two services. One of the Cardiff conclusions had been:

> The development of reservists with experience of the media or other relevant knowledge should be encouraged but, with the possible exception of the Royal Navy, these reservists should be seen as staff to augment Press Information Centres or at Command headquarters rather than as escorts.[23]

Almost all the RNR PAB members were to be recruited from those regular officers about to leave or having recently left the Royal Navy or the Royal Marines. As wide a range of experience as possible was required and personnel were appointed to the PAB from all branches of the regular service. In a few cases serving reserve officers with relevant media experience also joined.

The PAB had one further advantage. Lieutenant-Commander Christopher Lee RNR was not only a serving member of the Royal Naval Reserve (Intelligence Branch) but also a BBC defence correspondent who, in the latter capacity, had been extremely critical of the Royal Navy's PR performance during the Falklands Conflict.[24] As the natural head of the new Branch he was promoted to commander and appointed as such. During his leadership, and that of his successors, the PAB has evolved training programmes designed to retain service expertise and enhance media understanding.

The use of reserves has obvious advantages and disadvantages. Reservists do not have to be paid on a full-time basis. They are used as and when needed, ideally in the situations for which the PAB was created. Furthermore, because reservists do the job for pleasure they do not quite have the same perspective of a naval career as other officers. When regulars realise this it leads to a slightly different relationship, if anything for the better.

Reserve officers, however, have their full-time commitments which may not allow them to be available exactly as required. One result of this is that when a requirement does occur at short notice it tends to be the same nucleus of people who offer their services. This in itself can lead to a wide and uncomfortable variation in experience. Training, as far as possible, has to compensate for this but it is very difficult to simulate operational conditions, especially in dealings with an institution as unpredictable as the press.

Following some five years of consolidation and development the Royal Navy's new branch of minders, along with its colleagues in the other services, was tested during the Gulf War of 1990–91. Operations 'Desert Shield' and 'Desert Storm' offered the chance to assess a number of the new media-minding techniques which had been introduced as a result of the Falklands Conflict, from the United Kingdom perspective, and other operations such as the invasion of Grenada in 1983 and the bombing of Libya in 1986, from that of the United States.

The American system of pooling journalists into easily controllable and manageable groups had evolved from the Grenada experience, where the Americans had almost deliberately tried to preclude any meaningful press coverage from the operation. Although in a rather different way this had led to a frustration not unlike that experienced by British journalists in the Falklands, it also resulted in some very mischievous reporting of the sort that frustration very often causes.[25]

Pooling journalists is a difficult process and can only be achieved successfully by adequate preparation and very careful diplomacy. In a national environment this may be difficult enough. In an international operation, with national media demanding priorities which lead to the growth of jealousies and general disharmony, the situation assumes nightmare proportions.

The nature of the Gulf War was not unlike the Falklands in a number of respects. The natural environment was not conducive to independence; the services themselves had a large degree of control over the means of communication; and the state of Saudi Arabia, by no means a liberal democracy, could vet those journalists entering and leaving the theatre of operations. Consequently, it was believed that journalists would remain in their allocated pools. Despite this, however, the pooling system was not popular among journalists especially when they were led to believe that other pools were being granted greater access, that operational information was being withheld and, as some began to believe, the system was actually designed to control the media, not assist them. This had a number of repercussions including the withdrawal from the pools of some journalists who, despite the other disadvantages, believed they could serve themselves and their media masters better by going alone (known as the 'unilateralists').[26]

The Gulf War was not primarily naval, certainly not in the way that the Falklands had been, where sea power was fundamental to the success of the operation. It had a maritime dimension both in the period of economic blockade and during the War itself, but the primary military operation to liberate Kuwait was undertaken by the land forces. Sea power did offer support through air attacks from American carriers as well as gunnery and cruise-missile support provided largely, and spectacularly, from American battleships. The Royal Navy played its part in these operations but the use of British warships in the offensive was confined to attacks on Iraqi patrol craft and minesweeping. The war did, however, give the Ministry of Defence in general and the Royal Navy in particular, the opportunity to use its new system of media-escorting for the first time in a situation leading up to and involving hostilities.

It is easy to say that from the media point of view the naval operation was a great success. It certainly was an improvement on the Falklands experience but problems did remain. Frictions between the Royal Navy and the Government Information Service were apparent but these were largely caused by personality problems. The senior naval officer in the Gulf at the time the crisis began was openly hostile to the media, and his senior PRO was notorious for his lack of tact. Later, a more careful selection of staff did much to alleviate this. By December 1990 both had been replaced by personalities far more able to approach the task sympathetically (including the present author!). Furthermore, the RNR Public Affairs Branch was deployed for the first time operationally. After some initial difficulties the system worked and, coupled with a competent pooling system arranged in the British Ministry of Defence, the media were generally, but not always, satisfied.

There were two discernible periods of the media operation. Before Christmas 1990 the Ministry of Defence (Navy) media relations operation consisted of little more than public relations facilities arranged either directly from London or, in some cases, in theatre itself. A variety of national and local press and television groups were hosted and programmes arranged.[27] Following New Year 1991, as the UN deadline approached, the emphasis shifted to the disposition of accredited war reporters onto particular ships. It was in this period that the Public Affairs Branch was particularly valuable. Of the four major surface warships involved (initially the Type-22 frigates HMS *London* and HMS *Brazen*, and the Type-42 destroyers HMS *Gloucester* and HMS *Cardiff*) each had media representation on board; on three of these the minder was RNR. In addition, the RNR provided the minder for the minesweepers which were operating off Kuwait City and there was an RNR officer ashore (initially in Dubai, then Bahrain), assisting the senior PRO (GIS) in the co-ordination of shore support, particularly the onward transmission of material, usually using the local television station.

The system had a number of advantages, not least of which was the establishment of useful personal contacts and relationships. As such a trust was born between media, minder and military which was never experienced during the Falklands. The media understood the operational parameters they were working under and, while demanding, were never outrageously so. Similarly, ships' companies began to understand that, not only could the media be tolerated, they could actually be liked. By the end of the operation, ships' companies were expressing disappointment if there was no mention of their ship in the national media. Some of the results were also dramatic, particularly from the ITN team (Mike Nicholson and Eugene Campbell) on board HMS *Gloucester* whose footage of the discovery of a mine, the destruction of several Iraqi patrol craft, and the launch of cruise missiles from USS *Wisconsin* kept TV editors in London happy in the rather quiet period before the land war began.[28]

While the most important relationship lay between the media and the minder, a slightly more surprising relationship grew between the civilian members of the Government Information Service and the RNR officers.

A number of the more experienced members of the latter were initially resentful that they remained subordinate to the GIS officers, and there was some justification for this attitude while the wrong personalities were in positions of influence. Once these people, on both sides of the fence, were replaced and officers with greater mutual sympathies appeared in theatre, the situation changed dramatically; and a logical distribution of responsibilities proved that good personal relationships could produce a much more efficient organisation, based largely on a much more pleasant professional atmosphere. This in itself reaped dividends in relations with the press.

The lesson of the Gulf War, from the Royal Navy's point of view, was that of personal relationships. A good working relationship can lead to a successful result, and that professional relationship can only be based on competence and mutual respect. This has to operate both ways if the minder is to fulfil the real purpose of his role.

THE ROLE OF THE MINDER

The job of the minder, as explained briefly earlier, is to act as the buffer between the military and the media. The experience of the Falklands Conflict told the Ministry of Defence that such a role can best be performed by an officer in uniform. That officer can retain authority and credibility within the particular operational environment in which he is serving if he is respected by both sides for his competence and skill. If solid personal relationships result from this respect then this can only enhance the credibility of the minder and, by implication, the credibility of the organisation being served.[29]

Of course the minder has terms of reference, and these are laid down and available as required. In peacetime circumstances he might be required to organise and provide press facilities in the time-honoured manner of a public relations officer, but in most circumstances this task falls within the remit of the full-time professional public relations staff. In wartime, or the build-up to conflict, the minder may be approached to provide press facilities of a more operational nature.

When the Royal Naval Reserve Public Affairs Branch came into existence in 1985 it spent many months trying to qualify or define the difference between public relations and public affairs. The Branch at times did not help itself in that it would quite regularly provide officers to fill public relations roles within Royal Naval Reserve units or within the Ministry of Defence PR structure itself. The public affairs aspect should only be referred to when the Branch is fulfilling the role for which it was

158

formed; that of providing escorts to the press at times of conflict and build-up to conflict. (There may be a grey area where media escorts are required for specific occasions, such as the many anniversary commemoration events of the Second World War which took place in the 1990s.)[30] In its real role, in common with its sister services, the RNR PAB provides a service, which relieves pressure on command and maintains service credibility in the eyes of the media. By devoting itself solely to this task it can not only gain the professionalism required to maintain that credibility but it can build up the personal relationships so important yet so controversial.

The naval environment does give the minder a few advantages which are not evident for the other services. A ship is a self-contained floating steel box. Within it are all the facilities required to complete its operational task. It works in a very hostile physical context and access to and from it, both physical and as regards communications, are severely limited and easy to control. Furthermore, in wartime the ship is an important target. The minder can quite easily ensure the approximate whereabouts of his charges, that they are not sending material ashore which may compromise the tactical situation and can persuade them that, should such a compromise occur, they are literally in the same boat as the rest of the ship's company.

The closed environment, however, may lead to other problems especially when a media team has been embarked in a small ship for so long that it becomes part of the ship's company. It is also impossible for the minder to accompany the media 24 hours a day, especially when the minder is on his own. In these cases it is his responsibility to remind the crew, gently, that the media are not one of them and should be treated with some circumspection.[31] Communications within a ship are also relatively open and the media may pick up information from a variety of sources which the command would rather they did not know. Again it is the responsibility of the minder to persuade the media that reporting such information may not be in everyone's interests even after the media have finally been landed.

Within these limitations, however, the creation of a constructive personal relationship can work to everyone's advantage, with the media having access to as much as possible of the information it requires and the facilities, within reason, for getting material ashore. The Royal Navy in general, and the ship in particular, may find itself projected in a positive light which should reap significant public relations and, possibly, political dividends later. If the command is also sympathetic the role of the minder can almost become a most pleasurable experience.

In an operational situation also, the accredited defence media will be as familiar with the rules of what can and what cannot be reported as the minder, so the invidious task of vetting need not be the acrimonious exercise it was during the Falklands Conflict. The command, however, will continue to exercise its prerogative in this area as certain innocuous facts can, quite innocently, when analysed in a military context, lead to a compromising situation.[32]

The trust that can emerge from such situations depends, obviously, on the personalities involved, and the minder should never forget that control over the media is lost as soon as the journalists leave the ship. The temptation to blame the minder for any reporting at this stage which the unit would prefer not to have been reported, is great but unjustified. If a unit exhibits problems which may be considered to have a public interest, and these are reported, that is the price of a free press. It is worth the minder, therefore, being fully aware of the nature of the embarked media. As mentioned above, the accredited defence correspondent may usually be trusted to remain objective. In a genuine emergency situation when journalists without any knowledge of – or sympathy towards – the services are embarked, trust may be rather more difficult to establish and to sustain. Recent experience, however, has given weight to the argument that the media have been so grateful for being accorded facilities, they have remained objective to a point which might be considered suspicious.[33]

It is in this context that the rules which govern the activities of the minder are superimposed. They are obvious and well known. The media must never knowingly be lied to; they must be kept as well briefed as possible; they must be provided with facilities as required within the security parameters of the operation. The media must also be treated well, again within the operational restraints. Members of the media must be briefed on safety, they must be accommodated in the best conditions the environment can provide and, obviously, they must be fed and watered. They are also granted officer status.[34]

Such housekeeping requirements and procedures are exercised regularly and professionally. A media serial is now built into the Royal Navy's operational sea-training exercises. In this serial a ship is given 24 hours warning of a media visit. It is expected to provide domestic services according to the requirements of the Director of Public Relations (Navy). It is expected to keep the media briefed and up to date on the exercise, and provide interviews with senior officers on its conclusion. (This evolution is valuable training for the minder in that often senior officers may not be quite as discreet as they should – such interviews should always be recorded!) It is also expected to provide communications facilities for the onward transmission of 'the story'. The media will arrive on board accompanied by a minder from the RNR PAB. Until the exercise is over the ship does not know whether the press is simulated or real. The directing staff produces a report on the serial as it does with all others and the ship awarded a grade as a result. A recent addition to this exercise has been a CNN-style fly-by using, if available, a civilian helicopter. The 'press' on board the helicopter will demand an interview with the captain of any of the ships involved. The captains have to comply. Similar serials are now incorporated into other exercises, as well as those which would naturally have a major public information input. Accidents in nuclear facilities are a particularly pertinent example of this.

Although such exercises are really orientated to the war scenario, the diminishing number of warships in the Royal Navy means that individual ships are now expected to be in areas of significant media interest much more regularly and may have to accommodate the press in a real situation. At present these areas include the Adriatic, the Persian Gulf, the West Indies and the South Atlantic as well as more mundane operations such as fishery protection. The Royal Navy is learning quickly that no longer can the media be ignored.

PERCEPTIONS: IS THE MINDER A FACILITATOR OR A CENSOR?

The perception of each of the sides involved in media relations in the military operation is coloured by misconception and personal experience. The journalist's view of the Royal Navy may have been formed out of a television programme, or a series of articles about homosexuality, women at sea and particularly interesting courts martial. The service's view of the press may be similarly jaundiced by articles written or programmes produced which reveal the service which the man (or woman) serves and respects in a less than encouraging light. It takes time, and experience, for such views to be reconciled. The time will very rarely be available unless both sides are willing to compromise to an extraordinary degree, or the operation is a particularly long one. The experience is available, however, and it is this experience which both sides look for in the minder.

The Falklands Conflict reminds us how important this experience was. The lack of experience in the minder coupled with the vagueness of the terms of reference produced a relationship which was to colour the media's view of the Royal Navy, in particular public relations in the Royal Navy, for years to come. According to Mike Nicholson:

> These men were not only unqualified, they were unwilling to help. They were afraid: they were looking over their shoulders: they were constantly worried about London.[35]

161

Tony Snow continues:

> I found the MoD PRs lazy, loath to agree to do anything that
> involved them having to do any work, obstructive ... and dishonest
> – I was lied to by them on a number of occasions.[36]

While Alastair McQueen believed that they were:

> Unable to drag themselves away from the cosseted environment in
> which they dealt with defence correspondents. They were unequip-
> ped for a wartime role. They did not understand the requirements
> of newspapers, or television organisations ... In my opinion they
> were totally out of their depth.[37]

During the Gulf War the journalist's view of the minders, certainly
in the Saudi theatre, was coloured less by their incompetence or lack of
experience and background than by the nature of their task, which was
perceived to be that of censor rather than facilitator. The reasons for the
objections to the Falklands minders had largely, but not entirely, been
removed. Virtually all the minders were in uniform and their credibility
was thus enhanced. However, those public affairs officers, particularly
the Americans, with the media pools were sometimes seen as being
officious, unhelpful and over-zealous with the blue pencil. On the latter
point, the main issue of contention was not the necessity for censorship
but the arbitrary nature of the way it was carried out. Procedures differed
widely between the various pools. According to Deborah Amos of
American National Public Radio, 'You could get an angel or a devil.'[38]
Journalists were generally very suspicious of their role, not least because
of reports of instructions allegedly issued to American public affairs
officers which stated that 'you're the one who keeps journalists out of
areas they shouldn't be in'.[39] A further bone of contention was that if a
report was published which higher authority did believe to be detrimental
to the war effort, it was the journalist, not the minder, who suffered most.
Whereas the minder might get a reprimand, in some cases the journalist
lost his membership of the pool.[40]

The task of the Royal Navy minder in the Gulf was easier. The
sympathy of the media was also gained by an early decision taken in Dubai
that the United States and British media facilities would be jointly pooled
where necessary and possible.[41] In reality this concession was meaningless
when, as soon as the war began, prearranged pools of national journalists
were despatched to national ships, but it did produce an atmosphere
which helped all concerned. In the shipboard environment issues of

censorship were generally straightforward and the ground rules accepted with little controversy. The media simply saw the minder as a person to whom they could turn when they wanted something: the interface between the ship and the media. Personal relations developed to the point at which some degree of trust was established. In other words, the minder was seen as the facilitator, not merely the person who would tell the press why they could not do something.

The perception of the media by the minder is perhaps not quite as important as that of the minder by the media. In this context it is perhaps relevant to compare the situation with that of a market. The media are the customers, the minder is the supplier. The supplier would not be required if the customers did not need the product. In other words the media are the reason for the whole relationship, not the other way round. The situation, however, does not bear a direct comparison with the sales desk. The supplier does not always wish to provide the product and by no means is the customer always right.

Even in the Falklands situation where the public relations staff were soundly pilloried, the fault did not only lie in one area. Graeme Hammond, one of the few PR officers in the Falklands who gained some respect from the journalists, states that the military were not always to blame for the poor relations:

> There were times when journalists and officers had stand up rows because they simply disagreed with each other. But the policy was to allow as much information as possible to be released. The overriding factor, however, was that information was not of help to the enemy. But they did make mistakes. And because we got the relationship wrong to start with, every time something went wrong for whatever reason the journalists believed that this was part of the overall conspiracy.[42]

Whatever the individual relationships are, the real requirement is to establish the relationships early and at formal and informal levels. If credibility can be thus established and respect gained the errors that occurred in 1982 can be avoided.

Despite this requirement wrong perceptions and prejudgements do occur. The military's view, and that of the minder, of some journalists will differ from others. Media people with whom the military have had a long and successful relationship will be trusted and probably accorded greater sympathy than those who are young, new and inexperienced. The defence-orientated journalist will almost always fall into this category, as they are more objective, more knowledgeable and more sympathetic to

163

the view of the serviceman, if not always that of the Ministry of Defence. The representative of the quality press will, rightly or wrongly, be taken more seriously than that of the tabloids whose objectives may be slightly different. Age also has its complications. Younger journalists may be out to prove a reputation. The visual and broadcast media bring their own problems and perceptions. To the serviceman the broadcast media means more than the written. Its immediacy and its prominence prompt a greater interest and awareness than reports in newspapers, even popular national ones. The broadcast media bring well-known names and faces if nationally prominent figures are involved. Such journalists would always deny that they would use their reputations and familiarity to their own ends. Experience, however, suggests that this is not always the case. Sometimes the development of a healthy cynicism by the minder can be useful.

CONCLUSIONS

It is difficult to discuss any aspect of the media and the military in the period since the Second World War without reference to the Falklands and Gulf Wars. It was in these two conflicts that the relationship between the two came of age. Lessons were learned and new guidelines drawn up. Following the Falklands Conflict, the House of Commons Defence Committee produced the report which was to lead to the Ministry of Defence producing its *Green Book*[43] which remains the British services' main reference on how to deal with the press in time of emergency. Cardiff's report, later published as *The Fog of War*, drew similar conclusions. Many of these conclusions resulted in a better relationship during the Gulf War where the media were much more sympathetic to the needs of the military, and the military to those of the media.

Some of this improvement is certainly due to the changing nature of the minder. Although, in the Gulf, civilians were still used in the role, the necessity for credible uniformed escorts had been accepted and largely introduced; although it was interesting to see how, for domestic 'political' reasons, the British Ministry of Defence still preferred to have civilian PROs at least nominally in charge. The situation may continue to improve, but the whole area remains a dynamic one in which personalities, situations and technology are subject to constant change. Such developments as instantaneous satellite links will add their own degrees of complexity to already complicated situations.

The Royal Navy has been particularly notorious in its attitude to the media.[44] It was the Royal Navy which underwent most examination following the Falklands and whose PR reputation could only improve.

Perhaps, as a result of the reforms of the Royal Navy's PR organisation and the formation of the RNR Public Affairs Branch, it has. The Gulf experience, and lower key exercises since, have proved this. But vested interest remains, as does a rather out-of-date attitude to the use of reserve forces (which will be seen to change, one presumes, with the passing of the new Reserve Forces Act), and will continue to exert its influence, as it has in former Yugoslavia. Increasing financial controls and restraints also do not help, as they disrupt already difficult and complex training patterns.

However, it may be a sign towards the future when the recently retired Second Sea Lord referred to the RNR PAB as 'the Jewel in the Crown of the Royal Naval Reserve'. This may have been merely a rather obvious attempt at PR in itself as it was part of an address that Admiral Sir Michael Layard gave to the PAB in 1995 at its annual conference at the former Royal Naval College, Greenwich.[45] It certainly caused some comment by the other 3,960 members of the Royal Naval Reserve, where the Branch has been criticised for being an organisation to itself ('a private Navy' according to one divisional commanding officer).

But it is gratifying to discover that PR in all its forms is now included in all officer, and some non-commissioned officer, career-training in the Royal Navy, something that certainly did not happen in the 16 years the author spent as an officer in the regular Royal Navy. Indeed there is now even a PR input into the School of Maritime Operations at HMS *Dryad*. The only depressing aspect remains the necessity for a continual process of education, as senior officers and commanding officers suddenly discover the need for all the PR help they can get in certain situations, only to lose enthusiasm when they pass to appointments with a far less obvious PR profile.

NOTES

1. On his first appointment as a ship's PRO the author spent a morning at the Ministry of Defence learning the importance of 'home town stories'. Since the Falklands, however, the Ministry of Defence has sent personnel on the week-long PR course at the Civil Service College, Sunningdale. A useful handbook is also now available for naval PROs.
2. In a warship a PRO can be any officer but is usually one with a less important operational task such as the supply officer or the education/met officer. During Operation 'Desert Storm', however, HMS *Gloucester*'s PRO was the senior pilot of the Lynx Flight. He was delighted to see a public affairs officer join the ship. Lieutenant-Commander Livingstone RN was subsequently awarded the DFC.
3. The United States attitude to reservists is significantly different from that in

the United Kingdom. Many are virtually full-time. A significant number of US Navy public information officers are reservists on long-term second-ments to the regular service.

4. Each reserve officer has a contractual commitment which requires him to fulfil specific training objectives. Courses are held in naval bases at weekends and combine updates on operational and technical matters with practice in writing such things as news releases and briefings on media developments. Normally, professional journalists are invited on such courses and invited to discuss their problems, requirements and experiences.

5. Michael Nicholson commenting on the claim made during the Falklands that a particular minder was an 'ex-journalist' wrote: 'They were mostly failed journalists rather than ex-journalists.' Nicholson had discovered that the person concerned had been the agricultural correspondent on a Midlands local paper. See R. Harris, *Gotcha! The Media, the Government, and the Falklands Crisis* (London: Faber & Faber, 1983), p. 28.

6. At the time of writing it is believed that some 58 journalists, almost all uncontrolled, were killed in the Bosnia Crisis 1992–95.

7. Anecdotal evidence suggests that some years ago the Army conducted an exercise on Salisbury Plain during which an officer was briefed to try to cause as much chaos as possible just using a mobile phone. The result, I believe, was impressive!

8. See P. Knightley, *The First Casualty* (London: André Deutsch, 1975), for an excellent and graphic account of the early history of the war correspondent.

9. P. Knightley is also useful for his coverage of the role of the media in Vietnam. In addition, see M. Herr, *Dispatches* (London: Picador, 1979), and T. Royle, *War Report* (London: Grafton Books, 1987). The feature film *Good Morning, Vietnam* provides a realistic reconstruction of the conditions appertaining at the time.

10. R. Harris, p. 30.

11. R. Harris, p. 48.

12. D. Mercer, G. Mungham and K. Williams, *The Fog of War* (London: Heinemann, 1987), p. 87 (hereafter D. Mercer).

13. R. Harris, p. 27.

14. P. M. Taylor, *War and the Media: Power and Persuasion in the Gulf War* (Manchester: Manchester University Press, 1991), p. 91.

15. The most important of these analyses was the report of the House of Commons Defence Committee entitled, *The Handling of Public and Press Information during the Falklands Crisis*, Command 8820 (London: HMSO, 1983).

16. For an analysis of the Army's experiences in Northern Ireland, I am indebted to my colleagues in the Communications Studies Department of RMA Sandhurst.

17. *Sailor* was among the first fly-on-the-wall documentaries, and covered the penultimate commission of the 1955 aircraft-carrier HMS *Ark Royal*. It received almost universal praise and formed the precedent for many similar programmes. It was filmed in 1975–76 and broadcast in 1977.

18. The author vividly remembers taking part in Exercise 'Teamwork 88' on board HMS *Intrepid*. On introduction to a very senior officer, without whose co-operation his job would have been almost impossible, he was greeted with the words 'I hate the Press'. The senior officer subsequently refused to have

anything to do with either the embarked UK media or the Norwegian media on arrival at Namsos. Media coverage was not very positive.

19. *The United Kingdom Defence Programme: The Way Forward*, Command 8288 (London: HMSO, 1981).
20. Nott's review, had it not been modified, would have led to the disposal of about 25 per cent of the Royal Navy's surface fleet, including the light carrier HMS *Invincible*.
21. Captain Jeremy Black of HMS *Invincible* was particularly forthright in expressing the view that he needed a competent person to advise him on PR. Captain Black subsequently became Commander-in-Chief Naval Home Command and was a very enthusiastic supporter of the RNR Public Affairs Branch. See D. Mercer, p. 112.
22. For a detailed analysis of why reservists are preferable in the context of minders, see D. Mercer, pp. 328–37.
23. See the conclusions of D. Mercer, p. 379.
24. Quoted extensively in V. Adams, *The Media and the Falklands Campaign* (London: Macmillan, 1986), for example, p. 151.
25. D. Mercer, p. 291.
26. For a full account of the media's perspective of the land war in the Gulf, see P. M. Taylor, *passim*.
27. Errors did occur. On one facility on board the hospital/aviation support ship RFA *Argus* the local UAE press had been invited but the BBC had been overlooked. 'Auntie' was not at all happy!
28. As a result of this the Ministry of Defence insisted that ships should make every effort to land film where possible. On one occasion HMS *Gloucester* steamed 50 miles south and transferred a cassette ashore using three other ships' flight decks. Such an effort made it possible to have film of the day's activities broadcast on early evening television. In the Falklands it had taken about ten days.
29. The use of service officers, such as Group Captain Niall Irvine, as spokesmen at high command level also gave the PR aspect a greater credibility in the Gulf War.
30. RNR PAB officers were involved in the anniversaries of the Battle of the Atlantic, D-Day, VE and VJ Days.
31. A number of journalists have played on their ability to move and mix around a ship. While it is possible to ensure information thus gained is not transmitted ashore from the ship, neither the Ministry of Defence nor the minder has any control over the journalist ashore.
32. One particular aspect of naval warfare which can be very sensitive is the weather. On one occasion during the Falklands Conflict a live broadcast inadvertently announced that the weather was very pleasant. The Task Force had to sail 50 miles at top speed to leave the only small area of good weather in the South Atlantic.
33. Colin Wills of the *Sunday Mirror*, quoted in N. Pierce, *The Shield and the Sabre* (London: HMSO, 1991).
34. This can cause acrimony as the standards of dress and behaviour of the press are not always what more traditional members of officers' messes and wardrooms would prefer.
35. R. Harris, p. 27.
36. Ibid.

37. Ibid.
38. P. M. Taylor, p. 52.
39. Telephone conversation of 12 January 1990 attributed to Louis A. ('Pete') Williams, Pentagon press relations spokesman to subordinates at the US Central Command's Joint Information Bureau in Dahran, quoted in J. R. Macarthur, *Second Front – Censorship and Propaganda in the Gulf War* (New York: University of California Press, 1992), p. 19.
40. P. M. Taylor, p. 53.
41. There was even an attempt to form a joint PR HQ in the World Trade Center, Dubai, but this was vetoed by both the Ministry of Defence and the US Department of Defense.
42. Quoted in L. Metcalfe, 'Controlling the Media', unpublished BA dissertation, University of Bournemouth, 1995, p. 21.
43. Ministry of Defence, *Proposed Working Arrangements with the Media in Times of Emergency, Tension, Conflict or War* (*Green Book*), including amendments up to 26 July 1994.
44. It still is, according to a conversation between the author and Mark Laity, BBC radio defence correspondent, April 1995.
45. M. Layard, 'The Jewel in the Royal Navy's Crown', *Despatches, The Journal of the Territorial Army Pool of Public Information Officers*, 5 (Spring 1995), p. 84.

12

Future Commanders Be Warned!
A Brigade Commander's View of the
Media in the Gulf War

MAJOR-GENERAL PATRICK CORDINGLEY

7TH ARMOURED BRIGADE

The first indication I had that the 7th Armoured Brigade could be deployed to Saudi Arabia, and that we might become the focus of mass-media attention, was during the course of a divisional study-day in early September 1990 in Wolfenbuttel, Germany. Time passed and rumours increased but no one made any further suggestions to me until 11 September when I was told that an independent brigade group, based on 7th Armoured Brigade, would deploy to the Gulf and that a public announcement to this effect was imminent.

From that moment on, the lives of all of us in the 7th Armoured Brigade Group were turned upside down. The stresses and pressures that the media put on us were soon to become part of the daily routine. Very early on, I was acquainted with the plan that the Director of Public Relations (Army) (DPR(A)) had made, and told that the details would be handled by my own Public Information Officer (PIO). At this stage the media themselves arrived. I had expected this intrusion but the manner of its coming was revealing. To prepare me for the first encounter I was not only called to 1 British Corps Headquarters to be briefed by the Commander-in-Chief BAOR (British Army of the Rhine) and the 1 British Corps Commander, but on the morning of the press facility DPR (A) and my divisional commander arrived at breakfast time to rehearse a question-and-answer routine. This coincided with my first malaria medication; I was promptly sick but I did feel well-prepared and briefed!

On arriving at Fallinbostel for the facility, it was interesting to note that my plan for the day had been overturned. I believed that we should show the British public a mass of armour, and, accordingly, had arranged the Royal Scots Dragoon Guards' tank park. The Public Information staff had all the tanks put back tidily in the hangars and one representative piece of equipment from each arm organised in a semi-circle, not dis-similar to a country fête. It was quite clear to me then that there was a small battle about to begin.

On 17 September, after another press facility, I flew with the oper-ational reconnaissance team to Riyadh. Our accommodation was to be the Intercontinental Hotel. The contrast between the white robes of the displaced Kuwaiti guests and our combat kit, gas masks and pistols, was stark. After the reconnaissance was complete I returned to my own brigade headquarters back in Soltau in Germany, eventually travelling back to Saudi Arabia with the advance party on 11 October.

SAUDI ARABIA

The problems that faced us on arrival needed to be prioritised: I identified four to which I gave precedence over all others. The third of these was to learn to handle the media effectively. In retrospect, I believe that the media plan had been well made in the Ministry of Defence and that the recommendations of the Beach Committee after the Falklands War (which had investigated the participation of the media in British military operations) had been scrupulously followed. But nobody could have foreseen the real extent of the problem. There were approximately 1,000 British and foreign correspondents living in Dhahran, 50 miles from the port of Al Jubayl. Quite rightly, their editors required a story from them daily. As a result, we laid on a major press facility every other day, for the first two months that we were in theatre. No media plan had been devised for such an invasion and, even if it had been, it could not have foreseen the stress that it put on commanders and the small Public Information (PI) staff that we had available to us.

It is interesting to note that during this time, very early on, ITV had written to me asking if they could give us a team on a permanent basis until the crisis was over. I offered this letter to the Ministry of Defence and heard nothing more about it. It was, of course, a similar idea to the Media Response Team (MRT) that was eventually used, and at the time it would have been very easy for me to set up because I had the vehicles available to me. It is also interesting but understandable that it was many months before such a system was effectively implemented. Clearly, negoti-ations with the media organisations over membership of the MRTs had to be conducted in London by the Ministry of Defence, rather than on the ground.

Almost immediately there was a set-back to the media campaign. We were presented with the front page of *The Times*, where there was a picture of two of our soldiers dressed, unmilitarily, in vests and underpants carrying their gas masks and rifles, and underneath it the caption, 'On Patrol in the Gulf'. Quite rightly, the Prime Minister Mrs Thatcher wanted to know what we were up to and asked the Secretary of State for Defence. It was not long before the question arrived with me in the sheds, and 40°C, on the quayside of Al Jubayl. I was most concerned that anybody should doubt our professionalism. The truth of the matter was that the incorrectly-dressed soldiers were not on duty when photographed but the damage had already been done. This was one of the hazards of encouraging openness with the media, but for every adverse story there were hundreds that were positive.

Then we had to tackle the problem of trivia in the tabloids. It became apparent that our soldiers were being offered up to £300 for a published letter: of course, those letters that were published tended to be of a derogatory nature. One went through the business of finding out whether it was possible to censor soldiers' letters, but when there were 10,000 of us in theatre, most of whom were writing one or two 'blueys' (letter forms) a day, the task was clearly going to be an impossibility and of questionable legality.

PUBLIC INFORMATION AND MEDIA PRESSURE

As a result of these problems we had to take dramatic decisions, and very soon the media were not third on my list of priorities but first on the agenda of the daily conference. It also became apparent that I had to strengthen my own Public Information team; I took one of my most experienced and competent majors from his unit and promoted him to temporary lieutenant-colonel, putting him in charge of the Public Information activities.

We were not only a curiosity for the media during this time: during our first seven weeks in theatre we hosted 112 military or civilian visitors of major-general status and above. While we were very keen to accept these visits, because it fell in line with the aim of projecting an efficient and well-organised brigade group, it was an extra burden when added to the already excessive attention from the press and television.

Even during our initial training phase in the desert I felt that the media were still concentrating on trivia rather than the major issues that were clearly at stake in the eastern part of the Gulf. It was the massive scale and unconventional nature of the warfare about to be entered into that concerned us: this didn't seem to find a place in the articles that were being published about the brigade group. So towards the middle of November I spoke to General Sir Peter de la Billière and discussed the problem with him, asking if I could address it to a team of visiting defence correspondents. He felt that I was not the right person to do so.

Towards the end of November these correspondents came straight from the Ministry of Defence to my headquarters in the desert. After briefing them for some 20 minutes I took their questions. The first that came to me was: 'We understand, Brigadier, that if you go into the attack now you will take very few casualties.' This did seem to me a ridiculous comment to make: the two armies that were facing each other were quite enormous! With my recent discussion with General Sir Peter in mind, and conscious that we were trying to answer questions honestly, I said words to the effect, 'When two armies of this size meet there are bound to be a considerable number of casualties'; but I went on to point out that although we were psychologically prepared for this, I didn't believe there would be many British dead or wounded because we were extremely well-trained and we had better equipment than the other side. I also said I wondered if the British public was similarly ready. And I thought no more about it.

At the end of the second day of the visit, I went to have dinner with the correspondents in Al Jubayl. Towards the end of the meal one defence correspondent leant over to me and said, 'It was a lovely trip, Brigadier, and we have been most impressed with what we have seen, but we're slightly sorry about what we might have done to you.' 'What do you mean?' said I, and he replied, 'Well, we have really made a little bit of a saga out of your comments on casualties.' As I drove back into the desert in my Land Rover his remarks began to prey on my mind and, as we had satellite communications up and running from the headquarters, I put through a telephone call to my brother. I asked him if there was anything that caused him concern in the newspapers recently and he said, 'It's funny you should ask that, but I have the *Evening Standard* in front of me and the headline makes interesting reading: "British Commander's warning as Gulf Forces go on alert; Prepare for a Bloodbath".'

During the course of that night I was woken up four times to be asked precisely what I had said to the press and on the following day I received the expected rocket from General de la Billière. While talking to him, I asked permission to continue with my proposed two-day visit to Bahrain. This had been organised for some time and, although there was work involved, it was also my first opportunity to have a break in three months.

When I arrived, I moved into a very comfortable five-star hotel and the first day was extremely pleasant. On the second day, Tuesday, the Sunday papers arrived and I bought several, which was a mistake. In one I was giving advice to the new Prime Minister Mr Major, who had been in power for only one week and I was not certain that he would be impressed by that, and in another it was demanded that I should be sacked. Rather moodily, I went off to lunch, and on returning I was given two messages, one to ring up the British Ambassador in Riyadh and the other to ring up General Sir Peter. I went up to my room to make these telephone calls only to find that neither gentleman would be available until the following day. The next 18 hours I can only describe as stressful. That is the sort of pressure the media can put on you.

Incidentally, during that same meeting with the journalists, I managed to get in a comment about our troops not being as well-supported from home as our neighbouring American divisions. This brought reaction from the *Daily Telegraph* and slight embarrassment to me as it seemed that I was complaining. However, the response from the British public towards Christmas time was quite dramatic and I did my best to make certain that the soldiers responded to all the letters and presents that came their way.

THE MRTs AND THE GULF WAR

On returning from Bahrain to the desert I discovered that Colonel David McDine, an old friend and Territorial Army (TA) officer, had arrived in Dhahran to help mastermind future Public Information programmes. His appointment was a classic example of finding just the right person for the delicate situation. His advice and the pressures of training helped me dismiss the kerfuffle over the casualty affair.

The arrival of the 1st Armoured Division and 4th Armoured Brigade should have taken the media pressure from us, and for a week or so it did. But then the MRT system came into being and we were back again with a constant concern as to what to show the media on a daily basis. However, having a television crew and a sound crew from the BBC with us as half of the team, and not just the press, was in many respects a relief; throughout the previous four months we had found that television and radio were, for obvious reasons, much more likely to report things as they were, as opposed to the newspapers which relied entirely on the journalists' interpretation and style of expression.

I could discuss at length the success of the MRTs but much of that has already been covered by experts more competent than me to comment and assess; but I do congratulate all those Public Information officers, both regular and TA, who made it work so well. The MRT members became friends like any other person in the brigade. The main problem lay in when to brief them fully on our operational plans; too soon and it would inhibit their ability to report truthfully, and leave it too late and it would cause frustration. I was also concerned over how casualties would be reported once the land war had started, but so were the journalists. However close we had become, I knew that their job and mine had, in war, different aims. I felt affronted for them afterwards when some of their colleagues suggested that their relationship with the forces had altered their ability to report truthfully. But of course the final phase of the media plan was never, fortunately, fully tested because we met with virtually no reverses during the four-day land war. Let us hope we will never put it to the test in future but be aware that this vital final phase must be studied in depth.

This study is so necessary because of the possible effects of the media on modern warfare. I detected, during the initial settling-in period, the belief among reporters that they should encourage emotion. If an interview could be turned to probe fear or shock, this seemed to win favour at home. The intrusion, if challenged, was justified as caring and in the public interest. But don't the public, and indeed the armed forces, shape their behaviour to the media's demands? Did we not confess in the Gulf, under this examination, to being frightened? Well, of course, we were – but was it not unpatriotic to ask us to say so? And then the reporting of the very clinical nature of modern weapon systems and their effects on the bunkers and buildings in Baghdad led the public, particularly the American public, to lose touch with the reality of war; a grim, ghastly and bloody affair. Such reporting also heightened the public concern over casualties. This is also a dangerous preoccupation. I wonder if commanders can now be ruthless enough, in a television age, to pursue the enemy to the limit, if the stakes are anything less than national survival.

Part Four:

The Media and Policy Decision Making

13

The Military and the Media
Past, Present and Future

PHILIP M. TAYLOR

Since the Gulf War of 1991, the relationship between the military, the media, the reporting of wars and of 'conflicts other than war' has attracted a considerable amount of professional and scholarly attention.[1] At the heart of this writing is an attempt to validate or refute the claims of such distinguished figures as Henry Kissinger, George Kennan and Boutros Boutros-Ghali that the media, and live television in particular, have become a significant driver of the diplomatic environment of the post-Cold War era. The argument runs as follows: officials are now being forced to respond to dramatic television 'real-time' images either in ways that they might otherwise have done or at a speed that they find incompatible with their traditional methods of working. Hence there is a danger of hasty or ill-thought-through decisions based on emotional responses to tragic images rather than rational judgements made in the cold light of day. This might even include the deployment of armed forces into situations that make it difficult for them to achieve their objectives because those objectives have been driven more by political factors than by military objectives. The media, having created the situation, now revel in the dramatic pictures which result, while their quest for 'infotainment' causes friction with the armed forces whose job is made even more difficult by their presence. This phenomenon has been termed the 'CNN effect' or the 'do something factor'.

Something must indeed be done to address this issue, which is in danger of becoming a 'given' in the next decade. Essentially we are talking about media effects. Now, although common sense tells us that the media must have *some* effect upon their consumers, even after decades of research in a variety of academic disciplines there has not yet emerged a proven causal link between observation and behaviour that satisfies everyone. Why certain individuals react at certain times in certain ways, and not at others, may have something to do with the media but only within a wider sociological, psychological and cultural context. With the supposed CNN effect, we need to be equally careful in rushing to conclusions about the impact of television; not least because it is in the interests of the media to promote the view that they have power to change things, and because it is highly convenient for those making the decisions in response to blame the media if things go wrong. The shadow of Vietnam looms large in this debate.

There are essentially four interlocking arguments presented here. First is that the actual historical record of military–media relations for the past 100 years has been characterised far more by co-operation than it has been by conflict. This has often been forgotten due to the widely held but erroneous assumption that the Vietnam War – the so-called 'first television war' – was lost not on the battlefields of south east Asia but due to the reception of hostile television coverage in the living rooms of middle America. Secondly, it is suggested that it has never been, and it is still not, possible for the media to convey the realities of warfare to a wider public watching from far beyond the scenes of fighting. This is only in part due to the existence of military censorship or official propaganda. Mainly, it is caused by the nature of the media beast. Live television and other new communications technologies, if anything, compound this problem. Thirdly, it is argued that, having lost their respective institutional memories, the military and the media are in danger of reinventing wheels and repeating mistakes that are no longer appropriate to the international environment of the next decade, in which inter-state conflicts might have become a thing of the past. Rather, the real challenge is to find a way of informing the public about the context of those now more characteristic and complex intra-state conflicts which produce such appalling pictures of human tragedy: the lines of refugees, starving children, ethnic conflict and genocide. These are the images which are assumed to prompt the cries that 'something must be done' by the international community to stop the horror before its eyes, when doing something is infinitely more complex than the images can ever convey. Finally, it is suggested that because the media are more event-driven than issue-driven, they cannot be relied upon to provide the context necessary for informing rational, as distinct from emotional, responses. Hence, more proactive informational strategies are required not just on the part of military authorities (many of which are in fact responding to the new circumstances) but also on the part of international and multinational organisations, especially the United Nations itself.

THE MEDIA AS PATRIOTS, HEROES, MYTHMAKERS AND PROPAGANDISTS

When nations have gone to war during the course of this mass-media century of ours, it is really an undeniable historical fact that their national media have helped the prosecution of those wars far more than they have ever hindered them. And the reasons for this lie not just in the development of ever more sophisticated methods for controlling and manipulating journalists. There is no need here to rehearse the processes by which first the press and then the mass media came to constitute a fourth estate in the body politic of democratic nations. Let us just say that one of the roles of the news media is to convey information from, and about, the few to the many. Whether or not they see themselves as representing the views of the establishment to the public or vice versa, in wartime the media are in the same boat as the rest of society. And if the many support the decisions of the few, the media would be committing commercial suicide not to support the war effort. Indeed, one lesson of the Falklands War of 1982 was that an over-zealous support, such as the *Sun*'s highly jingoistic campaign, could result in a fall in circulation. It may therefore be a truism that democratic nations cannot go to war unless they have the backing of both the public and the media.

The 'problem' in the 1990s has been that very few democratic nations are going to 'war'. Democracies anyway tend not to wage war against other democracies. But they are contributing to military interventions in ideologically adrift or collapsing states on behalf of the international community: northern Iraq, Somalia, Bosnia, Haiti, Albania. The role of the media in covering such crises is both erratic and unpredictable. Many of the planet's civil wars simply go unreported or are reduced to a few lines in the 'World in Brief' sections. Why the media focus on some of these conflicts and not others – Somalia rather than the Sudan, say – is beyond the scope of this chapter, but the difference is illustrated by the plight of Iraqi rebels in the wake of the Gulf War. To the north, the televised Kurds were helped by Operation 'Provide Comfort'; but to the south, the un-televised Shias received no equivalent assistance. But the complexity of this is also illustrated by the fact that despite months of shocking pictures from Rwanda beginning in April and May 1994, including scores of bodies floating down rivers and the hacking to death of a woman, for 12 weeks of terrifying tribal genocide both the Clinton administration and other Western governments 'actively resisted the flow of horrific pictures that documented the mass slaughter'.[2]

Once the decision is made to despatch troops on a humanitarian or

179

peacekeeping mission, media interest in those countries inevitably increases. This media spotlight however merely maximises the problem in one area while minimising issues in another part of the world. Further problems in media coverage then arise from the lack of clear-cut issues: who is 'the enemy', where is the 'battle-front', why cannot the peace-keepers open fire? In other words, conflicts other than war are infinitely more complex than conventional wars and do not provide the kind of ready frameworks in which traditional war-reporting has taken place.

What we used to call civil wars have always, of course, presented special problems for journalists from 'neutral' countries. If a journalist reports from one side of such a conflict, he becomes a spy or an enemy propagandist in the eyes of the other side. And if there are three sides to a dispute, as in Bosnia, then confusion reigns supreme. And because such conflicts are often fought with a brutality which borders on anarchy, they become extremely dangerous places for journalists, which is why their casualties were so high in Somalia and Bosnia. Being read is infinitely preferable to being dead. The safest place thus becomes alongside the intervening military forces, which in turn brings us back to the military–media relationship.

Many analyses of the military–media dynamic concentrate on the points of tension and criticism. This is perhaps inevitable but it is also misleading. As General Sir Harold Alexander, who took command of British forces in the Middle East in 1942, wrote:

> My own opinion is that the press correspondent is just as good a fellow as any military officer or man who knows a great many secrets, and he will never let you down – not on purpose – but he may let you down if he is not in the picture, merely because his duty to his paper forces him to write something, and that something may be most dangerous. Therefore he must be kept in the picture.[3]

Indeed, the record of most war correspondents in both World Wars is one of wholehearted support for the war effort, whatever side they were on. In Britain, for example, despite strict censorship procedures, the number of occasions on which the media clashed with the government in six years of total war between 1939 and 1945 was remarkably few.[4] After the First World War, Field Marshal Sir Douglas Haig even thanked the press correspondents for their coverage by presenting each of them with a Union Jack flag.[5] And when American correspondents after Pearl Harbor likewise encountered bad news, they often failed to report it, 'not because disclosure might help the enemy in playing to Allied weakness, but simply because it reflected negatively on the Allied performance'.[6] There are endless examples of this. Hence General Dwight D. Eisenhower could refer to the 500-strong press corps attached to his command in the Second World War as 'almost without exception ... my friends'.[7] And although he did not quite mean it in this way, it could be construed that this was behind Pete Williams' comment about the Gulf War coverage as being 'the best we've ever had'. Of course, this is where patriotism and propaganda coincide, and in wartime the record of journalists as patriots and propagandists is every bit as noteworthy in democracies as it is in authoritarian regimes. The difference is that in one the media volunteer to serve this role and in the other they are compelled to do so.

The system of voluntary censorship adopted in Britain and the United States in the Second World War did not however extend to combat zones where field censorship of what modern war does to real people was particularly tight.[8] The military argue that this is essential to prevent relatives and friends back home being offended by the sight in the media of their loved ones in anguish, but there remains an element of public morale in this argument. Too much bad news, especially too many casualties, is to be avoided in war reports because of a somewhat dubious assumption that a sanitised version of war via the media helps to sustain public support for it. Equally dubious is the converse assumption, now so prevalent among critics of the media, that if only the 'reality' of war could be shown, public support for it would be undermined (Vietnam again).

We heard much of this during the Gulf War with accusations about the 'video-game' nature of much of the coverage. Those with a fondness for counterfactual history often suggest that if television cameras had been present on the Western Front during the First World War, then that brutal conflict would not have lasted as long as it did. Yet this misses two fundamental points. In the first place, the military authorities would never have let such cameras anywhere near the scenes of human destruction. And second, it assumes that 'the camera never lies'. But there is also a third and much more significant issue. Despite wobbles in public opinion polls, so long as there is a widespread societal belief that the war being fought is 'just' and that the sacrifices are therefore 'justified', the media tend to be every bit as patriotic as the public they are serving. They are not uncritical in this support, but, when 'our boys' are fighting, the instinctive reaction of press and public alike is to support them. Hence retreats are turned into 'withdrawals', defeats into 'set-backs'. And huge numbers of casualties can be sustained, as in the World Wars. But these are 'our wars'. What might be termed 'other people's wars' in which 'our boys' are thrust into dangerous situations require a quite different framework of justification to 'our publics'. Hence, pictures of dead Americans being dragged through a Somalian street were all the more shocking

181

because the American people had only been subjected to a picture of American intervention as being one for peaceful or humanitarian reasons. The public reaction was swift: get 'our boys' out of there.

Interestingly, a professional journalist did not take those pictures. Somalia had become too dangerous following the deaths of several members of the Western press corps, and most had left by the time of this incident. Instead they were taken by a local 'stringer' and distributed around the world, in much the same way as the infamous 'Rodney King' footage. The arrival of new communications technologies such as the portable camcorder might suggest therefore that we have new opportunities for seeing the realities of war and conflicts like never before. But, just as the military sometimes fear what would happen to public morale if the 'whole truth' were known, so also do the media fear the risks of alienating their customers if the 'whole truth' were told. Slaughter has not only to be rationalised but it also has to be rationed. It is here that the interests of the war reporter and the soldier in the field coincide, although it is rarely acknowledged as such: perhaps because the military mind rarely grasps this and because the media dare not acknowledge it.

REAL WAR AND MEDIA WAR

Certainly, after Britain abandoned national service in 1963, and the United States abandoned the draft in 1973 the military found that when they went to war, journalists with no previous military experience were turning up with little idea of the realities of war fighting, making unrealistic demands that could not be accommodated, which in turn merely caused media criticism that was resented by the military. This increasing lack of mutual understanding has been the source of ongoing tension which, when combined with the experience of Vietnam, has poisoned military–media relations for the past 20 years and which is only now beginning to see some signs of improvement. This improvement is to some extent due to the enormous efforts that the military have expended on trying to understand the media, their needs and their practices. That the media have failed to understand the military in anything like the same way perhaps helps to explain why, outside conflict situations, the military only make the news when soldiers commit a rape (as with a recent case on Okinawa) or a murder (an equally recent case on Cyprus) or 'frag' new recruits (as in Canada), or admit overt homosexuals or women into their ranks. These are rarely the most significant issues facing the military in the post-Cold War environment. Those issues are really more concerned with what the actual role of the military should

182

be in a world in which democracies do not fight democracies, and where non-democracies are declining in number. And if, during Operation 'Desert Storm' in 1991, the military demonstrated that they have perfected the art of waging 'an information war' to their benefit, the 'bad news' stories about the behaviour of a minority of their members since then suggests the need to improve their information strategies at times other than war.

War, on the other hand, to put it quite bluntly, is good for the media business. Despite the excessive costs of sending foreign correspondents to distant lands based in expensive hotels, and using up expensive satellite equipment and air time, armed conflict between two or more warring partners is precisely the type of event on which the media thrive. Wars produce a stream of human stories of tragedy and heroism; they involve the deployment of troops and weapons in a manner which makes for exciting copy and pictures; they invoke heightened emotions of patriotism, fear, anger and euphoria; and they involve winners and losers. When a nation is at war, newspaper sales increase, television and radio ratings go up, while extremes of popular and media support can reach new heights of intensity, usually at the expense of dissenting or critical voices whose democratic opposition and disagreement are translated into forms of near treachery.

As one veteran foreign correspondent once remarked, 'Whenever you find hundreds of thousands of sane people trying to get out of a place and a little bunch of madmen struggling to get in, you know the latter are newspapermen.'[9] Today, we would add radio and television correspondents. During 'Desert Storm', an astonishing 1,500 journalists swarmed to Saudi Arabia, which was more than the troop contributions by most Coalition members, and three times the number of journalists present on D-Day in 1944; another 1,500 journalists were waiting for accreditation by the time the war ended. The globalisation and increasing competitiveness of the deregulated media would certainly appear to suggest that a new player had walked onto the fields of foreign policy and international conflict. But has the game been altered as a result?

After all, millions of people may be watching the same CNN report but they react to it differently, in accordance with the individual, cultural, political, historical and psychological baggage which each member of that audience brings to the newscast. Some scholars have identified this as being similar to the Heisenberg Principle in physics, namely that events are altered by the fact that the media are observing those events. This prompted the then British Foreign Secretary Douglas Hurd in September 1993 to assert that 'the public debate is run not by events, but by the coverage of events'.[10] The fundamental question therefore, which has exercised much political and military planning since Vietnam, is whether the media are good for the business of waging war.

Once a war breaks out, it is not always immediately apparent that very quickly two wars start taking place: what might be termed the 'real war', in which real people die, and what may be called 'media war', in which the realities of war, such as death and destruction, are both distant and distanced from a non-participating mass audience. This occurs not just because of such factors as official censorship but indeed because of the very nature of the media as mediator. Real war is about the sounds, sight, smell, touch and taste of the nasty, brutal business of people killing people. It frightens and appals most people, so much so that they would be repelled by its reality. Media war, however, is literally a mediated event which draws on that reality but which, in and of itself, is confined to merely an audio-visual, and therefore inherently desensitising, representation of it. Some theoreticians have labelled this phenomenon of war as a 'pseudo-event'; that is an illusion of war's realities disseminated, even manufactured, for the edification, almost in a gruesome way the entertainment, of a mass audience which can never experience its horrors at first hand but which participates in war as a spectacle, from a distance, via the media, almost to the point where the war becomes a manufactured figment of its imagination.

So, any media image of war is very much a flawed window on to the battlefield. This is because the very processes by which war reports are gathered at source, packaged by journalists and disseminated to a wider audience are subject to a wide spectrum of influences ranging from battlefield censorship to broadcasting standards of taste and decency in the newsrooms far beyond it. In between, they are subjected to fundamental factors such as where they are allowed to be physically located, self-censorship, the means by which information is communicated from the war zone to the outside world, deception and disinformation campaigns, official information policy and propaganda. These are indeed the pollutants which constitute that overworked idiom: the fog of war.

It is thus important to stress that whatever impression we gain of a given conflict via the media is not necessarily an accurate representation of what is actually happening while it is happening. The gap between war's image and war's reality remains extremely wide throughout its duration. During the process by which this image–reality gap is created, a third type of conflict also breaks out, namely the conflict of interests between, on the one hand, the military whose job it is to fight the war and, on the other, the media whose job it is to report on it. The former invariably disagree with the latter on how this can be best achieved, and

184

vice versa. The priorities of those responsible for fighting war and those responsible for reporting it are obviously quite different, epitomised in a sense by the difference between the equipment they carry. New technology may have replaced the sword and the pen with rocket launchers and portable camcorders, but soldiers are still trained to kill while reporters have appeared progressively to make that task much harder by virtue of the publicity they afford to an activity which no longer seems as 'glorious' or as 'natural' as it had once been. Because the media are felt to be largely responsible for exposing the brutalities of conflict to a population that once seemed happier to regard wars as events whereby individuals and nations earned their place in history, they have been invested with a critical capacity which supposedly fosters anti-war sentiment. If this is true (and there is much to question in it) then the camcorder has indeed proved mightier than the cruise missile. Yet, if this is more assumption than fact, there is a need to understand the fundamental dichotomy between real and media war in order to ascertain the source of such myths and to identify why and who the investors in such assumptions are.

Real wars are multifaceted, complicated and brutal events in which the participants themselves rarely have the full picture of what is going on while it is actually happening. An individual soldier, for example, might know what is happening in his segment of the battle area, but he is at a loss when it comes to events perhaps even only a few hundred yards away. Not even the commanders have every piece of information at their fingertips, although the struggle to maximise that situation is at the heart of modern planning in 'command and control' warfare. We cannot therefore reasonably expect the camcorders to do something which the commanders can not.

If truth, as is frequently asserted, is the first casualty of war, then one question we need to ask is: 'who is lying?' Without getting into postmodernistic theories about the relationship of 'truth' to 'reality', we do need to appreciate that no one journalist can report the whole truth, just as no single news story can cover the wider picture. Each constitutes one piece in the mosaic. It may be a truism, but, quite simply, if the journalist is absent, there is no story – at least until someone tells him about whatever has taken place. Then it has to be deemed 'newsworthy'. Equally, if two or more journalists are present at the same event, they will not necessarily report on it in precisely the same way. The emphasis, manner, tone and insight each journalist brings to bear on a given story is very much dependent upon the personality, experience, education and location of that journalist. For example, a film camera can only 'see' what it is pointed

185

at; whatever is going beyond the angle of vision does not constitute part of the image. The decision to point the camera at 'x' and not 'y' is a human decision based upon judgement derived from professional training and experience. Even the decision about when to start the camera rolling is a judgement call. Moreover, two cameras standing side-by-side, regardless of whether they are rolling at the same time or not, will create a variation. The operator will also be working for, or on behalf of, a news organisation which has particular institutional interests and emphases which may affect the angle adopted for the story. And if bullets or bombs are being fired at the camera operator, the human temptation to take cover is invariably greater than the journalistic imperative of keeping the camera rolling. There does exist footage by cameramen who did not take cover, and some of them were killed in the process. The resultant images are dramatic precisely because they are the exception to the norm. Robert Capa, the war-photographer, was fond of saying that 'if your picture wasn't any good, you're not standing close enough'.[11] It is worth noting that perhaps Capa's most famous photograph in *Life* magazine, that of a Spanish Civil War soldier 'the instant he is dropped by a bullet through the head in front of Cordoba' was in fact that of a soldier stumbling in training. That small detail aside, the essential point is that news stories, as distinct from graphic images whether faked, lucky or otherwise, have a life-span considerably shorter than that of human beings.

A news report, then, is by definition merely a slice of the action. The BBC's John Simpson has put it thus:

> It is rather like an account of a football match written from a seat near one of the goals. Whenever the play was down at my end I had a superb view of it. But when it moved to the far end of the pitch I only knew what was happening when I heard the crowd roar.[12]

One might retort that the journalist could always jump onto the pitch to follow the play, but on a battlefield that is a very dangerous business. Bullets and bombs do not discriminate between military personnel and journalists. Once in uniform, for example, the journalist has in the eyes of the enemy clearly aligned himself with the soldiers whose uniform he shares. He thus becomes a spy. It is for this reason that journalists are frequently prepared to exchange freedom of access for personal protection; and, thus protected, they have aligned themselves against the forces of the enemy. They accompany the troops sharing a good deal of their risks in order to get the best possible slice of the action they can. In the eyes of the enemy, this merely exposes them as propagandists for the other side.

A TECHNOLOGICAL REVOLUTION?

Today, it is technically possible to transmit information instantaneously from a battlefield using portable satellite equipment. But, once again, that equipment still needs to be set up, the satellite air-time booked, and all the equipment needs to be working: hardly ideal conditions to capture live images of war. For this reason, journalists invariably recognise that their reports will not be in real time, at least not from scenes of actual fighting, but rather will be recorded packages of the best available pictures combined with voice-over report, usually edited on the spot once the movement of battle has slowed down or stopped. Modern-day videotape and portable edit suites allow for this. But how those packages then reach editorial headquarters for consideration varies considerably. Theoretically, a print journalist can call his head office on a satellite phone and dictate his copy verbally. Better still, he can now type his copy on a portable laptop computer connected to a modem and, with a few keystrokes, a 2,000-word despatch can be downloaded to a news office in seconds; just a decade earlier it would have taken an hour's dictation on whatever public pay phone was nearest to the action. Audio and video material can be transmitted likewise. This is all a far cry from the days when a newsreel cameraman, having set up his heavy equipment and filmed his raw footage, would have to beg or bribe someone else leaving the war zone by the fastest available land, sea or air route to deliver his cans of highly flammable nitrate film to his home base, whereupon it would be cut, edited and given a commentary written by someone else: or is it?

During the 1991 Gulf War, a selected band of journalists was granted permission to accompany the Coalition forces into the field to cover Operation 'Desert Storm'. (The Iraqis refused any equivalent access for their 'mother of all battles'. Although they did, uniquely, permit journalists from Coalition countries to remain behind in Baghdad once hostilities broke out.) The American, British, and French forces – but only those out of almost 30 contributing nations – formed 'news pools' consisting of around 50 reporters and crews who would compile their reports for use by the rest of the world's media corps. Although the number eventually rose to about 200 pool reporters, this was but a fraction of the 1,500 or so journalists who flocked to the region to cover the war, but who instead were forced to stay behind in hotels in Riyadh and Dhahran. As US General Dugan maintained: 'Now, 1,500 is not an unmanageable number, but it is a number that cries out for management.'[13] Apart from the fact that the journalists did not like this arrangement because it ran contrary to all their traditional professional competitiveness to get a scoop over

187

their rivals, they went along with it because limited and shared access was better than no access at all. Even then, the pool journalists found that, despite all their modern communications equipment, there were still considerable problems in reporting the war. Mischievously, the military minders, the American Public Affairs Officers (PAOs) and the British Public Information Officers (PIOs), told the journalists not to use their mobile phones because they would 'radiate signals to the Iraqis',[14] thereby giving their positions away and thus making them all vulnerable as targets. When, during moments of calm, those journalists in pools which permitted them tried to set up their satellite equipment to transmit edited packages, they were told to do so well away from the encampments for the same reason. Although no sensible journalist in such a position would want to take risks for fear of losing his own life, let alone the lives of the very troops who were protecting him, another game was afoot. Most journalists were unaware of the technical possibilities of their high-tech equipment, especially its interface with military communications systems. Even if the Iraqis had been able to monitor such transmissions, the point was that the military were suspicious of journalists in their midst and wanted to influence the way in which the war was being reported. When, for example, a British television crew tried to escape their minders and transmit copy back to London unsupervised, their transmission was intercepted by an airborne AWACS electronic warfare plane, and they were promptly arrested.[15] The American forces simply refused to permit satellite equipment in their pools, prompting one reporter to claim that 'each pool member is an unpaid employee of the Department of Defense, on whose behalf he or she prepares the news of the war for the outer world'.[16]

The system for getting copy back from the pools for shared use in Riyadh was also fraught with delays. Once British journalists in the pools had filed their reports in the field, the reports were then supposed to be taken to the Forward Transmission Unit (FTU), in fact located well to the rear, which had direct satellite links with newsrooms around the world. But once Coalition ground forces, after weeks of preparatory air strikes, moved against the occupying Iraqi forces in Kuwait their advance was so rapid 'that the system of getting our copy back to the transmission unit's satellite phones 50 kilometres back broke down completely. It was days before London got the first battle reports from the [British] 7th Armoured [Brigade] and by then the war was virtually over and we had to hurriedly compose retrospectives.'[17] Accordingly, the Reuters correspondent, Paul Majendie, who was attached to the American 1st Armored Division, felt his assignment had been a 'total disaster' from a journalistic point of view because 'the problem was the totally inadequate method of getting the stories back'.[18] Likewise, Edward Cody of the *Washington Post* complained that 'you turn over control of your copy to them [the military despatch riders] and they don't care whether it gets there or not. It's not part of their culture.'[19] At another level, Colin Wills of the *Daily Mirror* found that the minders of his pool with the British 7th Armoured Brigade proved unwilling to improvise, instead relying 'on pressing bits of paper into soldiers' hands and hoping they would get there',[20] unlike those of the 4th Armoured Brigade who proved themselves willing to drive back to the FTU and hand in the copy personally.

OUR WARS AND OTHER PEOPLE'S WARS

For the most planned 'information war' in modern memory, this chaotic picture reveals that no amount of preparation for the next war by looking to the lessons learned from the last one can anticipate the precise circumstances of conflict. These problems are compounded a thousand times over in Operations Other Than War. But in 'our wars' at least, it reveals the extent to which, on the battlefield, soldier and civilian journalist are mutually dependent. The aims of the respective professions may be fundamentally different, encapsulated by the saying that 'when the military make a mistake, people die, but when the media make a mistake, they run a correction', but they are not mutually incompatible. Co-operation is infinitely preferable to conflict and usually that is the nature of the relationship that emerges. After all, despite considerable military–media tension over the Falklands War, the Ministry of Defence could subsequently find only one instance of press speculation that damaged British operations.[21]

'Our wars' are those which involve 'our troops' possibly fighting alongside 'our allies' against a clearly identified enemy and 'their allies'. But 'other people's wars' are different in that outside media coverage of them differs fundamentally in character. This is not to suggest that the media are above taking sides in other people's wars, but that there is a greater level of disengagement about the issues involved even though they may invoke a similar emotional response about the human suffering involved. All wars are nasty, brutal affairs but other people's wars are about other people's business which may have little or nothing to do with 'us'. 'Our wars' are wars of the greatest emotional engagement for the combatants – both military and civilian – involved. There is of course a further distinction between conventional warfare in which civilian participation is limited to observation of the conflict via the media as distinct from actual participation in the form of 'total war'. Then the sense of mutual identification between military and civilian combatants is intensified, as distinct from other types of war in which professional armies consisting of volunteers are watched most intensely by their civilian relatives and friends.

For such people, media coverage of limited wars can be intrusive, which is why there are guidelines in reporting pictures of the dead and injured casualties of war. Opponents of war who criticise the media for 'sanitising' such images of war miss this critical point. A rule of thumb in the two World Wars was to show only pictures of enemy dead; that way, watching relatives could not discover the loss of their loved ones from the media, although they could see that the war was inflicting casualties on the other side. People understand that in war, people die. Whether they want to see it on their television screens is quite another matter.

Equally, in 'our wars', the journalist walks a very thin tightrope attached to two cliff edges labelled 'objectivity' and 'patriotism'. His journalistic responsibility to stand back from a story and to analyse it objectively can prove incompatible with his audience's subjective desire to see everyone support the national war effort. Bad news about the progress of 'our side' invariably prompts calls to shoot the messenger. This critical capability in fact gave rise to the birth of modern military censorship. But democracies have evolved during the course of this century cherishing notions of freedom of speech and opinions. In wartime, most people accept the need for some restrictions upon those democratic 'rights' but the issue remains of just how far the military should go. Should they suppress all bad news in the name of patriotism, even though this often occurs in the name of operational security? Examples of this occurring in the past are numerous. Casualty figures have often been minimised and defeats simply omitted from the public record. Following the retreat from Mons in 1914, the British War Office withdrew the permits of film camera crews; in 1940, while still First Lord of the Admiralty, Winston Churchill refused to release news that HMS *Nelson* and HMS *Barham* had sustained serious damage.[22] Such instances are only possible when the military are in complete control of information reaching the public domain from the war zone. Modern communications technology has theoretically weakened that control, whereas modern political imperatives have increased the likelihood of access being granted to journalists.

THE QUESTION OF ACCESS

Access is, indeed, the key to all this. In Vietnam, the media were granted virtually unlimited access to go wherever they wanted to go, at their own risks. As a result of that coverage being perceived as being more and more critical, especially after the Tet Offensive in 1968, various and ever more controversial ways of influencing the outside perception of a crisis in a manner beneficial to its military–political conduct have evolved since the 1970s. These include the exclusion of the media altogether, as in Grenada in 1983; to delay their arrival, as in Panama in 1989; to make them totally dependent upon the military for their safety, transport and communications, as in the Falklands in 1982; or a combination of all these, as in 'Desert Shield'/'Desert Storm' in 1990–91. All have attracted controversy, but at least all have fallen within a military–media framework that is essentially historically defined within the democratic traditions of Anglo-American inter-state conflicts.

In other people's wars, if anything, the media often attempt to make such conflicts more of our own than would otherwise have been the case. In the Spanish Civil War (1936–39), for example, British Movietone's newsreel coverage of the bombing of Guernica showed pictures of the devastated city under a commentary which ended: 'This was a war, and these were homes – like yours.' The message then was that the aerial bombing of cities – then a new and terrifying weapon – was of concern to all citizens of all countries. The equivalent message today – at least from those wars which do command media attention – is that ethnic conflicts are the enemy of all civilised behaviour. Whereas in the past there was an acceptance, or 'fiction' as Harold Lasswell called it,[23] that nations did not interfere in the internal affairs of other nations, a principle encapsulated in the United Nations Charter, global television coverage of brutal events in foreign countries invites the very idea of intervention, not to take sides, but to help the people caught up in the conflict, the 'innocent women and children'. Humanitarian interventions are therefore considered acts of civilised behaviour; but the extent to which the media, with their ever-growing appetite for human interest stories, are able to relate the complexity of issues involved (matters of international law, geopolitics, military logistics and so on) tends to be quite limited. These are *issues* that cannot readily be compressed to three-minute news segments or 12 column inches. The world has changed so rapidly since the end of the Cold War that everyone, including the media, is still grappling with modes of behaviour appropriate to the new 'order'. There is no simple Cold War-type framework for analysing *events* any longer. And when you have 24 hours of air time to fill, that leaves a lot of time for speculation, talking heads, and erroneous or incomplete facts about what that order may be. Live television may be exciting, and it may appear to be more 'real', but the news still has to be 'packaged' and it still has to be entertaining if it is to keep the attention span of its audience. Complexity can be a turn-off for many people.

Media coverage of other people's wars is characteristically less susceptible to censorship by militarily non-participating governments. It is, however, still subject to manipulation by the warring parties. More recently, in another European civil war, the Wars of the Yugoslavian Succession, attempts to manipulate journalists were endemic in an effort by the warring factions to secure the moral high ground for their cause on the battlefront of global public opinion. Hence, in Bosnia-Herzegovina, the Bosnian Serbs attempted to portray themselves as the victims, rather than the aggressors: as victims variously of German, Albanian, Islamic fundamentalist but, above all, Croat and Bosnian fascist conspiracies. One might have thought that in a global information environment, it would be much easier than before to verify or discredit such stories, but when international journalists wanted to check for themselves on one alleged atrocity about necklaces made from the fingers of Serbian babies, they were quite simply refused access to the alleged scene. The famous ITN footage of emaciated Muslim prisoners-of-war, which caused an international outrage in 1992, was banned on Serbian TV. Similarly, the Croatians and Bosnian factions were keen to steer the media coverage in their favour, not just within areas under their control but on the international arena as well. The Bosnian Muslims, for example, provided increased foreign journalistic access to their civilians on the march from the fallen 'safe havens' of Srebrenica and Bihac in the summer of 1995 to demonstrate that they, indeed, were the victims in this conflict; Serb protests that they were merely retaliating for Bosnian army attacks (off-camera) were drowned beneath the sea of devastating footage of Bosnian civilian suffering. It took aerial photographs from American U-2 spy planes to identify the likely fate of the captured Bosnian soldiers at Srebrenica.

Regardless of whose war it is, therefore, the question of journalistic access remains critical. If a journalist is not present at an alleged defeat or massacre, it can only be reported second-hand, which minimises the impact of the story. The absence of pictures minimises it still further. The converse is equally true. Modern communications technology facilitates increased access to scenes of horror and destruction that would have been inconceivable a century earlier. The growing ability of the media to bring home such scenes has widened the arena of warfare beyond those directly involved in or directly affected by the fighting. The media make all wars to which they can get access a matter of wider public concern. This, in turn, makes it all the more essential for the warring parties to control that access because their battlefront is no longer confined to the battlefield itself.

The most effective way of censoring the media is simply to deny them access. But the advent of the war correspondent as a specialised profession made this increasingly difficult to justify, especially as such reporters seemed to be catering for a demand among a public whose support for any war effort could only be sustained by feeding its hunger for information. The watershed of the Crimean War (1853–56) was significant in that the public could no longer accept uncritically the official pronouncements of the military spokesmen. An increasingly literate, educated and enfranchised public demanded third-party mediation, and the press filled this demand as a watch-dog. This is not without its irony. During the Gulf War of 1991, surveys in the United States indicated that the public was more prepared to accept the announcements of military spokesmen than the versions provided by the press. Because the 1991 audience could see those spokesmen live on television in the comfort of their living rooms more than 8,000 miles from the scene of fighting, the military were actually by-passing the media's traditional role, established since the Crimea, as intermediary between soldier and civilian. The same surveys indicated a greater trust in what the military spokesmen were saying than in what the media were reporting, the media not helping themselves by being seen to ask stupid questions live in the same press conferences. Indeed, live television made such conferences public conferences, rather than press conferences, with the role of the correspondents reduced to that of question asker. This decline in public trust in the media's capability to report on wars 'in the public interest' is not confined to the United States. As was witnessed in Britain following the death in 1997 of Diana, Princess of Wales, public disquiet for the media's behaviour generally runs extremely high.

The same Gulf War surveys revealed another significant trend, namely that the public was prepared to tolerate military censorship of war reports, at least until after the war was over, if that would reduce the risk of casualties. Casualties of war fall into two categories for the media: military and civilian. Military casualties are to be expected, but if they are 'our' casualties, then the military feel that there should first be as few of them as possible and then that the media do not give undue attention to them. During the Gulf War, a news embargo was imposed upon the media coverage at the Norfolk naval base in Virginia, the point where body-bags arrived home. This again is very much a legacy of the Vietnam War. The point here is that there has been a growing recent trend that wars can only be fought with a minimum of military casualties for fear of undermining popular support. The public, it is frequently assumed, cannot stomach huge casualty figures, especially if the dead and wounded are given prominent media attention. Although one suspects that the validity of this assumption varies from country to country, in accordance with the history of their military experience, it remains at the root of military assumptions about the role of the media in wartime, namely that they are more of a threat than an aid to combat.

How valid this is depends very much on the degree to which the public base their support for involvement in a war upon 'just' reasons. If the war is felt to be 'just', then casualties are regrettable but 'justified'. This applies even to civilian casualties, although the extent of military nervousness concerning non-combatant casualties, especially 'innocent women and children', is even more marked. During the Second World War, for example, the Royal Air Force (RAF) strategic bombing offensive against Germany was deliberately couched in terms very different from the reality, as a campaign directed at military and industrial targets, rather than at civilian areas. The head of Bomber Command, Air Chief Marshal Sir Arthur Harris, wanted in 1943 a stark public admission that 'the aim is the destruction of German cities, the killing of German workers and the disruption of civilised community life throughout Germany'.[24] He was unsuccessful. The illusion had to be maintained that the RAF was an instrument of precision bombing capable of hitting precisely what it was aiming at, resulting 'in a more constant concealment of the aims and implications of the campaign which was being waged'.[25] Accordingly, news reports, photographs and films were poured out to illustrate 'successful missions' against factories and other military–industrial targets, rather than hits on the residential areas in which those targets were invariably located. This not only served as a justification for the huge number of bomber crews who failed to return home, but also provided a moral counterpoint to the British experience in the Blitz. Given that the British public had clearly been targeted indiscriminately by German bombers then, they might have suspected that the RAF's line about the discriminate nature of Allied bombing was as patently untrue as we now know it to have been.

Even so, during the Gulf War, great emphasis was placed upon the ability of high-technology Coalition bombing. Thanks to advances in military technology, it is certainly true that cruise missiles and laser-guided bombs could hit their intended targets with an accuracy unprecedented in military history. Moreover, thanks to new communications technology, those weapons could be equipped with video-cameras. For the first time, audiences could see for themselves how 'smart' weapons honed in on military targets with uncanny accuracy prior to the screen going blank. Such footage not only gave the impression that the Coalition could hit precisely what it was aiming at, but that it could thereby discriminate between military and civilian targets. This fitted well with the line pursued by Coalition leaders that this was a war fought not against the Iraqi people

194

but against the regime of Saddam Hussein and those forces which supported him. The problem was that, of all the bombs deployed during the Gulf War, the 'smart' ones formed only about 8 per cent of the total. The remainder, old-fashioned 'dumb' weapons of indiscriminate destruction, were not seen on television screens. No journalist was permitted to accompany a bombing mission during 'Desert Storm', while the Iraqis refused journalistic access to those areas subjected to mass bombing.

Air power is a notoriously difficult phenomenon for the media. On the one hand, it contains the raw material of spectacular reportage, from the air aces of the First World War to the helicopter gunships of Vietnam and the Gulf. Aircraft-mounted cameras can produce the kind of exciting footage matched by no other war technology, as anyone who has seen William Wyler's 1943 colour documentary film of a bombing raid over Germany, *Memphis Belle*, will appreciate. On the other hand, by its very nature, most coverage has to consist of interviews with pilots and crews before and after missions, aircraft taking off and landing and, if camera crews are permitted, bombs being released. The Gulf War saw cameras mounted on the bombs themselves. But none of this allows for images of the impact of the bombs once they have exploded; when the bomb hits its target, either from a distance of 30,000 feet, or after honing in through cross-hairs, the screen goes blank. Thereafter, there is little indication of the sheer destructive power of high explosive until after the smoke has cleared. The time between the moment of impact and the scrutiny of bomb damage can never be captured on film; and it is in that space, after all, where people die. That reality of war evades media war.

SOME DEFINING MOMENTS

The Iraqis did try something unprecedented in the history of war reporting when, following the outbreak of the air-war phase of 'Desert Storm', they allowed journalists from belligerent countries to remain behind in Baghdad. Saddam Hussein also believed in the Vietnam syndrome. He believed that once the bombing began, it would result in massive devastation to civilian areas which, if filmed, could cause a public outcry in the very countries responsible for the bombing and lead to the cessation of the war. Captured pilots were accordingly paraded on Iraqi television declaring their disapproval of the war, which was duly retransmitted around the world by CNN. Iraq's solitary baby-milk manufacturing plant was destroyed by callous bombing, putting paid to the myth that the Coalition was not fighting the people of Iraq, and images of the bombed installation were retransmitted by CNN. The war would

195

thus be won in the hearts and minds of world public opinion rather than on the killing fields of Kuwait. But Saddam miscalculated. The Coalition decided not to carpet bomb the Iraqi capital but only to use precision weapons, and these invariably hit their targets. The captured-pilots ploy enraged public opinion, while the baby-milk plant was, the Coalition claimed, a chemical warfare factory. CNN was accused of spreading Iraqi propaganda rather than of reporting the war. But doubts remained. The Coalition said that it was only targeting military installations, and the Iraqis refused to accompany Western crews to such sites. Why should the Iraqis suddenly change that tactic now with the 'baby milk plant' if it really was a chemical weapons facility?

One new element of camera-mounted bombs combined with television crews inside enemy territory was bomb-damage evaluation. As one pilot stated:

> It certainly was interesting for us to come back and land and watch the [television] replays of what it's looking like from another perspective. Knowing where some of the broadcasts were coming from, and seeing the skyline ... we could actually pick out who some of the bombs belonged to ... There was some good in having good old Peter Arnett on the ground.[26]

Arnett, a veteran war reporter from the Vietnam era now working for CNN, was only too conscious of the Iraqi attempts to manipulate him. But, like the other Western journalists in Baghdad, he was put to his greatest test on 13 February 1991 when two laser-guided bombs crashed through an installation in the Al-Amiriya suburb of Baghdad, killing about 400 people. All Iraqi censorship restrictions were lifted that day and the journalists were told that they could say, hear and film anything they wanted to. Because the badly burned bodies being brought out of the charred building were clearly civilians – 'innocent women and children' – here was the crucial test of whether the Coalition line about minimising 'collateral damage' to the Iraqi people could be sustained. In the space between the reality of war and the media image of war, it was *the* defining moment. For the first time, the Iraqis had the kind of images which fuelled their belief in the Vietnam syndrome, all the more effective for them being taken by Western, rather than Iraqi, television crews. Because those crews arrived within hours of the explosion, there were no clumsy efforts at blatant propaganda as with the freshly painted 'baby milk plant' signs in English three weeks earlier; and there was no censorship. The problem was that the images were so graphic that Western broadcasting standards of taste and decency militated against their full use. As the pictures were beamed around the world by satellite, most editorial rooms bred on a Western tradition realised that they would have to take out the close-up images of horribly burned children prior to transmission. They would not show comparable images of a motorway crash or air disaster, so why should war be any different? Despite such self-censorship, however, the shock of what was shown still created an outcry, with the *Daily Mail* the next morning accusing the BBC of being the 'Baghdad Broadcasting Corporation'. Coalition spokesmen attempted to control the spin: they had hit what they were aiming at; it was a military bunker, not a civilian shelter; they did not know why civilians were inside. But the press attacked the messenger. Television was the enemy, just as it had been in Vietnam. However, as in that war, public support for prosecution of the war remained in the majority.

The premise of the media showing the realities of war while it happens so that it might adversely affect morale and promote anti-war sentiment therefore remains largely to be proven. It has, quite simply, never happened. Daniel Hallin has effectively debunked the so-called Vietnam syndrome.[27] More generally, if the censors do not get to the offending material first – and new technology has now made this so difficult that it is hardly worth trying anymore – broadcasters tend to self-censor graphic material on grounds of taste and decency. Again this varies from country to country and from broadcasting organisation to broadcasting organisation. But even in other people's wars, really graphic images, such as from Sarajevo's market-place, also tend to be edited out. Nonetheless, the images that remain can still shock; but how much the audience then clamours to do something to stop the slaughter depends very much upon the context in which those images are perceived.

THE CNN EFFECT

Here is the rub of the problem. Images of death and destruction that often appear suddenly on the nightly television news programmes shock precisely because their context is rarely understood by audiences generally disinterested in foreign affairs. Over-exposure to such images may lead to desensitisation. One suspects therefore that the clamour to 'do something' is among a relatively small elite, including officials and politicians, who fear that a wider public reaction might occur if they do nothing. It is known that they use live television as an additional source of information because sometimes it is faster with a breaking story than traditional diplomatic channels. Marlin Fitzwater, President George Bush's press spokesman, claimed that in international crises:

We virtually cut out the State Department and the desk officers ... Their reports are still important, but they don't get here in time for the basic decisions to be made ... The normal information flow into the Oval Office was vastly altered by live video images.[28]

However, the problem of this disturbing admission is that 'once CNN is on the story, the media drumbeat begins, public opinion is engaged, and a diplomat's options recede'.[29] We have to ask whether this happens because officials recognise that the media really have become participants, or because they fear that they might become so. Moreover, does this fear say more about them than it does about television? Douglas Hurd has said that, 'like it or not, television images are what forces foreign policy makers to give one of the current 25 crises in the world greater priority'.[30] Likewise, Boutros Boutros-Ghali's view was that, 'Today, the media do not simply report the news. Television has become a part of the event it covers. It has changed the way the world reacts to crises.'[31] If television really is being allowed to set agendas for diplomatic initiatives,[32] again given its limitations, this is a recipe for disaster. 'We are under no pressure to do something about crises that are not on TV', one British official has admitted.[33] Yet if it is difficult enough for psychologists to establish a direct causal link between television and human behaviour generally, how can we talk with certainty of a 'do something factor'? One might only conclude that television's 'power' to set the agenda is determined more by those taking notice of it – or who are afraid of it or who are willing to grant access to it – than it is by any inherent qualities which it may possess as an instrument of mass communication and persuasion.[34] There is evidence that such people are more likely to be the politicians and the officials in the audience than members of the general public at large. And despite the argument that decision-makers simply do not have the time to watch television, and are therefore not influenced by it,[35] (how many busy diplomats and politicians have the time to sit and watch the evening news?) no matter how hard they try television does intrude into their daily routines. If wives, sons or daughters do not tell them over the dinner table about the shocking pictures they have witnessed in that night's news programmes, their press officers almost certainly will the next morning. It doesn't matter whether the reports were accurate, balanced, contextualised or even significant – which they might not be – but rather that they have been transmitted and that they might have provoked a reaction. George Stephanopoulis gave the game away when he admitted:

In the White House ... we have 24 hour news cycles ... CNN assures you that you are forced to react at any time, and that's going to happen throughout the time of the Clinton Presidency.[36]

The journalist Nik Gowing has written that 'officials confirm that information often comes to them first from television or text news services well before official diplomatic and military communications channels can provide data, precision, clarification and context'.[37] President Bush even went so far as to say that 'I learn more from CNN than I do from the CIA'.[38] Here, then, is the real source of the change. The speed at which modern electronic news-gathering can – though not always – occur places increased pressure on the decision-making process, which in turn complains that it cannot cope sensibly with the kind of knee-jerk solutions demanded by the pictures.

This is in fact more a lasting testament to the impact of the Vietnam syndrome than it is a statement about the impact of television. Vietnam created a myth about military–media relations which is belied by the 150-year record of war correspondents. It also forgets the record of the democratic media as instruments for the maintenance of the *status quo*, or as the fourth estate. As the first television war, Vietnam left a legacy that wars and television do not mix to the benefit of either those doing the fighting or those who have ordered them to do so. But, given the type of circumstances outlined here, this is a red herring. The real problem arises out of the changing nature of conflict now that the Cold War no longer provides us with a bipolar framework in which heroes and villains, friends and enemies, can be identified. The enemy now appears to be 'chaos' while the international community – interlocked now as never before through the globalisation of the political economy, communications and international organisations – is expected to restore some kind of stability to intra-state conflicts that threaten the new world order. This apparent contradiction of an increasingly interdependent world avoiding recourse to conventional wars being 'chaotic' is partly explained by the media's random and 'spot' coverage of crises. Hence, other people's wars appear to erupt from nowhere on our television screens until the crisis subsides, and the media lose interest. The causes and consequences of those crises rarely command media attention. This leaves the impression of a chaotic or turbulent world when, in reality, there is an 'order' functioning in the invisible background of daily global life. But order is hardly newsworthy. It is the crises, the coups, the famines, the earthquakes, which make the headlines.

This is the principal challenge not only for democratically elected governments but also for international organisations such as the United Nations: how to first interest and then educate the global media as to the importance of relaying to the public the complexities and contexts of international relations. Until they address this issue, international organisations will always seem to be slow in responding to dramatic, instantaneous media coverage of crises randomly selected by the availability of television pictures. Instead of responding, they need to initiate more proactive informational and educational strategies. It might well be argued in reply that foreign affairs rarely commands the interest of the general public, and so even if the horse was led to water it could still refuse to drink. But the alternatives of not doing something in this direction could well mean that the international community is subsequently forced by media pressure to do something in response to short-term coverage that is either inappropriate, ineffective and indeed more dangerous. That, indeed, is a recipe for chaos.

NOTES

1. See M. Shaw, *Civil Society and the Media in Global Crises: Representing Distant Violence* (London: Pinter, 1996); P. Seib, *Headline Diplomacy* (New York: Praeger, 1997); W. P. Strobel, *Late Breaking Foreign Policy* (Washington, DC: United States Institute for Peace Press, 1997); and P. M. Taylor, *Global Communications, International Affairs and the Media Since 1945* (London: Routledge, 1997).
2. See N. Gowing, 'Real-Time Television Coverage of Armed Conflicts and Diplomatic Crises: Does it Pressure or Distort Foreign Policy Decisions?', working paper 94-1, Joan Shorenstein Barone Center on the Press, Politics and Public Policy (Cambridge, MA: Harvard University, 1994).
3. Cited in T. Hoyle, *War Report: The War Correspondent's View of Battle from the Crimea to the Falklands* (London: Grafton Books, 1987), p. 38.
4. See P. M. Taylor, 'Censorship in Britain in World War Two: An Overview', in A. C. Duke and G. Tanse (eds), *Too Mighty to be Free: Censorship and the Press in Britain and Netherlands* (Zutphen: de Walburg Pers, 1987).
5. S. Badsey and P. M. Taylor, 'Images of Battle: The Press, Propaganda and Passchendaele', in P. Liddle (ed.), *Passchendaele in Perspective: The Third Battle of Ypres* (London: Pen & Sword, 1997).
6. F. Voss, *Reporting the War: The Journalistic Coverage of World War II* (London: Greenwood Press, 1989), p. 24.
7. A. Challener (ed.), *The Papers of Dwight David Eisenhower: Volume 4 The War Years* (Washington, DC: Johns Hopkins University Press, 1970), document 1999.
8. G. H. Roeder, *The Censored War: American Visual Experience During World War Two* (New York: Yale University Press, 1993).
9. Cited in M. Rosemblum, *Who Stole the News?* (New York: John Wiley & Sons, 1993), p. 1.
10. Speech at the Travellers' Club, London, 9 September 1993.
11. Cited in T. Hoyle, p. 15.
12. J. Simpson, *From the House of War* (London: Arrow Books, 1991), pp. xv–xvi.
13. M. Dugan, 'Generals versus Journalists', in H. Smith (ed.), *The Media and the Gulf War: The Press and Democracy in Wartime* (New York: Seven Locks Press, 1992), p. 60.

14. As told by Ed Cody, pool reporter for *Financial Times*, 16 March 1991.
15. G. Meade, 'Hard Groundrules in the Sand', *Index on Censorship*, 20, 4 and 5 (April/May 1991), p. 6.
16. M. Massing, 'Debriefings: What We Saw, What We Learned', *Columbia Journalism Review* (May–June 1991), p. 23.
17. C. Wills, in *Reporting the War* (London: British Executive of the International Press Institute, 1991), p. 6 (a collection of experiences and reflections on the Gulf War).
18. Ibid., p. 7.
19. *Washington Post Weekly Edition*, 18–24 February 1991.
20. C. Wills, p. 6.
21. V. Adams, *The Media and the Falklands Campaign* (London: Macmillan, 1994).
22. See P. M. Taylor, 'Film as a Weapon in the Second World War', in D. Dutton (ed.), *Statecraft and Diplomacy* (London: Liverpool University Press, 1995), p. 144.
23. H. Lasswell, *Propaganda Technique in the World War* (London: Macmillan, 1927), p. 6.
24. Air Chief Marshal Sir Arthur Harris to the Under-Secretary of State for Air, 25 October 1943, Public Record Office (PRO) File AIR 14/32.
25. N. Frankland, *The Bomber Offensive Against Germany* (London: HMSO, 1965), p. 97.
26. T. B. Allen, F. C. Berry and N. Polmar, *CNN: War in the Gulf. From the Invasion of Kuwait to the Day of Victory and Beyond* (New York: Maxwell International, 1991), p. 236.
27. D. C. Hallin, *The Uncensored War: The Media and Vietnam* (London: Oxford University Press, 1986), and *We Keep America on Top of the World* (London: Routledge, 1994).
28. T. McNulty, 'Television's Impact on Executive Decision-Making and Diplomacy', *The Fletcher Forum of World Affairs*, 17 (Winter 1993), p. 71.
29. J. Neuman, 'Ambassadors: Relics of the Sailing Ships?' (Washington, DC: The Annenburg Washington Program in Communications Policy Studies, 1995). http://www.annenburg.uwu.edu/pubs.
30. Cited in N. Hopkinson, *The Media and International Affairs After the Cold War* (London: HMSO, 1993), p. 11.
31. Cited in P. Brock, 'Dateline Yugoslavia: The Partisan Press', *Foreign Policy*, 48, 1 (Winter 1993/4), p. 155.
32. M. E. McCombs and D. Shaw, 'The Agenda-Setting Function of the Mass Media', *Public Opinion Quarterly* (1972), pp. 176–87.
33. N. Gowing, p. 17.
34. This assertion, derived from audience research findings, recognises that television can have an impact on *some* people at any given time, say, in advertising or on violent behaviour or on Bob Geldhof; but that, despite 30 or more years of research it is still not possible to determine how, and how many, of the audience will be affected. Many watch, but few act. This is as great a problem for democrats wishing to increase electoral turn-out during elections as it is for politicians trying to get people to vote for their party as distinct from another, let alone advertisers getting people to buy one brand of soap powder rather than another.
35. This is essentially Nik Gowing's thesis (see note 2 above), although it might

be noted that the author spends most of his time in this paper documenting occasions when the reverse was true.

36. Cited in F. J. Stech, 'Winning CNN Wars', *Parameters* (Autumn 1994), p. 38.
37. N. Gowing, p. 5.
38. L. Friedland, *Covering the World: International Television News Services* (London: 20th Century Fund Press, 1992), pp. 7–8.

14

Media Coverage: Help or Hindrance in Conflict Prevention?

NIK GOWING

THE MEDIA'S ROLE IN CONFLICT PREVENTION

The media's role in the new generation of regional conflict and sub-state violence is ambiguous, unclear, and often misconstrued. Journalists and policy-makers alike tend to assume that media coverage has an undefined yet pivotal role in helping conflict management or prevention. Indeed, a role for the media in conflict prevention is routinely assumed at conferences, seminars, and gaming sessions without question or any clear understanding of what that role is. Frequently, there is an undignified rush to judgement. The instinctive assumptions made by policy-makers, diplomats, and the military are often wrong. Their instant, superficial analysis of the media's role is usually skewed by the emotion of anecdotal comments as opposed to rigorous analysis. Frequently, the media are blamed both for what does and does not happen.

It is regrettable, some argue, that more real-time technology and capability to report from the world's zones of conflict have not necessarily been matched by a qualitative improvement in journalism or information flow, however they are measured.[1] Instead, the trend is towards super-ficial, less-than-well-informed reporting, often based on second – or third – hand information, as opposed to primary data. The growing drift towards comment and opinion journalism is also identified as an obstacle to clear, impartial comprehension of a conflict and its root causes.

No reasonable person questions the emotive power of vivid, gruesome television images from a developing conflict. Senior politicians and government figures refer candidly and without reservation to the 'some-thing-must-be-done' pressures created by television in particular, *when it is present*. But off-the-cuff, apparently well-informed references to what is widely referred to as the 'CNN factor'[2] are not always helpful in under-standing the precise dynamics of this relationship. Often such references are conspicuously ill-informed and based on false assumptions, not least because CNN no longer has its original market-place dominance. Under-standable, superficial emotional responses by political leaders who make decisions to engage (or not) in a conflict are not the same as a fundamental political will to act in the national interest.

This distinction is crucial. Despite the conviction of many journalists about the powerful influence that their reporting has on policy,[3] ministers and government officials instinctively doubt the veracity of such report-ing. Evidence confirms that this loose talk of a 'CNN factor', with its implicit cause-and-effect relationship between media coverage and political action, is exaggerated. This author identified that 'only in occasional moments of policy panic' might there be a significant policy change.[4] Warren Strobel further refined this; he identified how media coverage affects the *process* of policy making 'more than policy itself'.[5] Therefore, rather than acting impulsively, most (though not all) officials treat what they see or read with considerable caution, if not scepticism. This doubt is often used by governments as a convenient justification for doing nothing.

This is a crucial corrective to the conventional wisdom that a direct correlation exists between media coverage and political (and therefore probably military) action in conflict prevention and management. Most important, the result is a government decision to commit itself publicly to the *appearance* of action by way of palliative humanitarian operations, rather than through a firm political commitment to do everything possible to prevent or end a conflict, using military force if necessary. As the controversial five-volume findings of the Committee for Joint Evaluation of Emergency Assistance to Rwanda concluded: 'War was the extension of failed diplomatic effort. Humanitarian aid was a substitute for political action in Rwanda.'[6]

THE MEDIA OR THE MEDIATOR: WHICH COMES FIRST?

Like the misplaced assumptions of the power of the CNN factor in conflict management, most people readily assume that there is, or must be, a direct cause-and-effect relationship between media coverage and the chances for either preventing, pre-empting, or limiting a conflict. The emotions created by vivid, gruesome television images add weight to this assumption.

Again, the evidence suggests otherwise. Conflicts are now pre-dominantly of a sub-state and intra-state nature, in what are described as 'sick state' cases.[7] Rarely is there media coverage of a conflict that is about to explode. It is war, and the images of fighting, that catalyses television coverage, in particular, and not the vaguer possibility of a conflict breaking out at some indefinable moment. When it comes to prevention, media coverage is usually too late to help.

Overall, there is now a growing body of analysis and research that questions the conventional wisdom of a direct cause-and-effect relationship, although more case work needs to be done. Livingston and Eachus, for example, debunk the conventional assumption that emotive television coverage of the humanitarian disaster in Somalia in late summer and early fall 1992 was pivotal in forcing United States President George Bush to approve an American involvement. 'News coverage trends do not support the claim that news attention to Somalia led to the Bush administration's decision to intervene', they conclude.[8] As the journalist Lindsey Hilsum confirmed, after reporting whatever she could manage to see of the horrors unfolding in Rwanda in April 1994, 'I couldn't stop the smallest part of it. I am only slowly beginning to understand it. At the time I could only watch and survive.'[9]

PRESSURE TO 'DO SOMETHING': MEDIA PRESSURE AND
NATIONAL INTEREST

Ultimately, the vital national interests and strategic assessments of governments hold sway over emotions. Usually those national interests are far more limited than most people assume, unless national security is threatened. Sovereignty and the limitations of Article 2(7) of the UN Charter are also severely limiting factors.[10] However appalling the television pictures and newspaper reporting, in the United States (and probably in many other Western countries, as well) 'severe human rights violations, including genocide' are most unlikely to constitute a vital national interest.[11] Conflicts in Bosnia 1992–93, Chechnya 1994, the Great Lakes of Africa 1996–97 and Kosovo until 1999 all underline this point in a vivid and harrowing way. The official working view of the new generation of sub-state conflicts further minimises the chance of a significant intervention. They will have 'no immediate, substantial impact upon the interests of the great powers' and 'the international response to such crises will rarely be decisive'.[12]

The approach of governments appears to follow a clear trend to be non-interventionist, regardless of the power of media reporting. United States President Bill Clinton's Presidential Decision Directive Number 25 on Multilateral Peace Operations (PDD 25) of 5 May 1994 defines clearly those limits of United States national interest beyond which it is highly unlikely that the country will ever commit itself, certainly militarily and on the ground. The directive came at a time when most leading European governments were exasperated by what they saw as the lack of both understanding and leadership on the Balkans crisis of 1992–95 from the United States government. Eventually, there was a period when the Clinton administration belatedly tried to portray an image of assertive presidential engagement in foreign crises. The high-profile American action on crisis management in Bosnia in the summer of 1995, which led to the Dayton Peace Agreement, is the primary example. This commitment was born out of a fundamental reassessment of United States national interests at the time, not because of media coverage. The United States envoy Richard Holbrooke has since detailed how it was presidential alarm at the likelihood of American ground forces being required to enter Bosnia to oversee withdrawal under Plan 40-104 during 1995 that ultimately catalysed political action which resulted in the Dayton Agreement.[13]

Privately, however, senior European officials remained sceptical as to how deep any American commitment might really go in such crises and how long it would last. In March 1996, US National Security Adviser Anthony Lake announced a seven-point, 'tough-love' checklist of national interests that might lead to an American use of force.[14] Implicitly, the checklist apparently ignored any emotive power of television and media coverage. Under the new Lake doctrine, defining a clear exit strategy seemed to carry more importance than any immediate urgency for an American commitment to enter conflict-prevention operation. A commitment that might prevent the conflict from exploding in the first place is most unlikely, whether reported by the media or not!

The Lake principles and the definitions of national interest in other capitals of the world help to explain the negligible response to most media coverage of conflicts, whether the conflict is looming or already being fought. Except in rare and unpredictable circumstances which can occasionally lead to policy panic, television pictures frequently create political impotence. This is despite any personal emotions that the images create among ministers, government officials, or members of the public who have anything more than a fleeting interest in the horrors that they see or read about.

An example of this occurred during a showing of the vivid television pictures of the massacres in Rwanda in 1994. At a diplomatic banquet in London, the then British Foreign Secretary Douglas Hurd (later Lord Hurd) movingly described the conflict as a 'true heart of darkness' whose details 'I can barely bring myself to watch'.[15] But, for the British government, as with almost all others (except France), such horror and emotion did not translate into a proactive switch in policy designed to end the fighting. It is a United Nations failing that continues to haunt UN Secretary-General Kofi Annan (who at the time was head of UN Peace-keeping).[16]

NATIONAL INTEREST: THE MEDIA'S COMPLAINT

Many in the media despise the minimalist view implicit in government calculations of national interest. For reasons either of self-interest or conviction, many journalists who risk their lives to report on a looming or exploding conflict will not be deflected from the view that the CNN factor either directly influences policy, or, if it does not, then it should.[17] Martin Bell, the BBC's distinguished former foreign affairs correspondent (and from 1997 an independent Member of Parliament), complained that most wars he covered were the result of failed politics and diplomacy. 'The Bosnia war', said Bell, 'has left me with the conviction that a foreign policy based only on considerations of national interest, and not at all of principle, is not only immoral but inefficient.'[18] Others continue to argue that without television coverage, looming conflicts and humanitarian crises would be completely ignored by the international community. Underlining the chasm between governments of leading world powers and the likes of Bell, Douglas Hurd wrote:

> Martin Bell's principle cannot surely be that we should intervene against horrors only when they are televised? ... Bosnia is far from unique. I can think of eight civil wars raging at this moment, with others simmering. Britain cannot be expected, even with allies, to intervene each time.[19]

Often the international community, once it sees the images, turns away, invokes international law, and declares that the conflict is an 'internal matter' for the 'sovereign government'. Such non-responses are the hallmark of what Martin Bell complains is the 'nothing can be done club'.

The record suggests that despite emotive and often brilliant reporting, the government negativists have prevailed. Except in a few rare moments of policy vacuum and panic, politicians by and large take a starkly different view to that of journalists. Both in Chechnya in November–December 1994 (claimed as part of the territory of a former superpower) and in Burundi in July 1996 (a tiny independent nation with no strategic importance to any great power), the international determination to respect the right of a sovereign nation to reject offers of outside assistance overrode any personal ministerial revulsion at the unfolding horrors being reported by the international media.

FEAR OF CASUALTIES AND LIKELY MEDIA COVERAGE:
A JUSTIFIABLE ANXIETY?

Fear of casualties, and the effect of media coverage of body-bags on political legitimacy, is assumed readily to be a key political consideration that restrains military intervention to contain or prevent a conflict. But is the predicted emotion and fear of body-bags justified by reality? Despite understandable domestic political fears, the spectre of even small numbers of casualties may not be the factor that many, especially the media, readily assume it to be. The prima-facie evidence from the United Nations Protection Force (UNPROFOR) 1992–95 and Implementation Force (IFOR) 1995–96 experience in Bosnia – especially the high number of casualties sustained by French forces – suggests that public opinion in Europe at least, is far more robust on the issue of casualties than many politicians instinctively fear it to be. Commanders from several nations, including those at the highest levels in the United States forces, have expressed privately to this author their irritation with political paranoia about the possibility of casualties and resulting media coverage. They say it restrains unnecessarily their military effectiveness. After all, they argue, any military operation must plan for casualties. In Bosnia, under the first year of IFOR's peace operation, non-American forces were contemptuous of the United States paranoia about casualties. It was a paranoia which manifested itself in large amounts of body armour being worn on a 'peace mission' in an environment of little hostility. Political preparation of the electorate in advance, along with vigorous ministerial handling of any casualties, should be enough to prevent a major public backlash that can undermine a military deployment. The casualty issue only becomes a problem when there are weak, diffident political efforts at belated damage limitation.

After searching for other evidence of significant fluctuations in public support for American peace support operations in Lebanon and Somalia, Professor James Burk of Texas A&M University has also questioned the conventional wisdom that the public is intolerant of casualties. He concludes that public opinion backed both operations and was 'neither volatile, overly sensitive to casualties, nor obviously irresponsible', even after incidents like the deadly firefight in Mogadishu in 1994.[20] Fear of casualties did not influence policy as many assumed it would, especially politicians and many in the media.

In separate research, Larson has further shown that public support for United States military operations and public tolerance for casualties is related directly to clear, unequivocal bipartisan political approval for 'compelling' missions.[21] Failure to secure such agreement will inevitably lead to questioning a mission's merits. As a result, the need for unity – whether inter-state or intra-state, and especially in the European Union (EU) – has been seen consistently as the overriding prerequisite for policy. The best way to achieve unity is by way of a minimalist, low-risk response that has virtually no chance of preventing or halting conflict. This is not what most of the media coverage might seem explicitly to demand.

THE MEDIA AND NGOS IN CONFLICT MANAGEMENT

Media involvement in conflict is further complicated by their new relationship with non-governmental organisations (NGOs). These have learned to harness the power of intense television coverage of a conflict, as a way to generate significant cash flows from both governments and the public. This is especially the case in the new environment of increasingly strapped financial circumstances, where generosity is squeezed and national donor agencies are retrenching.

But, at the same time, there are signs that NGOs and humanitarian organisations are belatedly coming to terms with the inherent limits and distorting influence of television coverage on conflict management. An urgent reassessment of priorities and likely responses is taking place. 'Rapid and radical shifts in the nature of international disaster response have left agencies reeling', concludes one new assessment.[22] In the view of one leading NGO figure, the kind of military response prompted up to now by television coverage in particular is not the most cost-effective. Indeed, while such operations carry the kind of high profile demanded by politicians to satisfy the need to 'do something', they are no longer effective or appropriate. Impulsive intervention prompted by a conscience-driven political response to television pictures is considered counter-productive, despite the valuable boost it gives to fund-raising.[23]

For the time being, however, most NGOs continue to fight hard – both subtly and blatantly – to persuade television news organisations to cover conflicts or looming catastrophes like Afghanistan, Burundi, Sierra Leone and Liberia. They believe, or at least assume, that high-profile media coverage of a simmering crisis will prevent much worse. But often the outcome is despair at the media's indifference or inaction. So great is the increasing desperation of some NGOs to get worldwide attention and funding for forgotten conflicts that they tempt journalists into the conflict zones with offers of transport and logistics support. But to what effect? Do the big nations really care about Afghanistan or Liberia? Do international mediators have the kind of political or military leverage that will persuade determined warlords or sub-state leaders to consider peace rather than the kind of military campaign for hegemony they have long planned? The evidence is not encouraging.

THE UNPREDICTABLE NEWS CYCLE AND THE TYRANNY OF REAL TIME

It is important to understand the nature of the news cycle. Its wavelength in this age of real-time reporting from conflicts becomes ever shorter. The consequence is that the media's attention span is diminishing proportionately. The news cycle has a voracious appetite for new information. It shows no mercy. It is uncharitable and ungenerous. Data and video are updated and replaced rapidly. Information becomes stale more rapidly than ever, unless freshened up regularly. The absence of new details, material, or angles means an issue drops swiftly out of the news cycle, replaced by something fresher.

Prima facie, vivid coverage will only create major international political resonance if, by chance, it hits a critical, often unpredictable void in the news cycle. Alternatively, there will be impact if it creates a moment of policy panic when governments have no robust policy and charts a clear course.

News editors have to search constantly for a new story that departs significantly from what has become a stale old news story, whether domestic or international. A lull in the news cycle, often reinforced during vacation time when politicians are away from their legislatures, can also mean that there is no home political story to compete with international news. Resources, personnel, and satellite dishes can then be deployed abroad, but selectively and only if media organisations see the chance for high-profile editorial impact. Hence the fickle nature of the media. It is impossible for an aspiring 'conflict preventer' to predict with any accuracy when these factors will converge. Often the relentless news cycle and the pressure of vivid domestic issues will conspire to prevent a pending conflict from making an impact as a lead or close-to-lead story to which ministers, civil servants, or the public will respond.

For governments with little interest in making a more positive engagement in a conflict, it seems that media indifference is an increasingly convenient alibi for doing as little as possible. Alternatively, diplomats, military officers, or civilians must live with the expectation that at some time they will wake up with 'big bruises' inflicted by emotive television coverage that unexpectedly creates strong public emotions and resonance without warning.

IS MEDIA COVERAGE A *SINE QUA NON* FOR CONFLICT PREVENTION?

The evidence is contradictory. There may be a strong argument that media coverage is counter-productive for effective diplomacy aimed at conflict prevention or management. Too often during discussions or negotiations, the protagonists or delegations perform somewhat theatrically for the press corps, thereby apparently stiffening their positions and compounding the problems of mediation or confidence building. In late 1995, one exceptional BBC television documentary by Michael Ignatieff on the work of the UN Secretary-General included a unique insight into the effectiveness of unseen diplomacy by the UN special representative in Burundi, Ould Abdullah. Abdullah's effectiveness was partly due to the absence of any media coverage that would probably inflame tensions and polarise positions rather than assist in conciliation.

Although journalists want a story, the wiser, more seasoned conflict journalists recognise that unseen mediation and diplomacy can play a more pivotal role than public posturing to the media. Witness the frustrations of Lord (David) Owen, Cyrus Vance, and others in the protracted Bosnian negotiations in Geneva, where the faction leaders indulged in public posturing at the microphones in the Palais des Nations before and after each session of 'peace talks'. But Ignatieff's film also highlighted the limits and frustrations of quiet, unheralded, unobtrusive mediation. However, some would argue that increased media coverage might have helped focus international concern on Burundi, thereby attaining a sustainable momentum and mediation-support mechanism.

The contention is debatable and possibly hypothetical. Because of the international lack of interest in Burundi, the media coverage never happened. Eventually, Abdullah asked to be relieved of his position because of his despair at the lack of political support and resources for his work. Then, to the delight and surprise of many conflict analysts, some governments expressed concern and even tried to do more. In a move apparently at odds with clear international indifference towards Africa's festering conflicts, the US government proposed a UN preventative force whose aim would be to stop Burundi from turning into another Rwanda-style mass genocide. Two months before the murders and coup that fleetingly put Burundi on the world's television screens, the then United

States Ambassador to the UN, Madeleine Albright, pre-emptively described Burundi as 'a car driving in slow motion over a cliff'.[24] She also chided France for vetoing a plan reportedly backed by President Clinton to prepare a UN rapid-intervention force for Burundi.

Why the sudden United States interest to do in Burundi in 1996 what it conspicuously refused to do in Rwanda in 1994? In no way can it be said that media coverage was the reason. Diplomacy was taking a lead politically. On Burundi's catastrophe the international print media and television had been virtually silent, despite a near constant level of killings and the many warnings in NGO reports of increasing violence reminiscent of Rwanda before April 1994. Again, no obvious cause and effect between media coverage and diplomatic action can be detected. In Burundi in early summer 1996, it was the opposite.

WESTERN NEWS MEDIA AND CONFLICT: THE NEW COMMERCIAL REALITIES

It is misguided for diplomats, the military, and NGOs to view the 'media' as a single, homogeneous grouping of journalists and broadcasters who act in a predictable, uniform way. The media are neither monolithic nor homogeneous. They are a diverse, highly competitive, unpredictable lot. Except in the most cataclysmic events – like an air crash, a disaster with high levels of instant death, or a political upheaval – there is no automaticity to a uniform, international news response. Indeed, the response of news organisations at all levels has become increasingly variable and unpredictable. Treatment of stories will vary according to national and regional agendas. A crisis in one part of the world can easily be viewed elsewhere as irrelevant.

The level of coverage (or refusal to cover) will often be a function of national interest and distance from the event. The lower the national interest and the greater the distance, the less likely it is that news organisations will have anything more than a passing interest in the developing story. There is no uniform media response that defies international borders and national identities. Responses to conflicts depend on considerations like editorial perceptions, the nationalities of those fighting and the forces being engaged to stop them, calculations about the interests of their audiences, and cash-availability in the news organisation. Gatekeeping theory has narrowed the media trends in conflicts that are a fickle and nationalistic process.[25]

Henceforth, commercial pressures are likely to predominate. The overriding pressures for budget discipline in media operations will be a harsh reality that cannot be overstated. Conflicts that explode at a moment of overspending or budget-stretching in a news organisation are unlikely to receive first hand coverage, however pressing the threat. As the sharp drop in media coverage of IFOR's military success in Bosnia illustrated during 1996, coverage of 'unsexy' nation-building and development projects, or the kind of economic regeneration efforts required to avoid conflict, is likely to be negligible at best.

None of these factors offers any comfort to those working to improve international awareness of conflicts to be prevented or resolved. The outlook is increasingly gloomy. Former US State Department spokesman Nicholas Burns has publicly acknowledged a trend that other insiders are less willing to express candidly. From his perspective of promoting and explaining United States foreign policy, Burns has described what is now a 'sorry minimum of foreign coverage, reflecting current prevailing public attitudes', especially on American television news networks.[26] The EU's Commissioner for Humanitarian Affairs, Emma Bonino, has expressed the new challenge in more caustic terms:

> What does it take for a humanitarian crisis to make it into prime time slots on radio or television? Deaths are essential, preferably hundreds of them in places that have not captured media attention before. News is by definition new ... I became aware that for every humanitarian crisis that made it into the headlines, there were dozens that went unnoticed.[27]

One reason above all else generates such pressure: the information and media business is experiencing a technological and commercial revolution of seismic proportions. The revolution's ultimate direction cannot be predicted, but current signs indicate that it will disturb the business of conflict prevention. The ultimate paradox will result: there will be increasing and overwhelming volumes of information, but less interest in harnessing the information commercially unless a profitable revenue stream can be generated. The conflict between journalistic instincts and commercial realities in the increasingly tough information market-place will be profound. The relentless push for news that entertains ('infotainment') seems unstoppable, with a trend towards the 'trivial and mediocre'[28] and news that is predominantly domestic with scant reflection of foreign crises. The leading journalists and producers at the 1996 awards ceremony of the One World Broadcasting Trust were warned of the 'danger of apartheid of the communications world', between media coverage of developed and the developing world: 'We [as broadcast journalists] can raise consciousness or retreat.'[29]

213

Many fear that commercial realities have already forced the retreat. 'Television and radio coverage of humanitarian issues outside the main news bulletins is dwindling throughout Europe', EU commissioner Bonino concluded. 'The sidelining of documentary and current affairs programs about humanitarian issues is also due to lack of interest among the owners and directors of broadcasting companies.'[30]

On the positive side are programmes like 'Channel 4 News' from Independent Television News (ITN) in London and the output of quasi-state-funded broadcasters like the BBC and the two German channels, ARD and ZDF. They are proud to retain a significant news-gathering infrastructure worldwide that is well funded. (The BBC, for example, retains a network of approximately 250 foreign correspondents in 50 bureaux.) The aim remains to broadcast comprehensive news, current affairs, and documentary coverage worldwide. The journalistic mission is still to cover international issues and conflicts, even for high-profile, low-audience programmes that the commercial sector considers too marginal to support.

However, audience shares for news programmes are falling, with increasingly fragmented and transient viewing patterns across a fast-increasing proliferation of channels.[31] Cash remains a constraint, but not because of any threat to profits: the real value of licence fees and state revenues is being cut. We must therefore ask what political impact such programmes can really be expected to have, unless there is a resulting rare public outcry about a conflict that the politicians cannot dare ignore. The chances of this happening are low, and – again – probably negligible.

On the negative side are the new commercial realities. Much to the regret of many (though not all) journalists, their editorial instincts to cover a conflict are increasingly being heavily constrained by the ever-tougher conditions in the media market-place. For commercial television-news organisations, the ratings or circulation figures produce revenue. The conventional industry view is that coverage of domestic issues will buoy up flagging sales and public interest, even though advertising agencies say well-researched documentaries, including those covering international issues, generate good revenue streams.[32] The typical commercial view is that only in exceptional circumstances will coverage of an international crisis raise circulation or viewing numbers.

In addition, the new data and news software embraced by information technology has an ominous potential power to distort the integrity of information. The Internet and multimedia products like CD-ROM are in the infant stages of challenging the monopoly of news organisations to disseminate 'news'. It seems likely that they will further fragment the market in a way yet to be charted with any certainty. The proliferation of unchecked and uncorroborated 'facts' circulating on websites in cyberspace may also serve to distort the perception of conflicts. When reading a newspaper or watching most television news programmes, the average reader or viewer assumes that the output has been checked and verified by editors and skilled journalists. In the future, with unfiltered Internet access to cyberspace, the typical consumer is unlikely to have the skill to discriminate between 'facts' and carefully disguised propaganda or polemics.

Meanwhile, on the commercial side, information technology is slicing the market into ever-smaller portions. As a result, revenue at the marginal end of each market is being cut. To preserve profit, newspaper and broadcast groups have to drive costs down. Thus the high costs (and risks) of committing editorial manpower to a conflict in a distant country in which there is no national interest to become involved will increasingly militate against conflict coverage. In mainstream daily journalism, senior editors and managers have been heard to say: 'If we don't cover it, no one will know the difference, so let's not bother.'

As a result, for both text and video-reporting of conflict, the international news and video agencies like Reuters, the Associated Press, and Worldwide Television News (WTN, now merged with APTV to become APTN) have become the conscience of many (though not all) large broadcast and newspaper organisations. The agencies provide the words and pictures for a fixed annual contract price. This satisfies the accountants because it ensures that there are no financial surprises. Editorially, it ensures rapid, real-time coverage of a story well before a correspondent and crew can be scrambled and sent to the airport, at a considerable extra cost. The agency material is assembled at base in either a television edit room or on a journalist's video display. In this way, above-the-line costs of such coverage are rock bottom, if not negligible. A degree of editorial honour can be retained, allowing editors to claim correctly: 'But we covered the story.'

To the purist, the sight of a company's own correspondent *in situ* is what field reporting of conflicts is all about. But for many organisations, the cost of securing that image and presence is disproportionate and of questionable value. No great compensatory revenue is generated. Regrettably, most viewers and readers cannot tell the difference between a company's experienced correspondent on the spot and a cheaper (though not always) credible journalist sitting in a head office merging text and images into a convincing, if not always accurate, package. To reduce costs and preserve profits, the commercial news organisations are

215

prepared to risk the disaffection of the handful of readers or viewers who notice the difference, along with any errors in interpretation of the second-hand information. The risk is more than offset by the big saving made by not dispatching the company's own staff and resources. The bottom line is that having a named, recognised journalist on location increasingly carries a high marginal cost that many news organisations will not pay.

Naturally, many editors will reject indignantly this kind of analysis as inaccurate or unduly cynical. In many countries, news organisations remain answerable to regulators or oversight boards which continue to insist on extensive coverage of international news, which invariably means conflicts. The regulators have the power to censure those organisations which fail to live up to their mandates. By and large the impression is one of public praise for foreign reporting by news companies, even those claimed by some critics to be falling short of their international news coverage responsibilities. However, insiders in some commercial news organisations are not convinced. Journalists detect a carefully crafted editorial sleight of hand designed to give the impression of a greater commitment to on-the-spot foreign coverage than is actually the case.

This is the new reality. There is no point taking a moral view and expecting matters to change. It is virtually impossible to see how they can. A yearning for the plentiful days of international coverage in the late 1980s and early 1990s is now only for nostalgic dreamers. Now the dominant question in deciding whether to commit increasingly scarce resources to a conflict tends to be: 'what's the *value added* by going there ourselves?' Often the answer is: 'nothing worth paying for'.

REAL-TIME TECHNOLOGY AND CONFLICT COVERAGE:
THE OMINOUS PARADOX

The developed world has more real-time technology and capability than it has ever had to cover crises and conflicts in the developing world. The contrast with the time-scale of conflict reporting, say, 50 years ago, is profound. Coverage of the Bosnian War from 1992 onwards was remarkably different to coverage of the Gulf War a year earlier. Notebooks and pencils have been replaced by laptop computers, with modems and communication cards that can transmit instantly by satellite phone. News organisations have highly mobile satellite television transmission systems that can broadcast from anywhere. Television news pictures can now be broadcast on telephone lines, albeit at present slowly and not yet in real

216

time.[33] Journalists from the richer news organisations travel with satellite telephones the size of a briefcase. There is more ability, mobility, and technology to cover and beam back more sub-state horrors in this world.

As a result, television news coverage suffers from a 'supermarket of war video'.[34] The proliferation of Hi-8 video cameras (small, highly portable, and easily hidden) and a new generation of low-cost digital video (DVC) hand cameras, means that the information no longer has to be provided by expensive professional sources. From a matrix of incoming video on their desktop video-screens, journalists in a television news room can pick and choose, just like walking down the supermarket aisles: one day, Nagorno-Karabakh; the next day Tajikistan, Georgia, Chechnya, or Afghanistan; then a bit of Angola, Liberia, Yemen, or perhaps Algeria, if we are lucky. On many days, all of this streams relentlessly into the television news machines from agencies. The task of filtering it all quickly is mind-boggling, given the mass of video and the short time usually available. As news organisations and audiences become more domestically oriented (or is it numbed and dulled to the misery of people in whom they have no interest?), there is also growing evidence of an inverse relationship between the wealth of raw television coverage and how much of it is actually transmitted as anything more than a few seconds of subliminal video with no context or detail. There is more video available from more conflicts but less editorial interest in transmitting it, except on continuous news channels like BBC World, CBC's NewsWorld, CNN International, or specialist, non-mass market programmes like 'Channel 4 News' in Britain or the 'NewsHour with Jim Lehrer' on PBS and Ted Koppel's 'Nightline' on ABC News in the United States.

Although not yet proven conclusively, there may be a further ominous trend. Technology has facilitated the globalisation of the news business. In television, international news channels like CNN, BBC World, and NBC Superchannel are lined up for battle on the new Wild West broadcasting frontier via satellite and cable. In theory, this situation should allow comprehensive coverage of global issues. Again, in theory, this coverage should include early warning of conflicts and any efforts at prevention, along with detailed reporting of conflicts that have erupted in defiance of all diplomatic efforts (assuming there were some!). However, with the explosion of media outlets wiring the world, information technology experts believe we may now be experiencing an unexpected phenomenon, namely, that except for the elites, globalisation promotes greater parochialisation in public perceptions and interests.[35] If correct, this is likely to further limit media coverage of conflicts. The fears are there, but the evidence either way is inconclusive so far.

217

PARTIALITY IN CONFLICT REPORTING:
THE MEDIA'S SECRET SHAME?

There appears to be one cancer above all that afflicts much of the reporting from wars and conflict. It is the virtually unspoken issue of partiality and bias in conflict journalism. The mere mention of it is usually seen as taboo and even heretical. Few media people want to discuss partiality and the resulting distortions. To do so would undermine the perceived integrity and objectivity of correspondents who report from battle zones. It would also challenge the motives of the organisations that print and broadcast their material in the name of objectivity and balance.

In Bosnia (1992–95), above all, there was more evidence than many media personnel care to admit that journalists embarked on crusades and became partial. They empathised with the Bosnian government because of personal outrage at Serb aggression. Prima facie, this partiality distorted the reporting and led either to a refusal to include certain qualifying facts in stories or to distorting the overall impression. Further evidence of partiality in reporting has emerged from the Great Lakes crisis of 1996–97.[36]

It is dangerous to generalise. There are reporters who cover conflicts at great personal risk and with the greatest degree of objectivity they can muster, especially given the often miserable conditions in which they find themselves. It is also professionally risky for a senior journalist to cast aspersions on the integrity of some fellow journalists' work. A few journalists have made great efforts to investigate and refute allegations of misreporting by news correspondents and misrepresentation by the UN military.[37] In the Great Lakes of Africa 1996–97 some reporters spoke with a mix of regret and pride at their 'Tutsi-tilt' in favour of the Tutsis who survived the massacres by Hutus in 1994. In Bosnia, there is compelling evidence that coverage was skewed due to both the personal emotions of correspondents and the corporate policies of some leading news organisations. Under the apparent veil of objectivity, they have taken sides, often unashamedly. Coverage has not been balanced, yet no 'health warning' or personal declaration has accompanied the coverage. As the BBC's television correspondent Mark Urban wrote, 'Few of the British-employed journalists – with some exceptions – seem to have been concerned with telling us the tales of the Serbian housewives blown away by Muslim snipers' bullets, or the Croat villagers whose throats were slit by the Muslim raiders from nearby villages in central Bosnia.'[38] What could be called the hypocrisy of governments – especially of the United States – has reinforced this cancer, along with a trend towards what might qualify as deceit.

A former senior United States commander in Europe, General Charles G. Boyd, wrote a remarkable exposé of the true perception of the Bosnian conflict by many American officers. The retired general's decision to go public was rare. His view directly contradicted the conventional political wisdom in Washington, which Boyd concluded was 'stunted by a limited understanding of current events as well as a tragic ignorance or disregard for history'. In his damning indictment Boyd added *inter alia*:

> Most damaging of all, US actions in the Balkans have been at sharp variance with stated US policy ... We must see things in the Balkans as they are, not as we wish them to be. We must separate reality from image.[39]

Boyd focused on the politicians and Establishment who, by intention or by default, went along with the conventional myths. In theory, a free and independent press should have been able to challenge and dispel the Establishment's myths by way of its on-the-ground reporting. By and large, the media failed. Instead they reinforced the myths.

Many military and civilian members of the NATO/UN operations who privately belong to the Boyd school of disillusionment have become increasingly angry with the media performance they witnessed.[40] Even if we allow for an instinctive institutional antipathy towards the media, the kind of complaints expressed by a pseudonymous UN official in Sarajevo, 'Kenneth Roberts', deserve detailed and serious attention.[41] With evident bitterness, Roberts complained of the deceptive picture of Sarajevo portrayed by the media. People were not starving, the city was neither besieged nor isolated; otherwise how would the markets be so well stocked – at a price? Like others, Roberts alleged that 'crusading' journalists succumbed to clever and ruthless Bosnian government tactics designed to ensure that the image of suffering Muslims was not undermined. He concluded by asking, as many non-journalists do, why there is no regulatory media body to exact sanctions on journalists who fail to report objectively. Now, well after the end of the Bosnian War, the emerging evidence confirms the correctness of that view.

It must be made clear that there is no shame in reporters who, having endured unspeakable horrors alongside fellow human beings, align their emotions and resentments with these victims and then write vividly about them. However, in the complex dynamics and politics of conflict prevention and management, the reader or audience must be made aware of the level of partiality of a particular journalist or news organisation. The new real-time pressures of continuous news channels further point up the dangers of confusing a reporter's personal opinions and his

219

relaying of facts. Yet it is virtually unheard of for any declaration of partiality to be made. Martin Bell's explanation of the emotional pressures in Bosnia, and latterly his call for a 'journalism of attachment', was a rare admission. 'All the reporters who work regularly on the Bosnian beat are, at least privately, interventionist', he wrote. 'Surrounded by so much misery and destruction, it is humanly difficult to be anything else.'[42]

Christine Amanpour, the British-born CNN reporter who exemplified gritty, gutsy, emotive reporting of the Bosnian horrors, and became renowned as the 'Queen of the Sarajevo Press Corps' gives a robust response to those who allege that she was not neutral:

> Whoa ... It drives me crazy when this neutrality thing comes up ... Objectivity, that great journalistic buzzword, means giving all sides a fair hearing – not treating all sides the same – particularly when all sides are not the same. When you are in a situation like Bosnia, you are an accomplice – an accomplice to genocide.[43]

Roy Gutman, who won a Pulitzer Prize for his revelations in July 1992 about Serb detention camps, has talked openly about the emotional difficulties of retaining the total objectivity that most people expect of a senior journalist. 'Some issues simply are not equally balanced, and we can't give the impression that for every argument on one side, there is an equal one on the other', he said in a discussion of his own shift from objectivity during his reporting of Bosnia. 'I do not believe the fairness doctrine applies equally to victims and perpetrators.'[44] Although claiming the high moral ground, few reporters or media corporations have openly declared their partiality in the way the *Guardian*'s award-winning war correspondent Ed Vulliamy was willing to do in 1994.[45] In no way did Vulliamy's honesty undermine his journalism. Rather, it made his writing more powerful because of his close affinity with the Muslims, a closeness born out of experiencing fear, horrors, deprivation and near death alongside them.

Would that others in the journalistic profession had matched Vulliamy's reasoned openness. As he says himself, he tried to be impartial in Croatia. In Bosnia he found it impossible to hold the line. 'I am one of those reporters who cannot see this as "just another story" from which I must remain detached, and in which I must be neutral', he wrote, 'I think that if I did require myself to be neutral, I would not understand the war.' He harboured contempt for the 'peace brokers and the men with clipboards who make cursory visits and treat the aggressors and victims as equals'. Like Amanpour, Vulliamy's commitment and disdain was absolute: 'These officials should please the "neutrals" in journalism – for they are the incarnation of the appeasers of 1938.'[46]

The trouble is that such emotive journalistic commitment was neatly exploited, especially by the Bosnian government. Ministers in Sarajevo ruthlessly harnessed such partiality to generate international sympathy for the government's fight against 'fascism'. It was a deft manipulation to which many journalists succumbed, either willingly or, more typically, without realising it. In the words of former EU mediator Lord Owen, the Bosnian government strategy, masterminded by Vice-President Ejup Ganic, was 'very credible but ruthless'.[47] Backed by public relations techniques honed in the United States, the Sarajevo government manipulated many of the international press who, like the Bosnian population, were enduring Serb shelling and a degree of danger and deprivation. Bosnian government ministers and spokesmen were always ready to comment or rush to the live satellite dishes to condemn the Serbs. They usually enjoyed a free ride, their increasingly exaggerated claims accepted as fact by callow interviewers and anchors in distant studios who did not have the knowledge or background briefings to know better. Frequently, Bosnian ministers made unsubstantiated claims that were untrue or grossly exaggerated. UN military personnel knew that the claims were untrue, but they were either forbidden or restrained from going public with the alternative version. Rarely were the Bosnian ministers and officials challenged, for example, about their policy of refusing to allow those of Sarajevo's population to leave who wanted to do so, or their claim that Sarajevans were starving, or their military policy of taunting Serb artillery with futile infantry attacks in order to incite Serb shelling, or their exaggeration of the predicament of the Bosnian population in Bihac and Gorazde.

Few, if any, journalists or news organisations sympathetic to the Bosnian position gave any public signal of the level of manipulation to which they were being subjected. Yet each day this kind of manipulation was skewing their news coverage, and with it the impression of the war abroad, especially among opinion leaders and journalistic elites on the East Coast of the United States. There is evidence that leading American newspapers, and television news in particular, had scant interest in running stories that did not fit a clear editorial line on Bosnia. They indulged in a pro-Bosnian Muslim campaign without openly declaring it, and the journalism was skewed unashamedly to serve that agenda. No one can deny any media organisation the right to campaign for the 'White Hats' (Bosnian Muslims) against the 'Black Hats' (the Serbs). But it can be argued that such 'reporting' should not be allowed to masquerade as balanced, objective journalism. Organisations gloried in Pulitzers and the baubles earned by prizewinning journalism. The impression was of a new generation of journalism's finest hours. But the record is less complimentary. Journalism suffered. Often, the high ideals espoused by media organisations were quietly set to one side.

This theme was taken up in a heavily criticised 1993 article in *Foreign Policy* entitled 'Dateline Yugoslavia: The Partisan Press'.[48] It detailed how, by late 1992, the majority of the media had become 'so mesmerised by their focus on Serb aggression' that any principle of balance and objectivity had evaporated. Shock waves from the article reverberated speedily through the American media establishment. The veracity of the argument was quickly destroyed by scathing attacks on author Peter Brock for alleged inaccuracies in some of the data he used.[49] Charles Lane, one of Brock's critics, agreed that there 'is legitimate room for self-examination by the Press about its performance in the supercharged Bosnian ethnic atmosphere'.[50] But critics also demolished some of the author's argument by questioning his analytical methods. As a result, the integrity of Brock's core argument about the partisanship of the foreign media in former Yugoslavia was swiftly undermined. The discussion withered and died quickly.

Evidence has been gathered from journalists that illustrates the determination of some media organisations to peddle one line to the exclusion of other evidence in a conflict that might undermine the line. One senior correspondent has described how 'balanced journalism has gone out of the window' because of what he calls a 'tyranny of victimology'.[51] Some of the difficulty of persuading American media organisations in particular to take a more balanced and less partial approach to a conflict like Bosnia was revealed fleetingly by Lord Owen in his book *Balkan Odyssey*. He described an 'explosive encounter' with the editorial board of the *New York Times* when he tried to impart to them some of the realities of Bosnia, including the fact that often the Bosnians were as deceitful and evil as the Serbs.[52]

However, the overall mind-set and editorial views of almost the entire journalistic elite, especially in the United States, did not change. For example, the Sarajevo market massacre on 5 February 1994 was instantly assumed to be the work of Serb artillery firing from the surrounding mountains. Without any question, the media swiftly reflected the conventional belief that Serb gunners were responsible for the outrage. However, a series of subsequent crater analyses by UNPROFOR ballistics experts from several different nations concluded otherwise. On a clear balance of probabilities, the evidence pointed to the fatal mortar being fired by Bosnian forces, as quickly became apparent in Sarajevo.[53] A finding to this effect was made public on 16 February, but the international press ignored it, because it did not fit the conventional wisdom. Senior officials have described how, at the time, it would have been 'politically unhelpful' to have undermined the case against the Serbs. Similar evidence was gathered by David Binder of the *New York Times*. The newspaper, however, declined to run the story. Instead, some six months after assembling the data, Binder published his own findings for a limited, elite readership in *Foreign Policy*.[54] The overall media lesson learned by those grappling with the challenge of preventing conflict is therefore disturbing: do not trust either the line or the coverage.

THE MEDIA AND CONFLICT: A SYNERGY FOR PREVENTION

Synergy is a medical concept, defined in the *New Shorter Oxford English Dictionary* as a 'combined or correlated action of a group of bodily organs', like nerve centres or muscles. It could be said that the media function as both a nerve centre and a muscle when it comes to the dynamics of conflict, and the international perceptions thereof.

Voices in the international community have also compared the developing science of conflict prevention to that of preventive medicine. For example, in a speech in 1996 on preventive defence, then United States Defense Secretary William Perry detailed how, in the same way that 'preventive medicine creates the conditions which support health, making disease less likely and surgery unnecessary', it can be said that 'preventive defense creates the conditions which support peace, making war less likely and deterrence unnecessary'.[55]

The medical analogy is a potent comparison taken up elsewhere by Lord Owen. Less optimistically, Owen, as a former medical doctor, outlined how the vast bulk of modern illness is not cured, but alleviated by the doctor's skills. The dramatic cure is the exception rather than the rule. Much the same limitation affects politicians dealing with conflict within a nation or internationally. Violence is part of daily living. We can deplore its existence, but we are not likely to root it out from our diverse societies. This author shares Lord Owen's conclusion that both doctor and politician 'have to accept, albeit with resignation, the limitations imposed by the structures in which they operate: the human body and the body politic'.[56]

The question for the business of conflict prevention is where do the media fit in to this illness and curative process? The media transmit information, but does the information help prevent the slide into violent conflict? When a patient informs a doctor of symptoms of an unknown condition, does that information mean that the doctor can either prevent deterioration from the illness or cure it? Or is that condition essentially incurable?

If the limited medical analogy is sustainable, then measured caution and pessimism remain justified. It seems that beyond the mere fact of reporting conflict, or signs pointing to a looming conflict, the media have significant limits on their influence. The same is true for big governments in the developed world. Beyond a certain point, they are powerless to prevent a conflict that at least one warlord or potential belligerent is determined to start and see through to its awful, premeditated end.

NOTES

This chapter is an updated version of a report to the Carnegie Commission on Preventing Deadly Conflict published in September 1997, and appears here with the permission of the Commission. The views expressed are the author's and do not necessarily reflect those of the Commission. Copyright 1997 by Carnegie Corporation of New York. The full study appears in a collection of essays on the media and conflict prevention published by the Commission.

1. See (Anon) *Report of Reporters Sans Frontières* (Luton: University of Luton Press, 1996), p. 3.
2. 'Report First, Check Later, James A. Baker III, interviewed by Marvin Kalb', *Harvard International Journal of Press/Politics*, 1, 2 (Spring 1996), p. 3.
3. See P. Mellor, 'The Dead and the Deadline', *Guardian*, 25 March 1996.
4. See N. Gowing, 'Real-Time Television Coverage of Armed Conflicts and Diplomatic Crises: Does it Pressure or Distort Foreign Policy Decisions?', working paper 94-1, Joan Shorenstein Barone Center on the Press, Politics and Public Policy (Cambridge, MA: Harvard University, 1994).
5. See W. P. Strobel, *Late Breaking Foreign Policy* (Washington, DC: United States Institute for Peace Press, 1997).
6. Abstract from *The International Response to Conflict and Genocide: Lessons from the Rwanda Experience* by the Steering Committee for Joint Evaluation of Emergency Assistance to Rwanda (Copenhagen: Danish Foreign Ministry, 1996).
7. Quoted with permission from a presentation by Cameron R. Hume, political adviser at the United States Mission to the United Nations, to a Fulbright Colloquium at the Centre for Defence Studies, Kings College, London, on 10 July 1996.
8. S. Livingston and T. Eachus, 'Humanitarian Crises and U.S. Foreign Policy: Somalia and the CNN Effect Reconsidered', *Political Communication*, 12 (1995), pp. 413–29.
9. L. Hilsum, 'Where is Kigali?', *Granta* (Autumn 1995), p. 148.
10. See Kofi Annan, 'A Reflection on Intervention', 35th Annual Ditchley Lecture, Ditchley, Great Britain, 26 June 1998.
11. Conclusions from deliberations of the Council on Foreign Relations conference, 'US National Interests after the Cold War', at Wye Plantation, Maryland, 14–16 December 1995. These have subsequently been codified into a checklist of 'Blue, Red, White and Translucent Chips' published in *America's National Interests* (Cambridge, MA: Harvard University, 1996).

12. From Hume's presentation to the Fulbright Colloquium (see note 7).
13. R. Holbrooke, *To End a War* (New York: Random House, 1998), pp. 66–8.
14. 'Principles Governing US Use of Force', speech by National Security Adviser Anthony Lake at George Washington University, 8 March 1996.
15. Quoted in N. Gowing, 'Behind the CNN Factor: Lights! Cameras! Atrocities! But Policy Makers Swear they are not Swayed by the Images', *Washington Post*, 31 July 1994.
16. Kofi Annan, 'A Reflection on Intervention' (see note 10 above).
17. See, for example, the editorial by M. Kalb and P. Norris in *Harvard International Journal of Press/Politics*, 1, 1 (Winter 1996), p. 1.
18. M. Bell, 'Conflict of Interest', an edited version of a speech to the Chichester Festival, reprinted in *Guardian*, 11 July 1996.
19. D. Hurd, 'Why Foreign Policy Cannot Be Dictated by Blind Emotion', *Standard*, 16 July 1996.
20. J. Burk, 'Public Support for Peacekeeping in Lebanon and Somalia', paper presented to Inter-University Seminar on Armed Forces and Society, Baltimore, 20–22 October 1995.
21. E. V. Larson, *Casualties and Consensus: The Historical Role of Casualties in Domestic Support for US Military Operations* (Washington, DC: Rand, 1996).
22. P. Walker, 'Disasters Debate: Whose Disaster is it Anyway? Rights, Responsibilities and Standards in Crisis', paper delivered to the World Disasters Report 1996 review conference, 23 May 1996.
23. N. Cater, 'Why Does the Media Always get it Wrong in Disasters: Stereotypes, Standards and Free Helicopter Rides', paper delivered to the World Disasters Report 1996 review conference, 23 May 1996.
24. J. Fitchett, 'US Aide Sounds Alarm Over Burundi', *International Herald Tribune*, 2 May 1996.
25. See S. Livingston, 'Suffering in Silence: Media Coverage of War and Famine in the Sudan', in R. I. Rotberg and T. G. Weiss (eds), *From Massacres to Genocide* (Washington, DC: Brookings Institution, 1996).
26. N. Burns, 'Talking to the World about American Foreign Policy', *Harvard International Journal of Press/Politics*, 1,4 (Fall 1996), p. 14.
27. E. Bonino, 'Bringing Humanitarian News Into Prime Time', *International Herald Tribune*, 28 June 1996.
28. Introduction to E. R. Girardet (ed.), *Somalia, Rwanda and Beyond: The Role of the International Media in Wars and Humanitarian Crises* (Geneva: Crosslines Global Report, 1995).
29. Remarks by Jon Snow, presenter of ITN 'Channel 4 News', to the 1996 One World Broadcasting Trust awards ceremony, London, 20 March 1996.
30. See note 27 above.
31. BBC News Programme Strategy Review, 6 October 1998.
32. J. Pilger, 'The Truth is Out', *Broadcast*, 10 May 1996, p. 20.
33. In October 1996, BBC television news and the television agencies transmitted news videos of the Afghan civil war by satellite phone at a speed equal to one-thirtieth of real time. Each two-minute news story took one hour to feed. The resulting video quality was adequate, but not perfect. The use of telephone instead of television satellite dish (with its transport and transmission costs) contributed to a significant cost saving.
34. N. Gowing, 'Lap-Top Bombardiers and the Media: Threat or Asset?',

225

presentation to the Royal College of Defence Studies, London, 20 November 1995.
35. See the remarks by Marcus Plantin of the ITV Network Centre to the Royal Television Society, 15 September 1995.
36. N. Gowing, 'New Challenges and Problems for Information Management in Complex Emergencies: Ominous Lessons from the Great Lakes and Eastern Zaire in late 1996 and early 1997', paper presented to the international conference on 'Dispatches from Disaster Zones: The Reporting of Humanitarian Emergencies', Church House, London, 27 May 1998.
37. T. Gjelten, 'Blaming the Victim', *New Republic*, 20 December 1993.
38. M. Urban wrote these remarks in a book review of *The Quick and the Dead* by Janine de Giovanni for the (London) *Sunday Times*.
39. C. G. Boyd, 'Making Peace with the Guilty', *Foreign Affairs*, 74, 5 (September/October 1995), pp. 23, 28; (Anon) *Selling the Bosnian Myth to America: Buyer Beware* (Fort Leavenworth, KA: Foreign Military Studies Office, 1995).
40. See R. Thornton, 'A Conflict of Views: The Press and the Soldier in Bosnia', reprinted without the author's permission in *South Slav Journal*, 15, 3–4, pp. 57–8, but contents confirmed as genuine to Nik Gowing.
41. 'K. Roberts' (pseudonym), 'Glamour Without Responsibility', *Spectator*, 5 March 1994, p. 12.
42. M. Bell, 'Testament of an Interventionist', *British Journalism Review*, 4, 4 (1993), p. 9.
43. Quoted in D. Rabinovitch, 'The Million Dollar Action Woman', *Guardian*, 6 July 1996.
44. S. Ricchardi, 'Exposing Genocide, ... an interview with Roy Gutman', *American Journalism Review* (June 1993), pp. 32–6.
45. E. Vulliamy, *Seasons in Hell* (London: Simon & Schuster, 1994), *passim*.
46. E. Vulliamy, 'This War Has Changed My Life', *British Journalism Review*, 4, 2 (1993), p. 5.
47. D. Owen, *Balkan Odyssey* (London: Victor Gollancz, 1995), p. 84.
48. P. Brock, 'Dateline Yugoslavia: The Partisan Press', *Foreign Policy*, 93 (Winter 1993–94).
49. See the letters published in *Foreign Policy*, 94 (Spring 1994), pp. 158–65.
50. C. Lane, 'War Stories', *New Republic*, 3 January 1994.
51. David Binder of the *New York Times*, quoted in Gowing, 'Real-Time Television Coverage of Armed Conflicts and Diplomatic Crises', p. 63.
52. D. Owen, *Balkan Odyssey*, p. 113.
53. Ibid., p. 260.
54. D. Binder, 'Anatomy of a Massacre', *Foreign Policy*, 97 (Winter 1994–95), p. 77.
55. Speech by William Perry to the John F. Kennedy School of Government, Harvard University, 13 May 1996.
56. D. Owen, 'A Clinician's Caution: Rhetoric and Reality', in K. M. Cahill (ed.), *Preventive Diplomacy: Stopping Wars Before They Start* (New York: Basic Books, 1996), pp. 305–17.

15

The Media, Megaphone Diplomacy and Disarmament

PHILIP TOWLE

THE MEDIA AND DISARMAMENT

Arms control and disarmament are considered dull but worthy by the Western media. Governments are expected by editorial writers to be committed to negotiating arms control and disarmament treaties and those like the Reagan administration which are openly sceptical of arms control have been harshly criticised as a consequence. But the media take little interest in the process of negotiation and the detailed issues at stake. Sometimes this is hardly surprising given the technical nature of the problems and the glacial pace of such negotiations. Ways of limiting chemical weapons were discussed for almost 100 years before real progress began to be made on banning their production in the 1990s. The talks on Mutual and Balanced Force Reductions (MBFR) in Europe continued for more than a decade without making any reductions. It would be hard for the media to make 'news' of such non-events.

However, the lack of media interest is due not only to the process of arms control but to its objectives, something which is suggested by the media's lack of interest in successful arms control agreements. The media relish drama, violence and confrontation. Arms control agreements are supposed to reduce the propensity for violence and to improve inter-state relations. The more successful they are, the less 'interesting' they and the world become as a consequence. They are the antithesis of the international scene viewed through the eyes of the media.

Only if arms control agreements are threatened by alleged cheating or by new weapons programmes do they become newsworthy. The general public had never heard of the Outer Space Treaty until the Strategic Defence Initiative (Star Wars) began to threaten its continuation. The arcane details of the Strategic Arms Limitation Treaty (SALT) were of no general interest until the US administration and its critics became concerned in the 1970s that the Soviets were not abiding by the agreement. Treaties which prohibit the use of specific weapons are useful in wartime, not for themselves, but because the enemy can be accused of breaching such international agreements and the general picture of a devilish and unscrupulous foe can be enhanced. The Geneva Protocol, which dates from 1925, banning the use of chemical and biological weapons suddenly became of general interest during the Gulf War because there were widespread fears that the Iraqis might use part of their vast chemical arsenal against allied troops, just as they had used them against the Iranians in the 1980s. Similarly, the Montreux Convention of 1936, which governs the passage of warships through the Dardanelles, was recalled only when the Soviets breached it in the 1970s by building aircraft carriers in the Black Sea and sending them through the Straits.

In peacetime, newspapers and television programmes filter out information on successful international conferences, which have negotiated new arms control agreements or strengthened old ones, leaving the public with an inaccurate and excessively pessimistic or over-dramatic assessment of the international situation. In April 1995, for example, the parties to the Nuclear Non-Proliferation Treaty (NPT) met to decide whether the Treaty should be maintained permanently, extended just for a brief period, or ended altogether. There was considerable anxiety beforehand amongst Western governments and academic analysts about the outcome of the conference because the NPT is the most important legal brake on the spread of nuclear weapons.[1] It is also, arguably, the most important single arms control treaty. Its collapse would have thrown the civil nuclear industry into confusion because the rules governing export of nuclear power stations would have been undermined. A breakdown would have been regarded as a massive set-back to all prospects for arms control over the next decade. It would have discouraged the United States and Russia from continuing to reduce their stocks of nuclear weapons. If the spread of nuclear weapons accelerated, so also would the proliferation of chemical and biological weapons, and the dispersion of missiles to deliver them.

Western governments considered the continuation of the NPT sufficiently important to make a number of concessions to the Treaty's critics. From the NPT's inception these had pointed out the invidious nature of an agreement which discriminates between the five powers having nuclear weapons and the rest of the world. Before the April 1995 conference the British government, therefore, took three initiatives to meet such criticisms. First, it announced that the free-fall nuclear bombs on British aircraft, which the Ministry of Defence had intended to keep in service until 2007, would be scrapped in 1998. It also said that it would no longer demand the right to 'bench test' nuclear weapons for reliability, so facilitating prospects for a Comprehensive Nuclear Test Ban Treaty. Finally, the then Foreign Secretary, Douglas Hurd, announced that Britain would stop producing fissile material for nuclear weapons, thereby helping achieve an agreement prohibiting the production of such material (a 'cutoff' treaty).[2] This would be particularly important because it would mean that the existing nuclear weapon states have made an irrevocable decision to end the expansion of their arsenals.

In the event, thanks very largely to intensive lobbying as well as strong economic and political pressure by the nuclear weapon states, the NPT Review Conference was an overwhelming success from the Western point of view with rapid agreement to perpetuate the Treaty. Yet the editors of *The Times* relegated the success of the conference to a small column on page 15. The editors of the *Daily Telegraph* dropped the story written by their defence correspondent altogether. *The Times*' policy was particularly noteworthy because it had previously published a number of articles and editorials on the threats to the NPT.[3] Successful arms control agreements lack drama. If the NPT Review Conference had failed, newspapers could have conjured up visions of a nuclear-armed world which would have caught the attention of the readers. Good news is by definition not considered newsworthy even if it is of major international importance. The success of the non-proliferation regime in discouraging the spread of nuclear weapons over recent decades is undramatic. The quiet diplomacy by which it has been achieved is unremarkable and unreported. Allegations that Iraq or North Korea have embarked on a nuclear weapons programme make much better copy, but the focus on such 'mavericks' gives a misleading impression.[4]

Two months after the NPT review conference *The Times*, the *Guardian* and other newspapers gave front-page treatment to a clash between Greenpeace protesters and French government vessels in the Pacific.[5] Television news reports also covered the story extensively. Here was an issue of no long-term international importance but with great personal interest and with drama. Whether or not Greenpeace managed to stop the French testing a few nuclear weapons, it was clear that, partly because of the success of the NPT Review Conference, France would sign a Comprehensive Nuclear Test Ban within two years as the French government was committed to doing.[6] But the clash with Greenpeace had the potential for causing casualties and a temporary cooling of relations between Paris and the Pacific countries led by Australia and New Zealand: thus, it was newsworthy. The success of the NPT Review Conference was vastly more important, but, because of the way it was handled in the media, it could have been easily overlooked even by readers of newspapers which carried the story. It was almost ignored by television news.

THE MEDIA, INFORMED OPINION AND DISARMAMENT

Western governments today provide a cascade of information on their policies through White Papers, ministerial speeches and briefings to journalists on and off the record. White Papers have become ever longer, statistical information on every aspect of national life has become more detailed. The annual statistical survey of British life, *Social Trends* runs to over 200 pages and, typically, the *Statement on Defence Estimates* to over 120.[7] This is a marked contrast to the 1950s when defence White Papers provided only a fraction of the information currently distributed and ran to about a dozen pages, without photographs or diagrams. The increased publicity is a reflection of the gradual opening of Western governments and of the greater wealth of the country. The expansion is in inverse proportion to Britain's importance and standing in world affairs, and the ability of British governments to act independently of Europe and the United States

Yet, the real paradox is that only a tiny fraction of this data is of interest to most citizens, who have a well-developed capacity to ignore the bulk of information which flows into their homes through television, radio and the newspapers. Some is filtered and condensed by journalists who write for the 'serious' newspapers but these are only read by minorities. Moreover, as pointed out above, the serious papers also focus on dramatic events, and ponderous analysis of the defence budget, the rationale for particular projects and the location of particular military units are rarely the subject of media interest. Television news suffers from the additional handicap of concentrating on what can be filmed. The necessary process of 'filtering' also forces ordinary citizens to rely on experts in each field, such as transport, health or defence, to assess the information supplied by governments. Yet, ironically, the public becomes ever more sceptical of the value of such 'expert' advice – not least because experts inevitably often disagree with each other, or change their minds at a later date – and the number of specialists employed by the serious press in the defence field and others is in decline.

Media handling of defence and disarmament reduces the flow of government information, which reaches the ordinary citizen from a cascade to a trickle. It has contributed to the lack of knowledge even among the politically aware elite. In 1988 the Institute for European Defence and Strategic Studies, based in London, carried out an opinion poll among Members of Parliament to see how they managed to sift the information they received on defence and disarmament.[8] The results were discouraging. A tiny minority of the MPs obviously took a close interest in defence issues: 13 per cent could name Manfred Worner as the (then) Secretary-General of NATO; and 7 per cent could name General John Galvin as the (then) Supreme Allied Commander in Europe. But the majority had concentrated their scarce time and energy mastering other issues. Altogether, 42 per cent of the MPs interviewed exaggerated the proportion of the GNP spent on defence and nearly one quarter had no idea of the proportion at all. Because there was a great deal of controversy over the purchase of Trident missiles at that time, the bulk of those questioned believed that the British nuclear force absorbed a much higher proportion of the defence budget than was in fact the case.

Most MPs were sympathetic towards disarmament measures: 98 per cent supported the proposal current at that time for reducing the number of US and Soviet nuclear warheads by 50 per cent, while 58 per cent went even further and supported Mr Gorbachev's proposal for abolishing nuclear weapons altogether by the year 2000. Only 2 per cent believed that the recent Intermediate Nuclear Forces (INF) Treaty removing Soviet and US intermediate range missiles was undesirable. On the other hand, many MPs lacked detailed knowledge of relevant defence issues: 75 per cent were unable to say whether either the US or the Soviet Union deployed anti-satellite systems (then a subject of some debate), while 58 per cent believed erroneously that the US deployed anti-ballistic missiles at that time.

MPs claimed that it was more difficult to find reliable and comprehensive information on defence than on any other subject. Yet, as pointed out earlier, governments have made a major and growing effort to spread knowledge about armaments and disarmament, although it is also true that the information distributed has tended to support their policies. During the Cold War years information was selected by Soviet and Western governments to blame the other side for the arms race and for the failure of arms control negotiations to make progress. In the 1950s, the Central Office of Information (COI) in London produced a series of papers on the disarmament question which, though reasonably unimpassioned, made clear whom British officials held responsible for the impasse. This was followed for more than a decade by the weighty annual White Paper *Further Documents on Disarmament* and from 1979 by the Foreign Office's *Arms Control and Disarmament* newsletter. From 1960 the US State Department distributed *Documents on Disarmament* which reprinted most of the important speeches made by Soviet and Western leaders on strategy and disarmament. In the 1980s, the USA produced an annual assessment, *Soviet Military Power*. The Soviets countered with *Whence the Threat to Peace*. Each contained glossy photographs of the weaponry prepared by the other side. Such publications were presumably aimed at opinion formers in the media and the universities. In his covering note to the first copy of the *Arms Control and Disarmament* newsletter, Mr Hurd, then Minister of State in the Foreign Office commented, 'these are not easy subjects and the newsletter will not be an easy read'. They have evidently not even been finding their way into MPs' reading lists, nor have the voluminous, balanced and well-informed publications by unofficial institutes such as the IISS or SIPRI.[9]

PUBLIC ATTITUDES

The public is understandably influenced by the tone of political speeches and the general feelings of national leaders rather than by arms control negotiations or agreements. Anxiety about nuclear weapons and the limited prospects for disarmament reached a peak among the public during the 1950s at the same time that government ministers were most concerned about these issues. Winston Churchill told the House of Commons in November 1953 that the 'fearful scientific discoveries' in the nuclear field 'cast their shadow on every thoughtful mind'. His public mood entirely reflected his private feelings, which oscillated between faith in deterrence and fear that mankind would be obliterated in a nuclear war. Ten years later, President John F. Kennedy told an audience at an American university that, in the event of an East–West war, 'all we have built, all we have worked for, would be destroyed in the first 24 hours'.[10]

This pessimism only started to disperse with the gradual abatement of tensions in the 1960s. Nuclear weapons largely disappeared from the consciousness both of government ministers and of the general public.[11] This changed mood was produced in no small part by the discovery that the East–West divide was not unbridgeable and that arms control agreements could be negotiated with the Soviets: the Partial Test Ban Treaty, the Hot Line Agreement, the Outer Space Treaty, the Seabed Treaty and the NPT. But the public knew little or nothing about these arcane agreements and, indeed, the strategic importance of some of them was very small. The Partial Test Ban Treaty removed the threats from the radioactivity produced by nuclear tests, but the Seabed Treaty was of limited importance when no state was seriously thinking of deploying nuclear armed missiles on or below the seabed. It was the tone of the statements made by national leaders which was picked up and reflected in the public mood. When the Partial Test Ban Treaty was signed in 1963, President Kennedy claimed, 'all mankind has been struggling from the darkening prospect of mass destruction on earth ... Yesterday a shaft of light cut into the darkness.' Interest in the issue of disarmament and in nuclear weapons rapidly faded away when they no longer appeared threatening.[12]

Political statements on defence and disarmament again started to have a major impact on public attitudes in the 1980s. Their effect was magnified because they coincided with a worsening of East–West relations as well as the introduction of SS-20 missiles into Europe by the USSR and plans by the USA to introduce cruise and Pershing missiles. President Ronald Reagan's comments on nuclear weapons were generally feared in Britain and the rest of Europe, and trust in the United States rapidly declined. This produced a revival of the Campaign for Nuclear Disarmament (CND) and massive public demonstrations against the stationing of US missiles in Western Europe. By 1987, 39 per cent of British people felt that the USSR and the USA represented an equal threat to peace; and 68 per cent of West Germans and 57 per cent of British people did not believe that the US genuinely wanted to stop the nuclear arms race. Only 17 per cent of the Italian people wanted US nuclear bases on their soil, against 33 per cent of West Germans, 35 per cent of the British public and 23 per cent of the French people.[13] Elite opinion in Britain was rather different with only 10 per cent of MPs polled believing that the USA represented an equal threat to peace with the Soviet Union. Nevertheless, the figures were disquieting for supporters of Trans-Atlantic links such as NATO.[14]

DISARMAMENT AND PUBLICITY

Statesmen usually behave as if the public is interested in defence and disarmament, and make bids for public support. Arguments between states about disarmament are conducted on a number of different levels. Statesmen and diplomats put forward the most palatable justifications for their policies even if the other reasons for their actions are all too clear. Western states long opposed a comprehensive nuclear test ban treaty on the grounds that it was unverifiable and might encourage cheating.[15] Nuclear weapons could indeed be tested in certain areas where it would be difficult to detect them or to distinguish them from earthquakes. But it was also obvious that the West wanted to test nuclear weapons because the USA and its allies relied upon nuclear deterrence to offset what they saw as the predominance of Soviet conventional forces. The Indian government has long denounced the NPT because of its overtly discriminatory nature, but it is also clear that New Delhi attacked the Treaty because it wanted to keep open the possibility of producing its own nuclear force. .

The media are hardly likely to be fooled by governmental rationalisations, although they are usually more sympathetic to their own governments' explanations than to those put forward by foreign statesmen. Only occasionally can the leaders of one country assist campaigns which actually embarrass other governments and encourage them to change their policies. In the 1970s President Jimmy Carter was genuinely embarrassed by attacks on his decision to produce neutron bombs. The Western European campaign against this decision might, in any case, have been effective. Those hostile to President Carter's decision claimed that the bomb was the ultimate 'capitalist' weapon, respecting property but killing people. But the anti-neutron bomb campaign was certainly encouraged by the Soviet leader, Leonid Brezhnev who said that the Soviets would not build such weapons and that US production of neutron bombs would make the use of nuclear weapons more likely.[16] Eventually, President Carter reversed his policy and cancelled the weapon.

More often foreign criticism either makes governments more entrenched or embarrasses them when they concede. If one state is being encouraged to sign an arms control agreement by a mixture of discreet pressure and incentives, the more attention concentrated on this process, the more difficult it will be for the government under pressure to give way. There was bitter anger amongst conservatives in West Germany over US pressure to persuade the Bonn government to sign the NPT in 1969.[17] But sign they did. Subsequently, President Carter's very obvious pressure on Brazil not to buy nuclear power stations and a reprocessing plant from West Germany in the 1970s alienated both Brazil and Germany. This time the Germans felt strong enough to ignore US pressure and the deal went ahead. In 1989, when the USA tried to persuade Bonn to prevent German chemical companies assisting with the construction of a Libyan plant, which US intelligence believed would produce chemical weapons, Chancellor Helmut Kohl accused Washington of treating his country 'like a banana republic'.[18] But it was Bonn which gave way and prevented its companies from involving themselves in the Libyan project.

Well-publicised accusations in the 1970s and 1980s that the Soviet Union was in breach of its arms control obligations had little impact on Soviet behaviour, although they increased distrust between the two sides. Such attacks also made it more difficult for US administrations to persuade Congress to ratify agreements which had been negotiated, and they produced a substantial body of opinion in the USA which believed that the whole arms control process had worked against US interests.[19]

Just as the negotiation of arms control treaties had played a major part in the development of *détente*, so the discrediting of such agreements was a major factor in turning US opinion against the attempt to improve relations with Moscow.

CONCLUSION

Important sections of the media have a natural but largely unconscious distrust of, even perhaps contempt for, arms control negotiations and agreements. Such processes conflict with the hard-boiled, 'realistic' appraisal of world affairs which is usually espoused by foreign correspondents. Successful arms control destroys news which is vivid, conflictual and dramatic. Editorials in the serious press may advocate arms control negotiations but the contents of the foreign news pages tell a different story. The editorials reflect the optimistic rationalism of the eighteenth-century Enlightenment, the news reflects the romanticism and hero worship of the early nineteenth century and the cynicism of the twentieth century. Neither picture is complete. When a total breakdown of order occurs in Bosnia, Cambodia or elsewhere the ensuing fight for survival can rarely be moderated by diplomatic niceties. Similarly, arms control agreements can only be negotiated when states are not bitterly opposed to each other. For most of their history, the Arabs and Israelis, or India and Pakistan have refused to negotiate with each other at all. It is when relations are improving that arms control can further this process and rational discussion can replace tension and confrontation. When relations improve beyond a certain point, arms control becomes much less important, as it has in negotiations with Russia since the end of the Cold War.

. Like the media, the general public ignores most of the efforts by governments and research institutes to provide information on defence and disarmament. Nevertheless, arms control agreements have changed the general public mood in the past when they have first transformed the outlook and assessment of the situation made by political leaders. This can work in various ways. The arms control agreements negotiated in the 1960s, technical and *recherché* as they were, laid the basis for the *détente* of the 1970s. Conversely, the accusations of cheating on these agreements, which were made during the 1970s, helped to undermine that same process of *détente* both in the United States and in the Soviet Union.[20] Pressure by foreign governments to alter arms control and defence policy is usually counter-productive once it is dramatised by the media, which often ignore the substantive issues at stake and evoke nationalistic sentiments.

Politicians are, therefore, wise to speak as if the public is interested in arms control, even though they know that for most of the time this is not the case. High-profile public campaigns well reported by the media can exacerbate international tensions, alienate foreign governments and make elected representatives less willing to vote for even well-balanced arms control agreements. The indifference of the media towards successful arms control agreements produces a distorted view of the world but it may assist the negotiators. By and large, vague public and editorial support for disarmament negotiations, combined with indifference to detail, may be the best that Western governments can hope for.

NOTES

1. See particularly 'Nuclear Treaty under Threat', *The Times*, 27 January 1995 and the *Programme for Promoting Nuclear Non-Proliferation Newsbriefs*, produced by the Mountbatten Centre for International Studies, Southampton University.
2. 'Britain to Stop Making Nuclear Arms Material', *The Times*, 3 April 1995; 'RAF to Lose Nuclear Role after 42 Years on Front Line', *The Times*, 5 April 1995; 'Britain Ends 40 Years of Nuclear Test Explosions', *The Times*, 7 April 1995.
3. 'Nuclear Perils' and 'Third World States Want Nuclear Treaty Altered', *The Times*, 17 April 1995; 'Hurd Backs Nuclear Pact Extension', *The Times*, 19 April 1995; 'Nuclear Treaty Wins Indefinite Extension', *The Times*, 12 May 1995.
4. 'Bomb Claim Increases Tension in Kashmir', *The Times*, 24 August 1994; 'Now It's a Nuclear World', *The Times*, 25 August 1994; 'Israel has Developed 200 Nuclear Weapons', *The Times*, 15 November 1994.
5. 'New Zealand and Australia Freeze Paris Military Links', *The Times*, 15 June 1995.
6. 'France to Call for Ban on All Nuclear Tests', *The Times*, 11 August 1995.
7. See, for example, *Social Trends 1995 Edition* (London: HMSO, 1995) and *Statement on Defence Estimates 1995: Stable Forces in a Strong Britain*, CM 2800 (London: HMSO, 1995).
8. *MPs and Defence: A Survey of Parliamentary Knowledge and Opinion* (London: Institute for European Defence and Strategic Studies, 1988).
9. *Arms Control and Disarmament*, Number 1, August 1979. This publication later became the *Arms Control and Disarmament Quarterly Review*.
10. Lord Moran, *Winston Churchill: The Struggle for Survival, 1940–1965* (London: Constable, 1966), pp. 493–4 and 504.
11. See the relative lack of interest in the issue in T. Benn, *Out of the Wilderness, Diaries 1963–1967* (London: Hutchinson, 1987), and B. Castle, *The Castle Diaries 1974–76* (London: Weidenfeld & Nicolson, 1980).
12. *Documents on Disarmament 1963* (Washington: US Arms Control and Disarmament Agency, 1963).
13. 'Europe and Defence: A Guardian Survey', *Guardian*, 16 February 1987.

See also 'Majority Disapprove of Britain Accepting Cruise', *Guardian*, 24 January 1983; 'Most People Opposed to Unilateral Disarmament', *Guardian*, 22 October 1983.

14. See note 8 above.
15. *Statement on Defence Estimates 1992*, CM 1981 (London: HMSO, 1992), p. 22.
16. 'US Doubts on Bomb Offer by Brezhnev', *Daily Telegraph*, 26 April 1978 and 'USSR Will Not Produce Neutron Bomb While US Also Desists', *Financial Times*, 26 April 1978; '"Weak" Brezhnev Takes Part in Intensive Talks', *Daily Telegraph*, 6 May 1978.
17. 'Brandt Overrides Opposition to Sign Nuclear Treaty', *Daily Telegraph*, 29 November 1969.
18. 'Bonn Investigates Blocked Libyan Export Deals', *The Times*, 11 January 1989; 'Bonn MPs Demand Full Account of German Role', *The Times*, 19 January 1989; 'US Wins Time to Toughen Chemical Arms Controls', *The Times*, 21 January 1989.
19. See, for example, the analysis of the Reagan administration's views in Strobe Talbott, *Deadly Gambits: The Reagan Administration and the Stalemate in Nuclear Arms Control* (New York: Alfred Knopf, 1984).
20. P. Towle, *Arms Control and East–West Relations* (London: Croom Helm, 1983).

16

The Media, the Military and Public Opinion

STEPHEN BADSEY

The fusion of ideas and practices about the media and international security which has been a feature of the 1990s has now gone beyond the first tentative steps of recognising the differences between the various professional cultures involved, which took place largely in the aftermath of the 1990–91 Gulf War. Already, one of its most productive results is that concepts which are commonplace in one discipline may often serve to unlock the problems of another. One excellent example of this, which has considerable implications for the use or threat of force in military operations, is the role of media studies in overturning the belief, still very strongly held in traditional international relations and in military Psychological Operations (PSYOPS), in the otherwise long-discredited 'Injection' or 'Stimulus/Response' model of mass social behaviour. In particular, David Morrison's classic study of British popular attitudes and the media during the 1990–91 Gulf War should have ended forever the glib military claim that the media or propaganda can dictate or control public opinion with any certainty.[1]

THE PARAMETERS OF THE PROBLEM

That the British armed forces should be concerned to have public support for their activities, and also concerned about their relations with the media, may appear only prudent and in keeping with their role. No matter what the ideological position or the evidence examined by those who have considered this issue, the one conclusion that is not found, and that no one ever expected to find, is no correlation, or utter public indifference

238

to military operations. This provides the obvious conclusion that the mass electoral public is in some way involved in the process. Whether foreign policy and the decision to commit forces overseas has ever been, in the words of Professor Lawrence Martin, 'an elite game' is highly questionable.[2] Certainly, this has not been true of Britain at any point in this century. Even in modern undemocratic states such as the Arab countries of the Magreb, a case can be made that such policies are of necessity highly responsive to mass popular opinion.[3] But it is equally clear that the link between public opinion and military operations is not a straightforward one. It is actually much easier to make out a theoretical case for the direct impact of electoral public opinion on the conduct of war overseas for Britain in the 1850s, when the proportion of the adult population entitled to vote was just 7 per cent, and the mass media consisted largely of *The Times* and the *Illustrated London News*, than it is for today. Such figures also warn against sweeping generalisations from media practice in the Crimean War (1853–56) to that of present times such as those made most boldly by Phillip Knightley's still widely-read book *The First Casualty*.[4]

It has become an established convention both of military thought and defence journalism in this country to see the operations of NATO forces, including those of Britain, as little more than those of the United States writ slightly larger. Since 1979 at least, it has been British government policy to align the structure and operating practices of its armed forces ever closer with those of the United States, to the point at which it is sometimes quite difficult to discern a separate British doctrine or mode of thinking, academic debates concerning 'the British way in warfare' notwithstanding.[5] By way of illustration, in a policy speech to the Royal United Services Institute in 1993, Malcolm Rifkind, then the British Secretary of State for Defence, listed criteria for the participation of Britain in overseas military deployments that were a recognisable copy of the so-called 'Weinberger Rules', the major American policy statement of 1984, without feeling the need to mention this fact.[6]

Equally, the trend in cultural studies in this country and throughout Western Europe has been to perceive, usually with various degrees of gloom, a Europe increasingly dominated by an Americanised media culture. Within the last two decades, technological and social developments have produced (probably for the first time in history) a genuinely international media, including news media dominated by virtually instantaneous global broadcast television. These international media institutions are also the media institutions of the United States writ slightly larger, with a strong secondary British element resulting partly from historical accident and the aftermath of Empire, partly from the coincidence of a shared language, and partly from the continuing high professional standards of the British print and broadcast media. Both the British military and the British media, therefore, stand in a curious parallel relationship with those of the United States. In making this comparison several caveats must, of course, be entered concerning the unique nature of the United States as the world's remaining superpower, which has many features to distinguish it from a country such as Britain. In particular, although they have become global and international in reach, the media of the United States remain national and even parochial in behaviour and content. But, since it is virtually impossible to exclude the United States from any discussion either of the British media or of British military operations, it is assumed of necessity that attitudes and practices which are known to exist in Washington as matters of public record (sometimes only though the Freedom of Information Act), will also be found in London and, to some extent, in Paris and Ottawa as well.

The idea that decisions regarding the use of military force, and even sizeable wars, could and should be undertaken largely independently of mass popular support enjoyed a brief vogue among political and military thinkers particularly in the United States in the two decades following the Second World War, playing a significant part in the theory of 'Limited War' most often associated with the work of Robert Osgood. The experience of the Vietnam War largely discredited this belief, leaving subsequent United States governments with the conviction that any military action must enjoy popular support to be successful. This change in attitude was incorporated into a number of policy statements in the 1980s of which Defense Secretary Casper Weinberger's 'Rules' are the most well known.[7] Largely in the period since then, developments in global satellite television broadcasting in particular have given the media and the public a potential new form of access into military operations. In present British military terminology, the effect of this new technology has been to collapse the Jominian 'Levels of War', so that operations and tactics have become potentially politicised in a manner not previously seen. The response of governments and their armed forces to this phenomenon has been to develop techniques of what Professor Jarol Manheim has called 'Strategic Public Diplomacy', more commonly known as 'news management' in the non-pejorative sense.[8]

While popular attitudes within the belligerent countries are an important part of the story of the two World Wars of this century, a further war on such a scale (which British military doctrine would at present call a 'General War') is at the moment only a remote possibility. It is also both a historically demonstrable fact, and a widely shared modern belief, that in cases of a direct and major threat to the country's survival caused by war the conventions which govern the relationship between government, military, population and media will undergo a significant change; direct military censorship of the media enforced by statute being one obvious example. As Winston Churchill put it in early 1940, 'In time of war the machinery of government is so strong that it can afford largely to ignore popular feeling.'[9] These facts argue once more against simplistic speculation as to whether the Second World War could have been won if reported by modern methods ('if CNN had been present on D-Day' and so forth). In fact, research into electoral mass public attitudes in the United States to the Vietnam War during its conduct has generally found little or no correlation with public attitudes towards the Second World War. Nor should any such similarity of attitudes have been expected by anyone familiar with the social history of the United States during either period.

Although everyday relations of the British media towards the armed forces, as with any other large and high-profile public institution, depend on mutual experience built up over considerable time, they are tested most strongly by the problems engendered in actual military operations. The last decade has seen a significant increase in British overseas deployments, which British institutional military thinking saw as coming largely within 'Defence Role Three' as defined by the 1993 *Statement on the Defence Estimates: Defending Our Future*. Even following a change of government, this trend has also been confirmed by the 1998 Strategic Defence Review. Such overseas expeditions are, virtually by definition, undertaken in pursuit of Britain's national interests rather than survival, although these interests can be very broadly defined to include an interest in peace and the ending of preventable atrocities. It is significant that some polling evidence suggests that a small majority of the British public views favourably the idea of armed British intervention in some circumstances to prevent barbarity, a view also taken by current international law. All these were factors in the British contribution to the intervention in Kosovo in 1999.

Tensions and disputes that have arisen between British governments and armed forces on the one hand, and the national media on the other, going back to the 1956 Suez Crisis and including the 1982 Falklands War, have often stemmed from the problem as to how far powers over the media and conventions of behaviour appropriate for a war of survival may be invoked by the military during such operations. However, the idea that some form of control over the media is necessary in any war also has wide popular support in Britain, on the basis that, as Richard Connaughton has put it, 'a soldier's right to survive transcends the public's need to know'.[10] This argument also carries considerable weight with most journalists.

MODELS OF PUBLIC OPINION AND MILITARY DOCTRINE

The term 'public opinion' itself has almost as many diverse meanings as it has users. Most commonly in military discussions of popular support it is taken to mean the mass adult population, or the electorate. In this model or hypothesis, which perhaps most resembles the ideals of representative democracy, the institutions of government are held to be highly responsive to electoral public attitudes, particularly in respect of the very serious matter of the threat or use of force overseas. By far the most important element of the media in communication between the government and the people in this model is therefore the mass medium of television, which for almost 30 years has been the dominant news medium in Britain as in other countries, providing the principal source of news for between 70 and 90 per cent of all poll respondents. In this hypothesis also, the interests and resources of the armed forces should be focused on television, and on developing good relations and understanding with its senior journalists and producers. Equally, if public support for a military operation wavers or declines, it is to television reporting that the military should look for the problem and a possible solution.

It is a curious feature of this hypothesis that while the mass medium of television is regarded as very important, the mass circulation daily tabloid newspapers are almost completely disregarded. It should first of all be noted that tabloids such as the *Sun* and the *Mirror*, with a total daily readership of about 17 million between them, are a specifically British phenomenon, not found in the newspaper markets of any other major European country, or in the United States. British academic research into the impact of tabloid journalism in this country, most obviously that of the Glasgow University Media Group, has largely focused on domestic issues, dealing with defence issues usually within a specifically domestic and popular context.[11] However, the idea that the tabloids play a significant part in military or military–political decision making, although often denied by the decision makers themselves, is supported by some anecdotal evidence and deserves further study. It is also usually forgotten that members of the British armed forces are themselves overwhelmingly tabloid readers, and that tabloid stories may have an effect upon them.

Nevertheless, poll evidence from the Gulf and earlier wars strongly supports the hypothesis that readers of the major British tabloids pay little or no attention to their foreign news content, do not necessarily share (or even understand) their politics, and that a significant minority of *Sun* and *Daily Star* readers in both the Falklands War and the Gulf did not share either their overt jingoism or their aggressive stance. The *Sun*'s suggestion that nuclear weapons should be used in the Gulf War was supported by only 21 per cent of its readers in one survey.[12] Evidence such as this calls into question the value of tabloid journalists in covering overseas deployments, and their right of access to military facilities and briefings. In practice, such access depends on the amount of political pressure generated by these newspapers at a much higher level than that of their readership.

Virtually since the start of polling, warnings have been issued and ignored concerning the limitations of statistics, and of opinion polls in particular. As the nineteenth-century wit Andrew Lang put it, such figures are too often used 'as a drunk man uses a lamp-post – for support rather than for illumination'. A single poll result proves nothing; a polling trend may prove very little, as was demonstrated by the surprise result of the 1992 British general election. Some polling results, interpreted through the complex mathematical models of psephology, may also strain the credulity of outsiders. One quite respectable model promoted by Professor John Mueller argues that public attitudes to war within the United States at the time of the Vietnam War align so closely with those found in the Korean War, during which there was virtually no television coverage and newspapers were still the dominant news medium, that television can have played no significant part in shaping American public opinion over Vietnam. Another model suggests that victory in the Falklands War, the alleged 'Falklands factor', played no part in Conservative Party popularity prior to the 1983 British general election.[13] Results such as these perhaps serve to foster the suspicion that statistics may be used to prove anything.

Under normal circumstances, there are many issues on which people genuinely have no opinion, or if asked will provide an opinion that is held weakly if at all, and 'public opinion' on these issues can scarcely be said to exist. The field of defence in general and the armed forces in particular is one to which the various publics of Western democracies are generally indifferent, with that of the United States leading the field. This phenomenon is quite easy to demonstrate anecdotally. Of the respondents to a 1981 *Washington Post* survey, 53 per cent identified the Soviet Union, rather than the United States, as the NATO member country. In 1983, the year of the Strategic Defense Initiative (SDI) 'Star Wars' initiative and the supposed height of the anti-nuclear debate, only 7 per cent of poll respondents in Britain could identify accurately their country's nuclear defence policy from a choice of three. Back in the United States in the same year, only 13 per cent of respondents knew which side their country was supporting in the civil war in Nicaragua.[14] The implication of this is that the mass of the public lack prior understanding of any crisis in which their governments might deploy military forces, and is therefore heavily dependent upon the media for perspectives and attitudes towards the military actions taken, a process usually known to the media themselves as 'framing' or contextualisation. A further implication is that if a crisis is too complex to be easily explicable by the machinery of television news, such as the events in Northern Ireland 1969–98 or former Yugoslavia 1992–95, then public attitudes will remain confused and ambivalent.

This importance of the media in 'framing' military events for the public may also be demonstrated quite clearly by opinion poll evidence. One survey conducted in the Kingston-upon-Hull area just after the Gulf War invited respondents to estimate the proportion of Coalition air sorties flown specifically by the British during the War. Relying on their impressions from television and newspapers, 97 per cent of respondents gave a figure above 5 per cent, and 42 per cent of respondents gave a figure above 30 per cent, against a true figure of approximately 3 per cent of all sorties. To nearly half of the respondents, the British media coverage had made the RAF effort appear almost ten times as large as it was.[15] Conversely, accounts of the Gulf War have been published in the United States that virtually omit the role of the British or the French (or for that matter the Arab states) from the war altogether.

Of the various theories of electoral response to the media reporting of military operations overseas, the one which has dominated the thinking of Western governments and their armed forces since the Vietnam era is the 'sandcastle' model: the belief that public support for the government will start at a high level and then gradually and inevitably erode over time, to the point at which a popular mandate for prosecution of military operations no longer exists. One version of this theory, still current in British military thought although declining in popularity, sees media coverage as the principal cause of this erosion.[16] The implications of this model are that positive steps are required by the government both to bolster and direct public opinion, and to restrict and control media coverage both at home and overseas on operations. This theory very largely governed the conduct of the United States government between August 1990 and February 1991 in practising a sustained campaign directed towards its own people and domestic media over its use of force against Iraq in the Gulf War. When undertaken for objectives based on interest rather than survival, the legitimacy of such actions may be politically controversial, and they are by no means value-free. In the words of one severe critic, Professor Hamid Mowlana, in the Gulf War, 'Conventional confrontation on the battlefield did not come until after the propaganda and communications strategy had succeeded both domestically and internationally.'[17] The question might be raised as to whether a similar strategy also succeeded in 1995 in former Yugoslavia, with the demonising

244

of the Bosnian Serbs before their being subject to American air attack and subsequent defeat on the battlefield.

Empirical evidence suggests that this 'sandcastle' model of the relation between military operations, the media, and public opinion would probably be accepted by most members of today's British armed forces, modified perhaps by what might be called the 'perturbation' model, which holds that public opinion will fluctuate on an almost daily basis depending on media reporting of military success or failure. This model reflects the greatest single fear of senior officials and commanders on military operations regarding the media. Often, if inaccurately described as 'the CNN factor', this is the perceived ability of live or near-live television coverage of a specific event to provoke a massive reaction at the highest levels of government, so distorting highly complex military plans. The earliest clear example of this effect may have been television coverage of the loss of 239 US Marines in Lebanon to a suicide lorry bomb in October 1983, identified by David Gergen, the Director of Communications for the Reagan White House, as a principal factor in the American decision to withdraw.[18] But with enhanced satellite television communications many more alleged cases have occurred, including the Anglo-French decision to promote the creation of 'safe havens' in Kurdistan in February–March 1991, the impact of Operation 'Irma' in August 1993 on British peacekeeping in Bosnia, and the pictures of a dead Special Forces crewman being dragged through the streets of Mogadishu in October 1994 which again played a significant part in the United States decision to withdraw its forces from Somalia.[19]

Early research into this phenomenon has failed to establish any convincing reason why these particular news stories should have produced such a dramatic reaction, when pictures of the fighting in Chechnya in December 1994 did not, and the extremely violent civil war in Liberia in the same period went virtually unreported. It is even possible to point to examples that apparently reverse the traditional wisdom of the 'CNN factor', such as the Belgian reaction to the loss of some of their peacekeeping soldiers in Rwanda in April 1994. The view that the media can in some way be blamed for doing their job, or that policy is being 'media led', is a particularly improbable explanation. The whole argument has also met a very effective counter from evidence that senior politicians seldom have the time or inclination to watch television. At present all that can be said is that such things as the 'CNN factor' undoubtedly happen, but that a very large random element indeed is involved in their generation.

A third possible model for public response to a military crisis, much admired by political scientists but little known among the military, is the 'rally round the flag' model. Based on the belief that in a stable democracy a large number of people will support the government whatever it does, this model postulates that as military action continues instincts of national solidarity will lead to an increase in public support. This applies to defeats just as it does to successes, and is sometimes known in the United States as the 'Pearl Harbor effect' for that reason (the British equivalent is, presumably, 'spirit of Dunkirk'). Study of British public behaviour in the Falklands War provides some support for this theory, although whether it played a part in such episodes as the political decision to attack Goose Green is by no means clear.

In reality the only three possibilities for any changing statistical trend over time is that it will either increase, or decrease, or fluctuate, and to this extent such models may appear as trivial. As might be expected, analysis of opinion polls from real wars provides only limited support for any of the three basic positions. That which has proved least convincing is the 'sandcastle' model, which also seems to be the most widely supported in military circles. In particular, the firm belief of the United States government in early 1968 that public support for the war in Vietnam had collapsed because of the Tet offensive, or more precisely media reporting of that offensive as an American defeat, often called the 'Vietnam syndrome', has now been so utterly destroyed by scholarly analysis that there would be little point in raising the issue had it not become an article of faith among the American military and the right wing of the Republican Party in the aftermath of the war. The impact of this belief, that, in the time-honoured phrase, 'the Vietnam war was lost on the television screens of America', on military–media relations is now well documented and understood, including its impact on British military–media relations in the Falklands and Gulf Wars. What is perhaps less well appreciated outside military circles is the manner in which the belief has affected the entire United States military organisation and thinking since Vietnam, and by extension that of Britain also. Not since the Franco-Prussian War of 1870–71 has a war in which Britain did not fight played such a large part in shaping its entire military posture. A preference for the use of overwhelming force in short wars, the fear of 'quagmires' and sensitivity to casualties on either side, a persistent overestimation of the enemy, and the employment of high-technology weapons systems, are all direct legacies not only of Vietnam but of the 'Vietnam syndrome' which have dominated British military thought, including much of British air power doctrine, and also the centrepiece of British Army doctrine, presently known as 'manoeuvrist philosophy'. Although military doctrine comes from many sources, and has erred for many reasons, this is also surely the first time in history that an error in media analysis has played so large a part in military affairs. Curiously, the British experience of relations between the armed forces and the media, first in the Falklands, and then in the Gulf War, and again in former Yugoslavia, has been very much better for both sides than those of the United States.

Meanwhile, much of the analysis of American behaviour in the Gulf War which has come from media and cultural studies in the last decade has been rendered almost valueless by a failure to appreciate the constraints under which the United States armed forces believed they were working, and by an ignorance of their operating methods. This criticism applies particularly to the assertion by Professor Noam Chomsky and his disciples that what happened in the Gulf in 1991 was not war but massacre.[20]

THE ELITES HYPOTHESIS AND ITS VARIANTS

Investigation of the role of the media in Vietnam, and the failure of opinion poll data to support any convincing model of a relationship between military operations, the media and public opinion, has led to the popularity among political scientists in the United States of what has become known as the 'elites' hypothesis. Ironically, this concept bears a remarkable resemblance to the 'dominant definition' model which has existed within the Marxist tradition of European sociology for some decades. As a model of public opinion it is closest to that envisaged by the founding fathers of both British liberalism and conservatism in the eighteenth century. According to this hypothesis the public opinion which matters is that which can be measured only indifferently by polling, the opinion of the various social and political elites for which the useful eighteenth-century term is the 'political nation'. Such elites are held to be highly influential in government, in the military and in the media, and indeed to form an important part of all three. Unlike most versions of the 'dominant definition' model, however, which is essentially class-based, this theory postulates a multiplicity of elites combining and re-combining to form constituencies on various issues. Given that the mass electoral public is so heavily dependent upon media 'framing' and contextualisation, if elite support of government policy is sufficient, broad news coverage and electoral public opinion will rally behind this policy, perhaps after some delay. But when elites dispute or oppose government policy, media coverage will tend to reflect this confusion. Therefore, the explanation for the alleged collapse of public opinion in the aftermath of the Tet offensive, which cannot be demonstrated from opinion polls, is that it was elite public support that collapsed, including a significant part of the elites within the government itself.[21]

In this model, the most important parts of the media in affecting military operations will be those that contribute to the forming of elite opinions. This devalues the role of television and enhances that of 'serious' or broadsheet newspapers, and in particular the role of specialist foreign or defence correspondents and editors. Agenda-setting is also very important to this model. It suggests a critical role for such radio programmes as the early morning BBC Radio Four 'Today', with an audience that is dominated by professional elites. Such programmes can often carry stories which will then influence the rest of the day's news quite heavily, filtering down into daily newspapers and evening television broadcasts. Indeed, the 'elites' hypothesis suggests an important but neglected role for radio in general, particularly in Britain. The implications of this hypothesis are that the government and the armed forces should direct their main effort not towards television journalists in the field, but towards the Whitehall lobby, which they are unusually well placed to influence, and that there is little practical reason to explain military events to the mass of the people. This attitude may help explain what is otherwise a very puzzling feature of the British military involvement in former Yugoslavia, given the importance placed on public support in recent military thinking. This is the virtual absence in the period 1992–95 of direct television pronouncements by either senior government or military officials seeking to explain Britain's role, and clearly aimed at the mass of the population.

Now gaining ground in the thinking of armed forces is a model of the interaction between the media, the elites and the military which apparently reverses the conventional 'elites' hypothesis. Popularised in particular by the Canadian Major-General Lewis Mackenzie, former commander of UN forces in Sarajevo, like most military hypotheses this appears to be entirely empirically derived, largely from the experience of UN peacekeepers in former Yugoslavia.[22] Unlike the 'elites' hypothesis, this model suggests that the media have little influence if the government presents a 'firm' policy (which is usually military code for the early use of force). However, if government policy is confused or ineffective, over time the media will generate their own policy and impose this on the home public, beginning with the elites. An early (if hardly auspicious) example of a government following this hypothesis may perhaps be seen in the attempts of the Nixon White House to generate a firm policy over Vietnam. This hypothesis once more makes the media into an enemy of the military. While their behaviour may be defended on the grounds that they are carrying out their historic role of criticising the home government, and bringing its shortcomings to public attention, they may also be criticised for making the conduct of delicate military operations impossible.

The implications of the 'elites' hypothesis are, to quote Professor John Zaller, 'a stark political world in which elites lead, masses follow, and the press does the bidding of the government'.[23] However, this view has been challenged by a rather more sophisticated hypothesis, advanced by Zaller among others, that politicians are genuinely much more responsive to electoral public opinion than any poll can possibly show. By this hypothesis, the public opinion to which politicians respond is that which they believe that the public will hold in the future. One example offered is the manner in which President Lyndon Johnson in 1964 took the United States into a major war in Vietnam for which neither he nor the mass of the people had any enthusiasm, in the belief that public opinion would *in the future* move towards greater commitment, and blame him if that commitment had not been made.

That political skill and acumen consist of trying to divine the public will of the future is to practising politicians, and to their associates and biographers, perhaps once more only a statement of the obvious. But the idea features very little in analyses of military–media relations and public opinion, and is useful in explaining some otherwise problematic phenomena. Most obviously, it explains the 'CNN factor' and arguments that policy is being 'media driven'. It also helps explain some of the anger directed at the media by decision makers who assume that when public opinion does not develop as they expected that it must have been diverted from its natural path. This hypothesis also suggests a much more important role in influencing British military operations for some otherwise neglected parts of the media, including local newspapers and radio, often with a greater penetration into the local community than the national dailies, and with considerable influence on constituency opinion for cabinet ministers.

A further implication of this hypothesis is that a priori the people who should be among those least able to predict or assess electoral public opinion should be senior members of the military. This is for well-documented sociological reasons. To quote a recent observation by a middle-ranking British officer studying at the Royal College of Defence Studies, the military are, or believe themselves to be, 'a society within society, drawn from it, reflecting it in part, but separated in culture and image by the needs of [their] unique purpose'.[24] As a matter of policy the British military, even more than those of other Western countries, have deliberately fostered such a separation between themselves and their parent society, for reasons which are of considerable interest both to military historians and sociologists. This factor should be a consideration in assessing any military opinion concerning the behaviour of the media or the public. Conversely, it should be remembered that the armed forces have a society and a culture of their own which it is particularly easy for outsiders to misunderstand.

Which of these various theories of the relationship between the media, the military and public opinion represents the truth is a question which may have no meaningful answer, particularly for those theoreticians for who the journey is more important than the destination. Although one of the more pressing needs in modern British military thought is for a coherent doctrine of the relationship between the armed forces and the media, this will, like all prescriptive doctrines, be as much a matter of faith, pragmatism and politics as of verifiable fact. But, perhaps it is neither trite nor naïve to suggest that the guiding principle for both the armed forces and the media should be that both, in their very different ways to be sure, are servants of the people.

NOTES

1. D. Morrison, *Television and the Gulf War* (London: John Libbey, 1992). For a discussion of the earlier models of response to the media, see S. Badsey, 'The Influence of the Media on Recent British Military Operations', in I. Stewart and S. L. Carruthers (eds), *War, Culture and the Media* (Trowbridge: Flicks Books, 1996).
2. Professor Lawrence Martin, quoted in *The Times Higher Education Supplement*, 20 November 1992.
3. S. Telhami, 'Arab Public Opinion and the Gulf War', in S. A. Renshon (ed.), *The Political Psychology of the Gulf War: Leaders, Publics and the Process of Conflict* (Pittsburgh, PA: Pittsburgh University Press, 1993).
4. P. Knightley, *The First Casualty, From the Crimea to Vietnam: The War Correspondent as Hero, Propagandist and Myth Maker* (London: André Deutsch, 1975).
5. See, in particular, D. French, *The British Way in Warfare 1688–2000* (London: Unwin Hyman, 1990); L. Freedman, 'Alliance and the British Way in Warfare', *Review of International Studies*, 21, 2 (April 1995).
6. M. Rifkind, 'Resources, Commitments and Capabilities: The Conundra of the Defence Debate', *RUSI Journal*, 138, 4 (August 1993), p. 4. Compare this with the 'Weinberger Rules', as cited in E. J. Carol Jr and G. R. La Roque, 'Victory in the Desert: Superior Technology or Brute Force?', in V. Britain (ed.), *The Gulf Between Us: The Gulf War and Beyond* (London: Virago, 1991), pp. 58–9.
7. See S. Badsey, 'The Doctrines of the Coalition Forces', in J. Pimlott and S. Badsey (eds), *The Gulf War Assessed* (London: Arms & Armour, 1992); B. Glad and J. P. Rosenberg, 'Limited War: The Political Framework', in B. Glad (ed.), *Psychological Dimensions of War* (Newbury Park, CA, and London: Sage, 1990); R. Brown, 'Limited War', in C. McInnes and G. D. Sheffield (eds), *Warfare in the Twentieth Century: Theory and Practice* (London: Unwin Hyman, 1988).

8. J. B. Manheim, 'Strategic Public Diplomacy: Managing Kuwait's Image During the Gulf Conflict', in W. L. Bennett and D. L. Paletz (eds), *Taken By Storm: The Media, Public Opinion, and US Foreign Policy in the Gulf War* (Chicago, IL, and London: Chicago University Press, 1994).

9. Quoted in C. Ponting, *1940: Myth and Reality* (London: Hamish Hamilton, 1990), p. 171.

10. R. Connaughton, *Military Intervention in the 1990s: A New Logic of War* (London and New York: Routledge, 1992), p. 55.

11. See, for example, Glasgow University Media Group, *War and Peace News* (Milton Keynes: Open University Press, 1985), and J. Eldridge (ed.), *Getting the Message: News, Truth and Power* (London and New York: Routledge, 1993).

12. M. Shaw and R. Carr-Hill, 'Public Opinion and Media War Coverage in Britain', in H. Mowlana, G. Gerbner and H. I. Schiller (eds), *Triumph of the Image: The Media's War in the Persian Gulf – A Global Perspective* (Boulder, CO, and Oxford: Worldview, 1992), pp. 150–4.

13. See J. E. Mueller, *War, Presidents and Public Opinion* (Lanham, MD, and London: UPA, 1985), p. 167, and J. Mueller, *Policy and Opinion in the Gulf War* (Chicago, IL, and London: Chicago University Press, 1994), pp. 100–2.

14. D. R. Gergen, 'Diplomacy in a Television Age', in S. Serfaty (ed.), *The Media and Foreign Policy* (New York and London: Macmillan, 1990), p. 52; P. M. Jones and G. Reece, *British Public Attitudes To Nuclear Defence* (London: Macmillan, 1990), p. 27; J. Zaller, 'Elite Leadership of Mass Opinion: New Evidence From the Gulf War', in W. L. Bennett and D. L. Paletz, p. 187.

15. M. Shaw and R. Carr-Hill, p. 152.

16. See C. Elliott, 'The Impact of the Media on Modern Warfare', *Despatches: The Journal of the Territorial Army Pool of Public Information Officers*, 4 (Autumn 1993), pp. 21–33.

17. H. Mowlana, 'Roots of War: The Long Road to Intervention', in H. Mowlana, G. Gerber and H. I. Schiller, p. 35.

18. Gergen quoted by H. Luostarinen, 'Innovations of Moral Policy', in H. Mowlana, G. Gerber and H. I. Schiller, p. 134.

19. See N. Gowing, 'Real-Time Television Coverage of Armed Conflicts and Diplomatic Crises: Does it Pressure or Distort Foreign Policy Decisions?', working paper 94-1, Joan Shorenstein Barone Center on the Press, Politics and Public Policy (Cambridge, MA: Harvard University, 1994).

20. N. Chomsky, 'The Media and the War: What War?' in H. Mowlana, G. Gerber and H. I. Schiller; see also R. Keeble, *Secret State, Silent Press: New Militarism, the Gulf and the Modern Image of Warfare* (Luton: Luton University Press/John Libbey, 1997). For a discussion of American and British war-fighting methods in the Gulf War and their relations to the media, see S. Badsey, 'The Doctrines of the Coalition Forces' and 'The Media War', in J. Pimlott and S. Badsey, *The Gulf War Assessed*.

21. See, in particular, J. Zaller, 'Elite Leadership of Mass Opinion'.

22. See, in particular, L. MacKenzie, *Peacekeeper: The Road to Sarajevo* (Vancouver: Douglas & McIntyre, 1993).

23. J. Zaller, 'Strategic Politicians, Public Opinion, and the Gulf Crisis', in W. L. Bennett and D. L. Paletz, p. 250.

24. Colonel Michael Charlton-Weedy, in his review of D. Chandler and I. Beckett (eds), *The Oxford Illustrated History of the British Army*, in *The Times Higher Education Supplement*, 25 August 1995.

Index